Transforming Christianity
and the World

Faith Meets Faith

An Orbis Series in Interreligious Dialogue
Paul F. Knitter, General Editor

Editorial Advisors
John Berthrong
Julia Ching
Diana Eck
Karl-Josef Kuschel
Lamin Sanneh
George E. Tinker
Felix Wilfred

In the contemporary world, the many religions and spiritualities stand in need of greater communication and cooperation. More than ever before, they must speak to, learn from, and work with each other in order both to maintain their vital identities and to contribute to fashioning a better world.

FAITH MEETS FAITH seeks to promote interreligious dialogue by providing an open forum for exchanges among followers of different religious paths. While the Series wants to encourage creative and bold responses to questions arising from contemporary appreciations of religious plurality, it also recognizes the multiplicity of basic perspectives concerning the methods and content of interreligious dialogue.

Although rooted in a Christian theological perspective, the Series does not endorse any single school of thought or approach. By making available to both the scholarly community and the general public works that represent a variety of religious and methodological viewpoints, FAITH MEETS FAITH seeks to foster an encounter among followers of the religions of the world on matters of common concern.

Faith Meets Faith Series

Transforming Christianity and the World

A Way beyond Absolutism and Relativism

John B. Cobb, Jr.
Edited and Introduced by Paul F. Knitter

ORBIS BOOKS

Maryknoll, New York 10545

The Catholic Foreign Mission Society of America (Maryknoll) recruits and trains people for overseas missionary service. Through Orbis Books, Maryknoll aims to foster the international dialogue that is essential to mission. The books published, however, reflect the opinions of their authors and are not meant to represent the official position of the society. To obtain more information about Maryknoll and Orbis Books, please visit our website at www.Maryknoll.org.

Published by Orbis Books, Maryknoll, New York, U.S.A.

Manufactured in the United States of America.

Library of Congress Cataloging-in-Publication Data

Cobb, John B.
    Transforming Christianity and the world: a way beyond absolutism and relativism / John B. Cobb, Jr.; edited and introduced by Paul F. Knitter.
        p. cm. — (Faith meets faith series)
    Includes bibliographical references and index.
    ISBN 1-57075-271-0 (pbk.)
    1. Christianity and other religions.   2. Religions—Relations.   3. Religious pluralism.   4. Religion and civilization.   I. Knitter, Paul F.   II. Title.
III. Series: Faith meets faith.
    BR127 .C558 1999
    261.2—dc21
                                                                                    99-31694
                                                                                         CIP

Contents

Introduction

PAUL F. KNITTER

In assembling this volume, John Cobb and I wanted to do more than collect his writings on religious pluralism and interreligious dialogue. In itself, that would have been an extremely valuable project, for though Cobb has been one of the major voices in the Christian discussion about how to understand and approach other religious ways, his many writings on this topic lie scattered across the theological landscape of the 80s and 90s. Still, we wanted to do more than assemble what was scattered. We wanted to interpret what Cobb has had to say about religious pluralism and dialogue and explore its significance for the present state of the world and of interreligious affairs. And as Cobb has stated and exemplified over the years, a sure path to interpretation is conversation.

So Cobb readily agreed when I suggested to him that I take on the job of gathering, selecting, ordering, and then commenting on his essays. This would make this collection of studies on dialogue into a dialogue itself. Without in any way tampering with or clouding the content of Cobb's writings on the many religions, I would try to identify different perspectives or emphases within these essays, suggest what seems to be an evolution in Cobb's central concerns, and also reflect on what his vision and evolution mean for the nature and necessity of dialogue at the beginning of the new millennium.

This dialogue about dialogue seems to have worked. In his concluding essay, Cobb responds to the way I have ordered and interpreted his essays, clarifying, confirming, and also correcting what I had to say. But he also admits that this conversation "has helped me understand myself better." As editor and commentator, I hope that our conversation will help others understand John Cobb's vision of interreligious dialogue better—and so keep the conversation going.

A VALUED VOICE

The editors of Orbis Books wanted to publish this collection because they are convinced that John Cobb's vision of religious pluralism is worth clarifying and exploring. In the international, inter-Christian, and increasingly interreligious conversation about *dialogue*, I honestly cannot think of any other name that is not only as broadly *known* but also as deeply *respected* as that of John Cobb. There are other theologians or historians of religions whose writings on religious pluralism may be more talked about around the world. (I'm thinking of names such as John Hick, Wilfred Cantwell Smith, Karl Rahner, Karl Barth.) But their writings usually elicit either a clear approval or firm rejection, depending on one's place in the spectrum of Christian approaches to other religions. In Cobb's case, however, the response is generally much more respectful and dialogical; one wants to listen more carefully to what John Cobb has to say about understanding other religions; one senses that his perspectives cannot be neatly categorized and are asking questions that others seem to miss. I guess what I am trying to say is that while others have helped construct *positions* within the academic discussion of religious pluralism, Cobb has fostered a *conversation* among those positions—which doesn't mean that he has hesitated to make his own views clear and firm. While others are "responded" to, Cobb is first of all "listened to." I think there are various reasons why this is so.

First of all, it has to do not only with the quality of Cobb's scholarship, but also with the quality of his person; he not only knows and studies what he's talking about, he also cares about whom he is talking to. A hard-nosed academician who did his basic training at the University of Chicago, he still expresses his ideas and convictions with an awareness of his own limitations and a respect for the views of others. True son of the South, he is a scholar and a gentleman.

Applying those same qualities to his Christian faith and practice, one would describe his approach to other religious ways as both firmly faithful to his Christian identity and at the same time genuinely open to totally different religious worlds. He is as committed to the specialness of the transforming Spirit in Jesus Christ as he is convinced that there may be other forms of transformation that are genuinely different from that worked by the Christ-Spirit. (For example, he found the transformation called "Buddha-nature" to be very different from that worked by the Christ.) Cobb wants to be truly open to whatever forms of transformation he encounters.

So he first calls on his fellow Christians to consciously and eagerly embrace what is always actually so: that they are looking at the universe of other religious worlds not with their naked eyes but with their Christian telescopes; there's no such thing as a direct-vision, mountain-top take of the universe of faiths. But he also shows that what is seen with this Christian telescope often has the ability to either thoroughly remodel the telescope or transform the viewer (here the analogy breaks down). This is what made his book *Beyond Dialogue: Toward Mutual Transformation* (1982) so influential and successful: he showed how deep commitment to one's own tradition, when understood as requiring dialogical openness to other traditions, can lead to a surprising transformation of everyone involved.

Furthermore, what gave this book its particular power and what makes Cobb's contributions to the discussion of religious pluralism all the more engaging is that his theory, or general claims, are grounded in and applied to a concrete dialogue with a particular religion. Buddhists have been John Cobb's particular dialogical partners and friends. Cobb's theology of religions has taken shape in the laboratory of a very real, particular dialogue. Though this collection does not include Cobb's writings on Buddhist-Christian dialogue, there are frequent indications throughout this book of how much this dialogue has inspired and directed his theory of pluralism and dialogue. In the main chapters of *Beyond Dialogue* he gives concrete, engaging examples of how the Christian sense of the self and the Buddhist perception of history can be transformed in a dialogue that is as faithful to one's own identity as it is open to that of the other. Cobb's theory is shaped by his praxis.

A final reason why Cobb's voice has been so influential—why he is not only responded to but listened to—has to do, I think, with the way he has tantalizingly fallen through the cracks of the often-used models for dealing with the reality of many other religions. As will become promptly clear in these essays, while Cobb is certainly not an "exclusivist" (only one true religion), neither can he be ranked with the "inclusivists" (among many true religions one outranks the others) or the "pluralists" (many equally valid religions). Cobb somehow wiggles between, or slips beyond, the neat categories of inclusivism or pluralism. That shows both the inadequacies of the models, but even more so, the creativity and care of Cobb's way of honoring and linking religious differences. If he's beckoning us "beyond dialogue," he's also inviting us beyond our usual models of dealing with religious others.

AN EVOLUTION IN COBB'S APPROACH
TO PLURALISM AND DIALOGUE

As the title of this collection indicates, there seems to have been, if not a transformation, at least an evolution in John Cobb's way of engaging the otherness of the many religious ways. It's an evolution that can help us understand not only Cobb but the challenges and potential of interreligious dialogue at the brink of a new millennium. I've described this evolution as a move from Cobb's concerns to avoid an *absolutism* of any one religion to one which seeks also to evade a *relativism* of all religions. The goal of each move offers a more positive description of this evolution: in avoiding absolutism, Cobb sought the transformation of *religions*, while his criticism of relativism aimed at the transformation of the *world*. In using the word "evolution," I don't mean that Cobb's concerns and goals for interreligious dialogue changed from one thing to another; rather they expanded. What came first was not left behind but broadened to include more.

To identify and understand this growth in Cobb's theology of religions and dialogue, we have to situate it within the wider movement of his personal and intellectual life. There seem to be two major periods in Cobb's efforts to combine his personal integrity as a deep-feeling believer with that of a hard-thinking scholar. The first phase was launched when he did his military service and so moved from the relative clarity and security of his Southern family's faith into the diversity and complexity of a fast-changing world. After the war, he decided to confront head-on his internal combat between piety and reason; for his battlefield, he decided on one of the citadels of reason, the University of Chicago. First he joined an interdepartmental program and exposed himself to most of the current clear-headed criticisms of religion; this exposure brought him to the brink of atheism. Then he searched for clear-headed responses to these critiques and enrolled in the University of Chicago's Divinity School. Though bludgeoned and bruised, and with ample aid from Whitehead's process world view (and God view), his Georgia Protestant pietism was reconstructed and so reborn into a faith that was nurtured by both spirit and reason. During these often painful but formative years—roughly between the late 40s and the late 60s—Cobb's primary concerns as a theologian were the relationship between faith and speculative philosophy.[1]

But in 1969, there occurred what Germans would call a *Wende*, a turning around. Like the fall of the Berlin wall, though it happened all of a sudden, it had long been in the making. Because Cobb went about his academic theology the way he had lived his Southern piety—in dogged openness to the wider world around him—he gradually woke up to the horrible and intrusive reality of how broken and endangered this world really was. In his own words:

> The danger to our future and that of our children struck me with almost unbearable force. It seemed to me then, and it seems to me now, that nothing can be more important than finding alternatives to the catastrophes toward which we are heading. I resolved to reorder my priorities accordingly.[2]

From that turning point onward, Cobb's scholarly pursuits would be marked, explicitly or implicitly, by this commitment to the ethical task of finding alternatives to the looming catastrophes of environmental collapse and social violence, which, more and more, Cobb identified as rooted in economic injustice. But around this same time, Cobb's academic and religious awareness experienced another shift, this time not a jolting turning-around but a stretching expansion. His long-standing interest in other cultures and religious viewpoints, which is evident in his *Structures of Christian Existence* (1967), was deepened, perhaps we can say galvanized, through a more intense and personal encounter with other religious thinkers and practition-

---

1. The contours of this stage are described by David Ray Griffin in "John B. Cobb, Jr.: A Theological Biography," *Theology and the University: Essays in Honor of John B. Cobb, Jr.*, David Ray Griffin and Joseph C. Hough, Jr., eds. (Albany: State University of New York Press, 1991), pp. 225-40, esp. pp. 226-33.

2. *Sustainability: Economics, Ecology and Justice* (Maryknoll, N.Y.: Orbis Books, 1992), p. 1.

ers, especially Buddhists. The year 1973 marks the first of his many inter-religious publications, this one born of a dialogue between Nagarjuna and Whitehead. These dialogical explorations into other religious worlds natu-rally led Cobb to a theological reflection on what he was doing. His first essay dealing with the challenge of religious pluralism for Christian theology appeared in 1982 (and is the lead chapter in this collection). His already men-tioned, ground-breaking book, *Beyond Dialogue*, which unlike most books of this genre explores both the theological theory and the actual praxis of dialogue, appeared in this same year.

And so Cobb can declare, in the concluding chapter of this book, that the "two important concerns [that] have shaped much of my work in the past thirty years" have been "religious pluralism" and the "global crisis." The way these two concerns have shaped Cobb's theology provides the heuristic framework, as it were, for the manner in which I am ordering and interpret-ing these essays on pluralism and dialogue. In his efforts to understand and learn from religious pluralism, Cobb, as we shall see, is resolutely submissive to his commitment to respect the particularity and the alterity of other reli-gious ways; in no way does he allow himself to hold up his, or any "univer-sal," perspective or criterion of truth as normative for all. But in his equally resolute submission to "find alternatives" to the global crises facing all humankind and all religions, he is also committed, personally and at least implicitly, to directing the dialogue toward the resolution of the global threats. In balancing these two central concerns, Cobb eventually reveals, I think, that his concern for the welfare of the planet has a certain existential and epistemological priority. How to prevent global catastrophes supplied the criteria by which, as he admits, he reordered all his priorities. The way this reordering took shape, perhaps even unconsciously to Cobb himself, in his efforts to balance his commitments to religious pluralism and to global concerns explains, I will suggest, the movement within Cobb's approach to other religions and to dialogue.

Let me briefly outline the movement I think I have detected in Cobb's the-ology of religious pluralism and dialogue.

BEYOND ABSOLUTISM TOWARD RELIGIOUS TRANSFORMATION

During the first stage of Cobb's efforts to carry on a dialogue with persons of other religious paths—and to figure out why and how a Christian should go about such a dialogue—a central concern for him seems to have been to urge everyone involved in such dialogues to move beyond what we are call-ing "absolutism." This would mean anything within a believer's or scholar's approach to others that might block a genuine openness to the other. Convinced as he was that interreligious dialogue is beneficial, even necessary, Cobb also was convinced that if such conversation between believers is going to take place, it has to start with authentic listening to each other. Whatever prevents such listening is what I'm calling an *absolute* position.

The absolute positions beyond which Cobb seeks to move are found not only in religious claims to possess the only true revelation or the truth to which all other truths must submit. It can also be lurking in scholarly claims to know where the dialogue is going, or should go, or in models for dialogue that lay out the common ground for the dialogue, or the underlying unity behind or ahead of all the diverse religious traditions. As we'll see in the following essays, Cobb can be just as critical of his fellow scholars as he is of his fellow believers when either of them claims to know it all. He is particularly pointed in the warnings he raises for his friends in the academy who endorse the so-called pluralist model for understanding religious diversity: in their proposals for common ground, or a common goal, or even a common Absolute, they are sliding down the slippery slopes of absolutism; they're fitting the diversity of the other into their own slots before they truly listen to and embrace that diversity.

During this period, as throughout all his theological labors, Cobb remained convinced of what had become clear to him during his early days at the University of Chicago when he sat at the feet of philosopher Richard McKeon: that every grasp of truth and every proclamation of what is so is always *facilitated*, but also *limited*, by the historical, cultural (later he would add, linguistic) context in which it is made. Place-bound as all truth is, we cannot absolutize the truth of one place over all others. There are many places, and thus many perceptions of truth. In this sense, Cobb was a resolute postmodernist before the term became fashionable.

But from the start, he transgressed the boundaries of contemporary postmodern proclamations when he went on to affirm the *full relativity* of all truth claims: every affirmation, every religious truth, is relative not only in the sense of being *limited*, but also in the sense of being potentially *relatable* to other truth claims. What we know may only be a piece of the truth, but that piece can be linked to, and therefore enhanced by, other pieces. But to make this linking possible, everyone involved in the conversation must be not only aware of the limitations of their own perspectives but also truly open to the limited perspectives of others. In fact, in one of the essays of this first period, Cobb makes the unusual (for him) assertion that the one "relatively objective norm" for dialogue that he would ask all participants to endorse before they enter the dialogue is to recognize that there's more to truth than what they already know. In affirming what one already knows, but in opening oneself to what the other knows, everyone can very well end up knowing more! To make this possible, however, Cobb tells us in the final essay of this book, there should be no "a priori limitation on openness."

And the envisioned results of such a conversation of religious believers who seek to move beyond absolutism in genuine openness to each other would be, Cobb hopes, the *transformation* of all members of the community of religions. He can even boldly speak of a "Buddhized Christianity" and a "Christianized Buddhism"; religious communities, like friends, will remain what they are but at the same time be thoroughly different because of the friendship. Such a transformation of religions, Cobb suspects, is necessary. It's necessary not only because from his process perspective we stay alive only if we change and we change through relationships, but also because after his 1969 "turning point," Cobb gradually came to the conviction that for religions to be able to respond meaningfully and creatively to the global challenges facing them all, they were in need not only of *interpretation* but of *transformation* as well.[3] Interpretation leads to a *deeper* understanding of oneself; transformation calls for *new* understanding and, especially, new ways of acting. Interpretation requires introspection, but for transformation, one needs conversation.

During this period, Cobb worked out the basic ingredients of a Christology that would support a dialogue seeking to move beyond absolutism toward transformation. The foundations for a more dialogical Christology were laid in his 1975 book, *Christ in a Pluralistic Age*.[4] Here he described "Christ" as the principle or lure of transformation pervading history and even the universe. Jesus was the incarnation of that transformative, creative energy. How such a Christology motivates and guides Christians in their confrontation with religious pluralism is spelled out clearly and provocatively in a dictum that Cobb formulated during this period: "Jesus is the Way that is open to other Ways." To be a follower of this Jesus the Christ is certainly to have a firm place to stand (the firmness of that place will become more important for Cobb in the following period); but it also means, paradoxically, that one is called to radical openness to others. "Securely rooted" but at the same time "radically open"—this is the difficult but exciting journey Jesus as the Christ calls his followers to embrace. Cobb presses the provocation when he goes on to say that the openness is to be so radical that a Christian must be ready, at least theoretically if not imaginatively, to give up Christ if one is led to do so by following Christ. As a Christian, Cobb can't imagine that happening; but such is the trusting, no-holds-barred openness to which Jesus invites his disciples.

BEYOND RELATIVISM TOWARD WORLD TRANSFORMATION

But the turning point of 1969 continued to turn—and to generate new energies and directions in Cobb's professional life. As he himself describes it, one of the most fundamental and enduring shifts in this turn originated from his jolting realization of a "dualism" within his own work as a theologian— a dualism between systematic theology and ethics. He had worked with a strict boundary line between his politics and his theology. While Cobb continued to make a clear distinction between ethics and theology, he came to see that to separate them was to pull the plug on both of them. What brought him to this insight was his head-on encounter with the suffering state of the

3. Griffin, p. 236.
4. Philadelphia: Westminster Press.

world: the recognition "that the whole human race was on a collision course with disaster shook me out of this dualism."[5] His 1982 book, *Process Theology as Political Theology*, was his effort to reveal and redeem this dualism; there must be an indissoluble bond between process thought and politics, between theology and ethics.

While Cobb's publications since the early 70s clearly show how much ethics both deconstructed and reconstructed his theology (during the 70s his ethical concerns were focused on ecology, whereas in the 80s the focus was broadened to include economics and politics), this animating union between ethics and politics did not, on the surface at least, become a similar union between ethics and dialogue. Both during the 70s and 80s, in his actual dialogues with others and in his theory or theology of dialogue, Cobb did not seem to detect, or announce, a similar dualism between the ethical and the dialogical. The necessary and fruitful links that he discovered between *process theology* and *political theology* did not reflect, it seemed, any similar links between an *interreligious dialogue* and what we might call a *political dialogue*.

This is not to say that Cobb went about his conversations with other religious persons in an utterly spiritual, theological, or a-worldly fashion. On the contrary, in the final chapter of this volume, he confesses that the central energy and purpose in this effort to reach out to the world of religious others has been a commitment to "the indivisible salvation of the world" as that salvation is represented in the key Christian symbol of the *basileia tou theou*—the Reign of God. Cobb's hopes were that the coming together of religions would be a determining contribution to diverting nations and peoples from their "collision course with disaster." But this was Cobb's personal, and Christian, motivation and goal. It was not necessarily shared by others in the interreligious conversation. And Cobb was careful not to suggest in any way that they had to share these ethical concerns for the ecological and social well-being of the world. He maintained his wariness about any effort to impose a common agenda, or a common ground, as the context or condition for the dialogue. Such wariness continued to be grounded in his twofold awareness: philosophically, of the historical conditioning of all knowledge, which rules out any absolute universal truth claims, and historically, of Christianity's track record of imperialism, which resulted from Christians' claim to have the common universal truth that would unlock the truth of all religions and cultures. The slippery slopes of absolutism remain a constant danger for Cobb throughout his life and career.

And yet, in his final remarks for this volume, he also confesses that his secret hopes that the interreligious dialogue would indeed promote the Reign of God were often realized without his non-Christian brothers and sisters realizing it. (Might Karl Rahner observe that they were "anonymous" contributors to God's Reign?) Cobb readily admits that it is not necessary that

---

5. *Process Theology as Political Theology* (Philadelphia: Westminster Press, 1982), pp. x-xi.

others share my hope for a world in which God's purposes are fulfilled in order to contribute to the coming of that world. Even without an explicitly recognized ethical agenda, even without a shared political or social common ground, interreligious dialogue can contribute to saving the world.[6] So even though Cobb's 1969 turning point, in which he tried to bond ethics and theology, did not explicitly extend to calling for similar bonds between ethics and dialogue, implicitly the bonding was taking place.

But toward the end of the 80s and beginning of the 90s, there seems to be a movement in Cobb's understanding of pluralism and dialogue in which what was implicit and hoped-for became more explicit and called-for. I'm not saying that this was a clearly conscious move on Cobb's part, but it does seem a quite evident, verifiable move. As the 80s became the 90s, Cobb begins to call for, or at least to work for, a closer link between interreligious dialogue and ethics, similar to the links he had been pursuing for the previous two decades between Christian theology and ethics. Though the reasons for this movement are not readily evident, I suspect that it was catalyzed not only by the worsening state of the world but also—maybe primarily—by what in Cobb's eyes was the worsening *state of the academy.*

The primary indication of this further turning of Cobb's fundamental turn of 1969 can be found, I suggest, in his December 1988 address to the American Academy of Religion. That one of his pupils and close friends could call this talk a "jeremiad"[7] indicates both how grave was the message and how uncharacteristic it was of someone whose criticisms usually come forth closer to the style of Gandhi than of Jeremiah. In his remarks, Cobb indicted his fellow scholars in the academy for not responding to "the fate of the earth." They were playing their scholarly fiddles while the planet and its sentient beings were perishing. The bedrock reason for this lack of responsibility has two strata: the debilitating and isolating fragmentation of the various disciplines within the academic community, and the ethically hamstringing effects of a postmodern awareness that so stresses diversity and social-construction that it undermines any effort for a common front.

This AAR "jeremiad," in its essential content, is found in chapter 6 of this collection; in it Cobb searches for "responses to relativism" and addresses his admonitions not only to his colleagues in the academy but also to his colleagues in the interreligious dialogue. He urges both academicians and religious practitioners to work together toward a "wide consensus as to [the] nature and importance [of global problems] and how they can be resolved." Adherents and scholars of religions can share, he suggests, an "ultimate concern that we leave to our descendants a habitable planet." This is why Cobb, in an essay published five years after his AAR address, could fundamentally endorse Hans Küng's "contribution to interreligious dialogue" insofar as

---

6. See chapter 11 below on Hans Küng's contributions in this area.

7. "Toward an Emancipatory Wisdom," in *Theology and the University: Essays in Honor of John B. Cobb, Jr.* (Albany: State University of New York Press, 1991), p. 127.

that contribution has taken recent shape in Küng's call for a "global project" that all the religions can communally endorse and share (though, as this essay indicates, Cobb has a number of tactical criticisms of the way Küng carries out his project).

That Cobb's approach to religious pluralism and dialogue was expanding from his concerns about absolutism to include equally virulent concerns about relativism is also borne out in the way he understands the Christian contribution to the dialogue. This is evident in the two christological essays from the first half of the 90s. If in the first part of this collection, he was worried about Christians swinging the club of imperialism, now he is concerned that they might have nothing to swing at all. If earlier, Christians engaged in dialogue didn't listen enough, now it seems that they are not talking enough; at least, they are not talking about what needs to be said. In an essay admittedly written mainly for a Christian audience, Cobb can sound downright evangelical: "We live in a time when the world needs Christ as never before." There are ingredients in the vision of the Nazarene prophet that our world, riddled with greed and injustice, is in sore need of hearing. Thus, Cobb now makes clear that to deny the absoluteness of the Christian message is not to deny its universal relevance. Or in more technical parlance, what is limited by its own "social-construction" can (sometimes must?) still be meaningful (if properly communicated) for other social-constructions.

But even though Cobb, since the 90s, is more sharply concerned about the connections between ethics and dialogue, even though now he is more aware of how a non-relativistic dialogue can transform the world (just as he earlier envisioned how a non-absolutist dialogue can transform the religions), still he points out in the essays of this second section (especially chapter 10) and in his final remarks that he has never himself proposed that ethics or a commitment to global issues be the sole common ground for interreligious dialogue. One deep-reaching reason for this is Cobb's recognition and reminder that if there is going to be an interreligious ethical commitment to help solve the woes of the world, that commitment is going to have to come out of the religious experience and traditions of each community; thus, to focus the dialogue too much on ethics and so forget the need to talk also about the religious convictions that sustain ethics is in the long run to pursue an unsustainable ethics.

Cobb's warnings not to limit the dialogue to any one common ground is also consistent with and faithful to what has always been his philosophical and theological conviction: that to insist on establishing common ground or common agendas for the dialogue *before* the dialogue begins is to put no trespassing signs on the total openness that all dialogue needs. To speak "outside of a confessional context" about truth or what is common is extremely dangerous. If there is to be any common ground or criteria for the interreligious dialogue, let it spring forth from the dialogue itself.

And that, to Cobb's candid surprise, is what has happened, or is happening! He admits this, happily and gratefully, in his concluding reflections.

What during the 70s and 80s might have been unthinkable or out of place around the tables of dialogue has taken shape during the 90s: in a variety of forms, in different contexts around the world, "dialogue among the religious traditions centering on the practical needs of the world is happening." More and more, religious people who give witness to an imponderable, uncontrollable, even incommensurable diversity of religious beliefs and practices are also, naturally and spontaneously, recognizing that a common ground on which to start, and a common source from which to guide, their interreligious conversation and cooperation is what Cobb described as a shared "ultimate concern that we leave to our descendants a habitable planet." Viewing such a turn of events that are calling religions to a shared globally responsible dialogue, Cobb admits with typical honesty and humility, "I should have called for this earlier...." One, however, wonders whether this natural movement of many religious communities toward a dialogue about the eco-human well-being of the planet has not resulted more from those who, like John Cobb, have respectfully practiced such a dialogue without expressly preaching it than from those who, like Hans Küng and myself, have often allowed our preaching to overshadow our practicing.

I leave to the reader, and to John Cobb, the final assessment about the way I have interpreted the content and especially the movement within his understanding of the plurality of religions and of their capacity to learn from and work with each other. Whatever the validity of my interpretation, these essays can stand on their own as both a monument and as a roadsign:

- As a monument, they attest to a man who, like few others within the Christian theological community, has explained and exemplified how dialogue among religions can transform both individuals and communities.
- As a roadsign, these essays show how John Cobb's thinking, both past and recent, continues to raise the key questions and indicate the promising directions that must be explored if the religious communities of the world are to succeed in avoiding both absolutism and relativism and so promote the betterment of themselves and the world.

PART I

Beyond Absolutism

Toward Religious Transformation

1

The Religions

Where We Are

In this opening essay, written from the perspective of the early 80s, Cobb offers a panoramic overview of Christian attitudes toward other religious communities. One is impressed, maybe even overwhelmed, by the diversity of these attitudes. All of them fluctuate, as Cobb points out, between the two poles of the brilliance of God's revelation in Jesus Christ on the one hand, and the evident energies and beauty of the non-Christian world on the other. Still, as one follows Cobb's tour through these Christian efforts to affirm the brilliance of Christ and at the same time recognize the "other lights" (Karl Barth's term), one can note how, for the most part, the light of Christ has either absorbed or, in the end, snuffed out the other lights. Those few Christian efforts that have not done this have landed on the other extreme end: they have diminished the distinctiveness of the Christian light.

For Cobb, this sets the agenda and the challenge for contemporary Christian relations with other religions: how to genuinely affirm and learn from the other without losing one's own identity and distinctive voice in the conversation. How to open oneself to the real possibility of being transformed in the process, without ending up deformed. Cobb ends this essay by recognizing that to move beyond "absolute claims" of truth toward transformation through the other is always to expose oneself to the dangers of deformation.

That such a dangerous process is, however, necessary and that the dangers can be avoided and overcome is the assurance that authentic faith in Christ provides the Christian. To question the security of absolute truth and to embrace the adventure of transformation through the others is integral to the following of Christ.

P.F.K.

This essay first appeared in Peter Hodgson and Peter King, eds. Christian Theology: An Introduction to Its Tradition and Tasks *(Philadelphia: Fortress, 1982), pp. 353–76.*

TO BE A CHRISTIAN seems to entail the judgment that being a Christian is superior to being anything else. To display this superiority has often been seen as the task of Christian apologetics. This has not necessarily meant a claim that Christians are morally or humanly superior to others, but it has normally meant the conviction that the God from whom alone salvation can be received is known or present to Christians as nowhere else.

Today this habit of thought is severely challenged by increasing awareness of the many impressive ways in which human beings are organizing their lives and seeking and finding truth, wholeness, or salvation. To more and more Christians, approaching others with the assumption of the superiority of their own religion seems false to Christian love. Is it not better to listen appreciatively to what others have learned and experienced than to assume that we already know better?

But this gives rise to problems too. Does it mean that we abandon the conviction that Jesus Christ is the savior or liberator of all? Do we become relativistic, accepting private decisions of others as beyond criticism? Does this charitable tolerance extend to everyone—to racists, for example? Or does our faith provide grounds to decide in advance what the limits of respect should be? If so, are we being truly open to those others whom we are called to love and who judge by other norms?

Prior to World War I, the problem was often formulated as that of the finality or absoluteness of Christianity. Can we appreciate the achievements of other religious traditions and still evaluate them from the Christian point of view? Has Christianity in principle already grasped the final truth, or must we recognize that Christianity is just one way of believing and living alongside others who have equal justification for their exclusive claims?

In the nineteenth century the problem was formulated in terms of Christianity and other religions. Philosophers of religion sought the essence of the universal human phenomenon of religion, and theologians undertook to show that this essence attained its purest and most perfect form in Christianity. The category "religion" thus became the basic context within which such matters were discussed. Theologians understood their task as explaining the beliefs of the Christian religion. Following this understanding, colleges and universities have developed departments of religion.

Nevertheless, this approach has become problematic in the period since World War I. Karl Barth, the most important theologian of this period, pointed out that faith has to do with what God has done in Jesus Christ and is not merely a particular expression of a universal human religiousness. Such religiousness is real enough, even among Christians. But to study Christianity as one form of religion among others is to miss its character as response to the unique act of God.

Since Barth, the category "religion" has become more and more problematic. Barth understood religion as the human effort to attain salvation, and he supposed that apart from Jesus Christ all people are engaged in some such effort. Hence he did not challenge the use of the category in relation to the great traditions of Asia. But representatives of these traditions have noted that religion is a Western category imposed upon them, often quite uncongenial from their point of view and grouping together quite disparate phenomena. If we continue to speak of "the religions," it is partly because of custom and partly because of the lack of consensus about a better way to communicate.

As a result of theological developments typified by Karl Barth, theology separated itself from the context of the academic study of religion and the religions. This discipline was pursued in colleges and universities as comparative religion or the history of religions, while theology was largely studied in seminaries. But theologians have recognized in recent years that they cannot continue to ignore the other religious traditions, and some historians of religion, notably Wilfred Cantwell Smith, have recognized that their discipline is impoverished when it turns away from the normative question of religious truth and value. As a result, the relation of theology to the history of religions is now in a healthy flux.

Christian reflection on "the religions" may come last in books, but it informs thought on all Christian doctrines. Awareness of living Judaism, for example, must influence the way we speak of Jesus Christ. Awareness of Buddhist saints who do not believe in God must affect the way we think of the relation of God and holiness.

In some respects these problems are new. The encounter with the great traditions of India and China alters the context in which Christians think, and this was not important before the sixteenth century. The nineteenth century introduced a new awareness of the sociohistorical conditioning of all thought. In the twentieth century, Westerners are finally abandoning the deep-seated assumption of the superiority of Christian culture.

But from the beginning, Christians have been aware of religious people who were not Christian. At least some of the available options for viewing these people were forged already in the early centuries of the church. The next section will deal with these classic formulations, while the following section will consider how the broadening of horizons and the rise of historical consciousness deepened the problem and called forth new solutions. Finally, we shall return to the present situation and suggest the character of faithful response today.

THE DOCTRINE IN ITS CLASSIC FORMULATION

There is no orthodox doctrine about the religions. Indeed, there is no classic position on the subject thus posed. This is partly because the category "religions" was not employed until modern times. It is also because reflection about most of the living movements we call religions was not central to Christian theology. The primary focus has usually been on people as individuals who believe, or do not believe, in Jesus Christ. Nevertheless, attitudes toward and beliefs about Judaism, pagan religions, and Islam are expressed in classical Christian literature. Moreover, in the early modern period the traditions of China, especially Confucianism, assumed some importance. The fact that these reflections were not subsumed under the common heading "religions" before the modern period may have been an advantage.

Determinants of Christian Attitudes toward Others

One element in shaping the attitudes of Christians toward others is a virtually universal tendency to divide the world into "us" and "them." Just as Jews opposed themselves to Gentiles and Greeks to barbarians, so also Christians have opposed themselves to the heathen or infidels. This fact and its expression in Christian history and contemporary society is of great historical and sociological importance. But theologically our interest is more in the ways in which Christian thought has given a distinct cast to this universal tendency.

Three themes are important here. First, Christianity has been an intensely missionary movement. Since the "us-them" distinction for Christians was not based on given characteristics such as ancestry, it could be overcome. "They" could and should join "us." Their ignorance of the salvation to which we witness can only be overcome as we carry the gospel to them. Hence Christians have at times engaged in heroic efforts to evangelize others. The ideal and goal has been one of the union of all people in acknowledgment of Jesus Christ as Lord and Savior.

Second, the same understanding that leads toward overcoming all natural barriers "in Christ" leads to disappointment and even anger when others who hear the word of what God has done for them in Christ are indifferent or reject it. When the distinction of "we" and "they" is established by race or even culture, "we" may feel contempt for "them," but we do not regard them as individually to blame for their condition. But when, as with Christians, "we" are convinced that once "they" have heard only stubbornness and willful viciousness prevent their believing, then the attitude toward them can become much more harsh. Christians have at times exercised great cruelty toward others in the endeavor to convert them or to make them suffer for their refusal.

Third, most Christians have recognized that there is much of value in the lives, thought, and culture of those who are not Christian. The earliest believers understood themselves to be the heirs of Abraham and the prophets, the true inheritors and continuers of Israel. As participants in Greek culture, most believers in the Mediterranean world affirmed much of that inheritance as well. Many Christians were convinced that their Savior, Jesus Christ, was one with the universal divine principle, the Word or Logos, that informed all people and all cultures. The prologue of the Gospel of John is the *locus classicus* for this immensely important aspect of Christian teaching. When this is emphasized, the person who is not a Christian is approached not merely as unbeliever but also as one in whom and through whom the everlasting Word acts and speaks.

These three motifs—readiness to extend Christian fellowship, enmity toward those who refuse the offer, and respect for the work of the Word even where Jesus Christ is not acknowledged—have produced varied and inconsistent doctrines through the centuries of Christian history. They serve primarily to relate Christians to other individuals who are not Christians, but they also affect Christian understanding of the religions.

Interpretations of Judaism, Paganism, Islam, and Confucianism

Theologically, the most developed understanding has been in relation to Judaism. At first the synagogue and the church shared a common scripture. Even when Christians canonized additional writings, they retained the Jewish scriptures as well. Christians and Jews viewed one another more as heretics than as adherents of different religions. That is, each saw the claims of the other as a false reading of the scriptures.

Central to Christian self-understanding was the view that the Jews were in error. Christians claimed to be the heirs of the promises of the shared scriptures, and that meant that the Jews could not be the elect people. The Jewish rejection of Jesus had to be shown as based on error and even sin. Christian theologians and preachers did not differ substantially in their denunciation of Judaism. They differed only in that some were more vitriolic than others. In relation to Jews, although the door to Christian conversion was always open, it was the second of the three motifs listed above that dominated. Christian theology encouraged the persecution of Judaism.

Theologians did not, however, support the extermination of Judaism. Whereas they often encouraged the annihilation of heresy and other competitors with orthodox Christianity, they supported a narrowly circumscribed legal status for Judaism. Jews were to exist in a condition of misery until the end as a negative witness to the truth of Christianity. At the end they would finally be forced to acknowledge the perverseness of their error. Of course such subtle limits to the approved persecution of the Jews did not prevent popular riots, Crusader massacres, and pogroms. And it was often Christian theologians and saints who then prevented the government from making reparations to the Jews.

Greco-Roman paganism required a more differentiated response. On the one hand, Christians joined Jews in refusing to participate in what they deemed superstition and idolatry. They would not, for example, acknowledge the deity of the Caesar. They opposed magical and occult practices, and when they came to power, they outlawed these practices.

They were more tolerant toward cultic acts of political religion. These were not outlawed at once, and there were even instances of Christian emperors participating in public ceremonies at pagan temples. Nevertheless, once in power, Christianity moved to displace these observances.

The great challenge lay in the philosophical schools, especially Neo-platonism. It was in relation to these movements that the doctrine of the universal work of the divine Word was employed most positively. Where Neoplatonism flourished in separation from magical and occult practices, as in Alexandria, Christian theologians recognized it as an admirable adversary, and it was allowed to continue under the Christian empire.

Today we might make the mistake of supposing that since Neoplatonism was "only" a philosophy it would not constitute a competitor to Christianity. This is to read back into the Roman world the fragmentation of our own. Philosophy is now one academic discipline alongside others, and Christian theology has largely accepted a role as another such discipline. But then philosophy and theology both claimed to offer the encompassing truth and to point the way to salvation. Among thoughtful people, Neoplatonism was Christianity's greatest competitor for total allegiance.

Christian theologians respected Neoplatonism and learned from it. Indeed, they incorporated much of it into their own theology. The Christianity that won the struggle for the mind of the later Roman world was a Neoplatonized Christianity. In the competition between Christianity and Neoplatonism, Christianity won because it was able to assimilate the wisdom of Neoplatonism, whereas Neoplatonism was unable or unwilling to assimilate the wisdom of Christianity.

The rise of Islam raised a different question for Christians. Whereas Judaism and paganism were internal challenges within Christendom, Islam was a powerful military threat which conquered half the Christian world. The chief Christian response was at first defense, and later the offensive reactions of the Crusades and the reconquest of Spain. In both defense and offense, Muslims were viewed chiefly as infidels.

Nevertheless, there was some theological response. The cultural and intellectual superiority of Islam over Western Christianity made it a conduit of scholarship to the West. Especially important for medieval theology was the new understanding of the philosophy of Aristotle. This philosophy seemed to embody a knowledge which could be common to Jews, Muslims, and Christians. For example, Christianity, Judaism, Islam, and much of Greek philosophy were seen as sharing a belief in the unity of God. This gave encouragement to the idea of natural theology, the view that human reason alone can establish many of the truths of faith. This idea was worked out most fully and influentially by Thomas Aquinas. For him, natural theology required completion by truths which could be known only by supernatural revelation. But in the seventeenth and eighteenth centuries the truths that are known by reason came to be regarded as all-sufficient and as the norm by which to judge the several positive religions. This normative natural religion is basically an ethical monotheism free from historical particularity and nonethical regulations.

The gradually increasing knowledge of China, beginning with Marco Polo, introduced Confucianism to the Christian consciousness. On the whole, the image of China in Christendom was quite positive. Hence the Christian attitude toward Confucianism was affirmative. Nevertheless, it was clear that Confucianism was not Christianity, and Christian faith was understood to call for the conversion of the Chinese.

In the sixteenth and seventeenth centuries, Jesuit missionaries achieved positions of influence in the Chinese court, and Catholic Christianity won a considerable following in many parts of the country. The success of the Christian mission posed problems analogous to those of the church in the Roman Empire. To what extent must Chinese culture and religious practice be rejected by converts to Christianity, and to what extent could they be assimilated? For example, could Christians participate in Confucian rites honoring the ancestors and especially Confucius himself?

Most of the Jesuit missionaries wanted to develop a Confucian Christianity analogous to the Neoplatonic Christianity that won the Roman world. In this effort they at times had support from the papacy. But during a century of struggle, beginning in the middle of the seventeenth century and continuing into the eighteenth (the so-called rites controversy), the papal position became more rigid. Confucian practices were proscribed, and tolerant missionaries were punished. Christianity in China was thereby limited to the status of a foreign religion.

It is interesting to see that in this struggle "religion" became a crucial issue. If Confucianism, with its pervasive influence on Chinese culture, was a religion, then Christians must refuse participation. If, however, the Confucian rites and practices so integral to Chinese life could be viewed as "political," then the church need not oppose them. The friendly Manchu emperor K'ang-hsi officially supported the Jesuit argument that they were political, and it was the refusal of the pope to accept this position that led to the loss of imperial support for the Christian mission.

These brief comments about the Christian relation to Judaism, paganism, Islam, and Confucianism should make clear that there was no one Christian view of "the religions." Each religious tradition posed its own problems for the church, and there was little effort to generalize. By the nineteenth century, however, the situation had changed. Christians understood themselves in a global context in which there were other religions. The understanding of these other religions became for many the central issue in the understanding of Christianity itself.

CHALLENGES AND CONTRIBUTIONS
OF MODERN CONSCIOUSNESS

Post-Enlightenment Views of the Religions

Immanuel Kant, who climaxed the rationalism of the Enlightenment, also effected a "Copernican revolution" in philosophy which paved the way for radical historical thinking. Whereas the other rationalists had thought of reason as a means of learning objective truth about an objective world, Kant argued that the mind has the more basic function of constituting a rationally ordered world. Although he generally thought of this constituting activity as that of human mind as such at all times and places, increasing knowledge of the diversity of cultures led his followers to see that in many respects human beings have constituted their worlds quite differently. The study of the ways the human mind has developed thus assumed primacy. The discussion of religion shifted from an effort to discover the universal rational religion to an evaluation of the actual diversity of religions.

G.W.F. Hegel undertook to read the entire history of religion as one linear movement. This did not mean that he failed to recognize the contemporaneous existence of a variety of religions, but he distinguished the creative moment of each from its sheer continuation. He saw in these creative moments a continuous development of spirit itself, which is at once divine and human. He discerned this creative movement as beginning in China, moving to India, Persia, Israel, Greece, and Rome, and finally coming to its fulfillment in Germanic Protestantism and Western European culture. One of the questions with which Hegel wrestled philosophically was whether religion itself, including Christianity, had like art now become "for us a thing of the past."

Although Hegel opened up whole new vistas for thinking about the religions and continues to be an immensely influential figure, few have followed him in his linear view of the relation of Eastern and Western religions. Others have also discerned patterns of progress in religion, but they have acknowledged the continuing and competitive validity of several forms more or less at the same level. Usually this is done by seeing all religions as expressive of a common essence. For example, Schleiermacher saw the essence of all religion in the feeling of absolute dependence. He could then distinguish primitive from developed expressions of religion in a linear fashion, but he could also recognize that there exists today a multiplicity of high religions, specifically Judaism, Islam, and Christianity. All these are marked by monotheism. Schleiermacher distinguishes them first according to their aesthetic and ethical orientations, classifying Islam as aesthetic and Judaism and Christianity as ethical. He describes the two religious forms in such a way as to imply the superiority of the ethical over the aesthetic, and then proceeds to display the superiority of Christianity over Judaism on the basis of idolatrous remnants in the latter.

By the end of the nineteenth century it was no longer possible so easily to relegate the religions of India and China to inferior status as having failed to achieve monotheism. If Christianity was to be shown to be the supreme form of religion, a much fuller wrestling with the self-understanding of other religious traditions would be required.

Ernst Troeltsch devoted extensive attention to the problem of what he termed "the absoluteness of Christianity." In his book by that title, he argues that religion, which he regarded as the manifestation of the divine life in human history, achieves its purest and most universal form in Christianity. He supports his argument by showing how expressions other than Christian are closely bound to particular nations or cultures, or are primarily philosophical in character. The Christian understanding of God's self-manifestation in persons breaks these boundaries.

However, Troeltsch himself could not rest with this formulation. His further studies of Christianity forced him to recognize the great diversity of Christian forms and the extent to which all of them are culture-bound. His studies also forced him to acknowledge the capacity of other traditions, especially Buddhism and Hinduism, to transcend national and cultural limits. Hence there was no longer any basis for persisting in the claim to Christian absoluteness. Although religion exists as a distinct element in each tradition, in its actual forms it cannot be abstracted from the culture as a whole. If we are to compare religions, we must compare the civilizations in which they are embodied and expressed. We have no criteria independent of the diversity of cultural values by which to make an objective judgment. We must accept Christianity as absolute for us, while recognizing that other religions may be absolute for other cultures.

Other scholars attempted to arrive at an understanding of religion on more objective grounds. Nathan Söderblom maintained that the idea of God or a supreme being is far more limited than the experience of the holy. Rudolf Otto came to a similar conclusion and declared the holy to be a universal category of human experience. Otto argued that Christianity expresses the holy in a distinctive and thoroughly ethicized way, thus making an argument for its superiority. Yet the effect of his work was primarily to turn attention from theological to phenomenological formulations. He illumined Christian beliefs by setting them in the context of the experience and beliefs of other religious communities. He also showed that religion is a necessary and universal feature of human experience, so that the question is not the justification of religion in a secular world but how it is best expressed.

It was the role of Karl Barth vigorously to reintroduce into this situation the perspective of the Reformers. More consistently even than they, he insisted upon a wholly christocentric mode of reflection. It is the task of the Christian to witness to what God has made known to us in Jesus Christ. This is both a "no" to all our human efforts to find saving truth apart from Christ and a "yes" to us as persons redeemed by Christ. Insofar as religion is to be understood as the human effort to attain salvation, it must be condemned. This goes as much for the Christian religion as for any other. Only as religion is understood as a human effort to respond to the divine self-revelation can a qualified affirmation be admitted.

In any case, Barth calls for a separation of theology from the study of religion. That study is completely justified just as any science is. Christians are free to study all human phenomena, including religion. Because in studying religion they have no need to show that one religion is better than another, the study of religion can attain a fuller objectivity and openness. But all this throws no light on Christian doctrine. The theologian looks only to Christ.

For two generations most Christian theology followed the direction pointed by Barth even when theologians have not agreed with him in detail. That is, for half a century the work of Christian theology was carried on outside the context of history-of-religions. Those theologians who against Barth's advice continued to attend to other religions usually did so only to display the contrast between the religions and Christian faith as response to divine revelation. Emil Brunner argued that either the Christian must deny that Christian faith is a religion at all, or else assert that it is true religion in sharp contrast to all others as false. Of those holding this position, Hendrik Kraemer engaged in the most detailed and responsible study of other religions in order to support this fundamental contrast.

The opposition of revelation to human religion could also function to ally Christianity with secularization. If religion as a human phenomenon expresses a lack of faith in Christ, then the de-religionizing of the world is, from the Christian point of view, a gain. Dietrich Bonhoeffer called for a "religion-less" Christianity and a nonreligious hermeneutic of scripture. A tradition of secular Christianity emerged. More recently there have been powerful calls for a political interpretation of the gospel which will make clear the concrete meaning of liberation from the actual oppressions operative in our world. Meanwhile, Arend Th. van Leeuwen has attempted to show what the association of Christianity with secularization has meant in relation to other religions. In his view, Christianity supports the movements for secularization against all the traditional religions of Asia, and it sees these movements as implementing its own message. For this strand of Christian thinking, it is typically Marxism rather than other religions with which dialogue is important and alliance appropriate.

Continuing Efforts to Locate Christianity in the Horizon of Religion

Until recently most contemporary professional theologians have been caught up in this nonreligious interpretation of Christianity. However, on the fringes of theology the tradition of viewing Christianity within the horizon of religion has continued, and the work done there has had a great influence on the habits of mind and modes of thought of Christians, especially in the English-speaking world. An important expression of this approach was that of William Ernest Hocking, a philosopher and lay Christian. He called for Christians to adopt "the way of reconception." He defined religion as "a passion for righteousness, and for the spread of righteousness, conceived as a cosmic demand." He then argued that all religions, while sharing this common essence, develop different apprehensions of the truth. As they meet each other, each has much to learn from the others and in the process needs to reconceive its own truth. Thus each can grow toward an inclusive form. He believed that Christianity has a peculiar capacity to develop into such an inclusive religion. Later he came to understand religion in a more mystical way.

The understanding of the essence of religion as mystical experience has probably been the most influential in recent times, at least in the United States, despite its lack of acceptance among theologians. Aldous Huxley and Arnold Toynbee did much to popularize the view that all religions express in diverse ways the unitive experience of mysticism. More recently, this esoteric core of religions has been distinguished from their exoteric manifestations by Frithjof Schuon, seconded and supported by Huston Smith. Meanwhile it has had an important practical effect on the way Eastern religions have been approached, especially by such Roman Catholics as Thomas Merton.

Beginning with Vatican II, Roman Catholics have taken the lead in relating Christianity to other religions both in theory and in practice. For the first time the church has taken an official stand toward other religions. It did so with specific reference to Buddhism, Hinduism, Islam, and Judaism. In all cases it expressed a positive and friendly attitude. It has been the responsibility of its theologians to clarify the relation between this positive stance and the continuing insistence on the supernatural centrality of Christ and the importance of the church.

Karl Rahner has been the most important thinker to take up this task. He has developed the doctrine that implicit faith can be found outside the church and has introduced the category of the "anonymous Christian" to refer to those who have received this faith apart from the church. Faith is no less the work of God among anonymous Christians than among the people of the church. Further, the religions of the world are channels for expression of this faith and for its encouragement. They are thus instruments of salvation.

This does not lead to a relativistic attitude on the part of Christians. What is anonymous, inchoate, and fragmentary has been fully manifest in Jesus Christ. When the opportunity presents itself to enter the church in which this full truth is celebrated, it is the duty of the anonymous Christian to do so. When the church arrives, the other religions are no longer needed. But the approach to these other religions should be dialogical rather than polemical. Christianity can learn from them as well as teach them. All can gain from their mutual encounter with the possibility of moving toward convergence.

Of particular importance are the specific statements of Vatican II on Judaism. Although the Catholic Church never officially taught the responsibility of all Jews for the crucifixion of Jesus, much Christian theology and preaching had stated that the Jewish people as a whole are guilty. The Council repudiated this teaching and rejected anti-Semitism. This paved the way for an important and badly needed dialogue between Catholics and Jews.

The shift from polemic to dialogue in the Catholic Church, and the corresponding shift which has occurred in much of Protestantism, could be supported from a variety of theological points of view. In some cases dialogue has been a means of better understanding the community from which converts were sought. In others it has been conceived as a subtle approach to the conversion of the dialogue partner. In still others it has expressed the conviction that all comparative judgments as to the respective merits of different religions are objectionable. But whatever its motivation, it has had a pervasive effect upon the Christian view of other religions and the self-understanding of Christians. To view representatives of other religions as partners in dialogue is, provisionally at least, to see Christianity as one religious movement among others.

Paul Tillich is an interesting embodiment of this development. In principle his theology was always open to viewing Christianity in the context of the history of religions, since he recognized a universal revelation of God in all cultures and all religions. Following in the tradition of Schleiermacher, Troeltsch, and Otto, he viewed Christianity as a concrete realization of a universal dimension of human existence. He described this universal dimension as ultimate concern. In principle he was interested in how ultimate concern is expressed in all religions, but in fact he gave more attention to the movements that were most important in Europe during his formative years: humanism, communism, and fascism. These he called quasi-religions. He also struggled to formulate his distinctive theological position in relation to the dominant Barthian rejection of religion as the context of theological study. In his later years, however, he developed this interest, made personal contacts with Asian religions (especially Buddhism), and expressed regret that he had not developed his theology more fully in the context of the study of the religions. He saw that as the task for the future.

Wolfhart Pannenberg also represents a movement toward reestablishing the religions as the context for the understanding of Christianity. For him the universal characteristic of human beings which expresses itself everywhere is the anticipation of an end which will retrospectively give meaning to all that has been. The confirmation of this anticipation and the revelation of what it entails are to be found in the resurrection of Jesus, so that the history within which that event occurred is of central importance. But because it is of central importance for the whole world, it needs to be displayed as such in the context of universal history. Such a history is primarily the history of religions, and the Christian affirmation can only be vindicated as the resurrection of Jesus Christ can be shown to be the proleptic fulfillment of what is anticipated in all religions. This, in turn, can be done only as objective rational inquiry into all religions supports this interpretation. Hence Christian theology in the context of the history of religions becomes the theology of religion.

Both Tillich and Pannenberg claim a certain superiority or absoluteness for Christianity, but they avoid the types of claims made during the nineteenth century. For Tillich, the criterion of absoluteness of a religion is the success of its central symbol in pointing beyond itself to the absolute. It is the particular merit of the cross that it does so. Hence there is no argument for the superiority of the actual institutions and beliefs or moral practices of Christianity, only the claim that the central symbol of Christian faith is transparent to the absolute precisely insofar as it refuses its own absolutization.

For Pannenberg, in a similar way, all religions are incomplete and unfulfilled; this is as true of Christianity as of any other. What is important is that this incompleteness be recognized and that a religion point beyond itself to the ultimate fulfillment of all. Christian eschatology, in its doctrine of the universal resurrection, meets this requirement.

The Critique of "Religion"

The pursuit of dialogue with other traditions has raised critically the question mentioned at the outset as to the usefulness of the category "religion." Attention to "religion" has led either to viewing Christianity as one among many embodiments of a common essence or else to the contrasting of Christianity with all the others as a revelation or a movement of secularization. In either case the traditions other than Christianity are grouped together under a common rubric on the assumption that they are all engaged in essentially the same task. Generalizations about this common task are sought through phenomenology or anthropology or metaphysics. These generalizations then provide the categories with which the several movements are approached.

Wilfred Cantwell Smith has been the most vigorous critic of the category "religion." He too has noticed that it is a Western category that imposes meanings on other traditions which are alien to them. He has seen how often these meanings are pejorative. Also, if we begin with Western ideas about religion, the relationship of religions seems inevitably competitive. The use of this concept compartmentalizes us into adherents of a given number of movements, ignoring the actuality of personal faith as faith develops in diverse contexts and cultures. He recommends that we encounter people in terms of their faith, talking with them person-to-person instead of as adherents of different religions.

George Rupp develops one feature of this direction of thought. He points out that the divisions within what have been called religions are often greater than the differences among the religions. Liberal Christians may find more in common with liberal Buddhists than with fundamentalist Christians. Although Rupp does not issue a polemic against the category of religion, he does call for a typology that cuts across the lines that have been established when we think of the religions.

The actual practice of dialogue raises another issue of equal importance. This is the problem of understanding. Our normal way of understanding is to fit what we encounter into the established categories of our thought. If, for example, we have a theory of the nature and function of religion and then categorize some movement as a religion, we can study it, or enter into dialogue with its representatives, in order to learn the particular way in which that movement expresses what are already assumed to be universal characteristics of religion. The problem arises if our dialogue partners find our questions inappropriate and try to explain something that falls outside our established categories. We must then decide that our dialogue partners have not understood us, that they are ignorant of their own movements, or that our questions are not appropriate. If we make the latter decision, we will either try again to work out the appropriate questions from our own resources or try to learn how to question by listening to the unanticipated answers.

The actual situation always involves some of both, if the dialogue proceeds effectively. We cannot break altogether from established habits of mind, but our ways of questioning and thinking will be gradually altered as we listen attentively to those who have different habits. Nevertheless, some who have participated long and seriously in dialogue despair of achieving any real understanding of the deeply different modes of thought and experience with which they are confronted merely through dialogue.

Two alternatives are then possible. First, people may participate in the spiritual disciplines of the other tradition and come through them to experiences more analogous to those that are being described. This is an approach in which Roman Catholics have taken the lead. There is a Catholic Zen center near Tokyo where many Catholics have participated in Zen-type experiences. In the United States both Zen and yoga have been practiced in Catholic convents and monasteries. Certainly the result is an improved understanding of what Hindus and Buddhists are saying.

The second possibility is the employment of speculative philosophy. Although the dominant Western tradition has organized the world of thought and experience in ways quite alien to those of India and China, there are some thinkers who have protested against the dominant mode and have pointed to radical alternatives. Schopenhauer is an outstanding example in the early nineteenth century. He interpreted the normal Western consciousness as one in which reality is organized by the will, and he saw the consequences as eminently destructive. Hence in his own quest for truth and salvation he developed the idea of the annihilation of the will as the route to serenity and truth. He believed that this was what happened in some forms of mysticism. When he encountered fragments of Buddhist literature, he saw in nirvana the realization of that extinction of the will to which his own speculations had led him. Although he never became a scholar of Buddhism, his grasp of Buddhist soteriology was far deeper than that of the leading scholars of the nineteenth century.

In the twentieth century, Martin Heidegger performed a similar service for the West. After he turned away from the typically Western understanding of existence developed in *Being and Time*, his thought moved more and more into an actual immersion in being. The rational conceptual approach of Western thought gave way to an openness to being which allowed him to experience himself as one through whom being is. The tendencies toward substantialism and dualism in his early thought give way to a mode of realization of what one is as an instance of being. This is remarkably similar to a Mahayana Buddhist realization of what one is as an instance of Buddha-nature. The approximation of Heidegger to Buddhism was recognized by Heidegger himself and has been frequently appreciated by Oriental Buddhists.

Although Arthur Schopenhauer and Heidegger have contributed greatly to the possibility of Westerners understanding Eastern thought, a price is exacted for accepting their assistance. One can understand Buddhism only at the cost of rejecting the whole structure of Western thought and experience. If one would continue to be a Christian believer, it must be in terms of a very different form of Christianity than any that has yet appeared, a form so different that one must question its continuity with our biblical roots.

For this reason another type of philosophical project appears more promising for dialogue, although it is not yet as influential. A philosopher may attempt not so much to shift from one thought form to another as to show how a multiplicity of thought forms are equally valid. Ludwig Wittgenstein's language games lend themselves to this type of use. Also in other ways Wittgenstein's thought is suggestive of still largely unexplored approaches through which Westerners may be able to understand an Eastern mode of thought without being removed from their own.

The first major book which systematically developed a complementary view of East and West was F.S.C. Northrop's *Philosophy East and West*. Northrop argues that human experience begins with a differentiated aesthetic continuum, that is, an experience of such things as colors, shapes, and sounds spatially arranged. From this starting point the Greeks and the West as a whole shifted attention to differentiating forms within the continuum. They abstracted these and reflected about them. This made possible the development of mathematics, science, technology, and a whole style of rational, conceptual organization. On the other hand, the East regarded these differentiating forms as superficial and sought the deeper reality in the undifferentiated aesthetic continuum. While acceptance of Northrop's position does not make it immediately easy to grasp the experience of the undifferentiated aesthetic continuum, or to understand the language in which it is expressed, it does make intelligible to Westerners what is being discussed. We can see why a different language is needed. In principle it enables Westerners to cross over to a strange world of thought and life without repudiating their own. Meanwhile it enables Westerners to view the two worlds as complementary rather than mutually exclusive. Those who participate in dialogue on this basis will understand why they have much to learn and will also be freed from the assumption that dialogue is possible only on the basis of a common essence or shared experience.

Although Northrop's book is important as providing a way in which different traditions can be understood as complementary, it is inadequate and even misleading in its accounts both of Christianity and of the several Eastern traditions. Hence the task of clarifying the complementary contributions of East and West largely remains to be done. Northrop's own teacher, Alfred North Whitehead, offers possibilities for this task which were neglected by Northrop and which are now being explored.

Theological Reconceptualization and Mission

As Hocking saw, the encounter of traditions leads to reconceptualization in all. He thought this was grounded in a common essence, which he described first in terms of moral passion and subsequently more mystically. Many have continued to suppose that dialogue and mutual influence can occur only between movements that are grounded in the same experience or have the same end. However, we have now seen that dialogue can also occur among movements which have complementary modes of experience. Indeed, the significance of the reconceptualization that follows an encounter with expressions of a radically complementary mode of experience may be even greater.

Today the encounter of Christians with Eastern traditions has already led to extensive experimentation with new meditational disciplines, as noted earlier. It has led to the incorporation of Oriental insights into Western psychology and therapy and has made its mark in Western literature.

In the early centuries of Christianity a vital faith was able to reconceptualize itself in and through its engagement with the wisdom of Greece. In the process it so assimilated the achievements of Greek thought that philosophers could become Christian without abandoning the truths to which their thought had led them. Today it seems that the dialogical relation with the religions of Asia offers a similar opportunity for reconceptualization in and through engagement with Eastern wisdom.

Thus far most Christian theological reflection has been stimulated by encounter with the other "higher" religions, but within American culture there is a new interest in "primitive" religions as well. American Indian religions have been reappraised as having much to teach us. Both African theologians and black theologians in the United States have opened to us the achievement and power of traditional African religion. In their quest to understand the religious experience of women, some feminists have forced a reappraisal of what has long been dismissed and berated as witchcraft. It seems that Christianity must not only learn from the great religious traditions of Asia but also come to terms with aspects of religious experience which it has repressed and suppressed in its rise to ascendancy. The task of understanding these manifold phenomena and reinterpreting theology in light of them has scarcely begun.

The process of such reconceptualization need not be viewed as antithetical to the concern for evangelization. Just as it was a reconceived Christianity which could win classical philosophers to the faith, so it may be a reconceived Christianity alone which can win those who have deeply tasted of the wisdom of the East or gained new appreciation for what was once dismissed as primitive.

There remains a still deeper question. Is there alongside the mission of evangelization of individuals another and different mission to "the religions"? This is suggested in Roman Catholic theology. Hans Küng, for example, has spoken of the church's task to be of service to the other "religions." The extensive missiological literature on "Christian presence" in non-Christian cultures suggests a similar stance. Perhaps through presence, service, dialogue, and Christianity's own rigorous reconceptualization, the process of reconceptualization in other traditions can proceed in a way that involves their progressive incorporation of that truth to which Christians have uniquely witnessed.

ISSUES AND PROPOSALS

Ours is a time of fresh opportunity. We can pick up the struggles of the nineteenth-century theologians to understand their faith in the global context, and we can do so with many advantages. Today we are much more ready to learn from other cultures since the assumption of the superiority of European culture over others no longer grips us. Both through scholarship and through personal contacts we have access to other traditions which our theological ancestors lacked.

Our advantages can also be our dangers. We may be so ready to learn from others, so ashamed of the imperialistic attitudes of our past, and so unsure of our inherited beliefs that encounter with new wisdom causes us to abandon our own inheritance. Often the issue is formulated as that of narrow faithfulness to our tradition or broad openness to the whole of human experience. Those who opt for the latter may feel themselves to be separating from the heart of Christian faith. Christianity comes to be viewed even by such Christians as most fully represented in its narrowest and most doctrinaire members, those who would continue the most negative aspects of our tradition. Conservatives see the vagueness and loss of rootedness that often follow from an open and receptive attitude, and build their defenses higher. Thus the encounter with other religious traditions, while it offers fresh opportunity for growth and vigor, can lead to the sterile choice of narrow-minded bigotry or lukewarm compromising liberalism.

The theological challenge is to make clear another option, specifically the option of faith. That requires once again clarifying what Christian faith really is as faith in Jesus Christ. We must show that faith in Jesus Christ is neither an attitude of rigid defense of inherited doctrines and attitudes, nor the pretense of standing on some neutral ground and supposing that from that perspective we can judge the merits of all the world's great religious traditions.

Insofar as we lack faith, we will try to establish our own security. We may do so either by absolutizing our relative heritage or by claiming neutrality and objectivity. If we do have faith, we will abandon the effort to establish our own security, and will trust Christ instead. That means we can listen non-defensively to what others believe and learn from them even when they deny Christ. The more deeply we trust Christ, the more openly receptive we will be to wisdom from any source, and the more responsibly critical we will be both of our own received habits of mind and of the limitations and distortions of others.

In the early church, faith led to the assimilation and transformation of Hellenic wisdom. In the process, the biblical heritage was itself transformed. Like all historical occurrences this one was ambiguous. Much of what has handicapped Christian thought in the twentieth century came from this incorporation of Hellenic modes of thought in the early church. But much of what was learned was of permanent value, and a church that failed to learn from the best thought of that day might long since have perished in its rigid isolation.

Similarly, we today confront the wisdom of ancient traditions, especially those of India and China but also of traditions that go back before the rise of civilization. These show their power of attraction through their penetration of Western culture. Faith calls us to assimilate and transform this wisdom. In the process we will again be transformed. Such transformation will not be the consummatory end of Christian history. It too will be ambiguous. There is danger that we will lose sight of important elements of our own tradition and uncritically ingest what should be radically transformed. But to fail to open ourselves to this process will be to declare our lack of faith, our insistence on establishing our own security on the basis of what has happened in the past, our refusal of Christ's future. It will have the practical result of making Christian faith merely one among many options confronted by the next generation, and one that looks peculiarly parochial and closed. Better to live by faith and take the risk of making many mistakes than to make the unquestionable mistake of trusting our ideas instead of the living Christ.

Of all the encounters with other religious movements, the most disturbing for Christians is the encounter with Judaism. It is most disturbing because for so long we have falsely supposed that we have already adequately assimilated and transformed the wisdom of Judaism, and we have treated the ongoing Jewish community more as a fossil than as a living movement. It is disturbing also because of the growing awareness of the enormous suffering we have inflicted upon the Jews in the name of Jesus Christ. The one who for us is the symbol and bearer of liberation, transformation, and reconciliation is for the Jew the symbol of oppression, abuse, and persecution. The Jew knows the underside of our history, the half that we have repressed.

We have much yet to learn from Jewish wisdom. But what we have especially to gain from our encounter with living Judaism is a realization of our own collective evil. We cannot be healed until our active memory integrates the vicious anti-Semitism of our saints, our repeated pogroms against Jewish communities, and the Holocaust itself. And unless we are healed, the Jews will have reason to fear the repetition of our depraved behavior.

Still we will do no favor to the Jews by abandoning all talk of Christ because it is offensive to them, for it is only in Christ that our healing can occur, and it is only as we are healed that Christ can cease to be their enemy. Indeed, Christians who seek understanding across the lines of religious traditions do themselves a disservice if they minimize the distinctive character of their own faith. Of course, there must be openness to change, and in the course of time we may find aspects of our traditional teaching which can only be repented and rejected. But if we are to learn from others and be transformed through them, we must bring into the encounter the full richness of our heritage. Christianity can grow broader and more inclusive only as it revitalizes its relations with its own deepest roots.

2

The Meaning of Pluralism
for Christian Self-Understanding

Though this essay, like the first one, offers a line-up of Christian perspectives on other religions, it is shorter on description and longer on critique and proposal. Cobb offers a fast-moving review of the three models he finds among his fellow-theologians: 1) The kerygmatic approach typified in Karl Barth and Jürgen Moltmann, which lifts Christian revelation or "the liberating Kingdom" above all religions (including Christianity). 2) The salvation-history approach, found typically in Karl Rahner and Wolfhart Pannenberg, which emphasizes the historical character of all religions but affirms the pre-eminence of Christianity among them. 3) The pluralistic approach of "liberal theism" (John Hick and W.C. Smith) which affirms the validity of all religions on the basis of a divine reality or faith common to, but expressed differently by, them all.

Interestingly, Cobb expressly identifies himself with "the perspective of the history of salvation" (but finds salvation in secular, and not just religious, history); yet he also calls himself a "pluralist" insofar as he agrees with the third group that no religion is so absolute that it cannot learn something extremely important from another religion about "the indivisible salvation of the world." Cobb finds himself, as it were, with a foot in each camp because he has to straddle a twofold opposition: toward those who hold up an absolute truth within one of the religions, and toward those who claim that there is something common within all of them. He sides with the pluralists in his wariness about absolute claims, and with the "historicists" (my inelegant term) in his reservations about something common that hovers within historical forms.

So let all religions start talking without anyone claiming to have the "final word" or the "common ground." And from such a conversation, Cobb believes, there will begin to take shape a transformation of all the participants—what he calls, for example, a Buddhized Christianity and a Christianized Buddhism.

But is there any "higher goal" to this individual transformation of religions—
something they can all affirm and that might animate and adjudicate the
process of religious transformation? That's my question, not Cobb's. Though
he doesn't pose the question, I think he begins to answer it when he agrees
with Moltmann that interreligious dialogue is a "part of the wider frame-
work of the liberation of the whole creation for the coming Kingdom," or in
Dorothee Sölle's vision of "the indivisible salvation of the whole world." Is he
suggesting that all religions might affirm the vision contained in such Christian
language?

P.F.K.

This essay first appeared in Leroy S. Rouner, Religious Pluralism *(South*
Bend: University of Notre Dame Press, 1984), pp. 161–79.

THE FACT THAT THERE is a plurality of other religious movements in the world
besides Christianity has always been obvious to Christians. That some of
these have some positive value has rarely been disputed. What is new is the
idea that in a plurality of religious movements each deserves respect in its own
terms and that Christians should not make claims for their doctrines of a sort
that they do not accept as equally legitimate for others to make about theirs.

For persons who are not committed to any one community or tradition, to
view all such movements as on the same level is far from new. This attitude
characterized the court of Frederick II in Sicily with respect to Jews, Christians,
and Muslims. Moltmann contrasts this "skeptical tolerance" with what he
calls the "productive tolerance" of Lessing.[1] But both these forms of tolerance
stand outside Christian theology.

Ernst Troeltsch is the great thinker who forced the issue of religious pluralism upon the attention of theologians. He gave enormous scholarly and
intellectual effort to justifying the claim of Christianity to absoluteness, and
he finally acknowledged that he had failed. He accepted pluralism. But for
him the acceptance of pluralism was connected with the abandonment of the
theological vocation.

The task of this essay is to wrestle with the theological legacy of Troeltsch.
How is one to understand the Christian faith in light of the challenge to its
claim to absoluteness constituted by Troeltsch's life work? To what extent
can it acknowledge the pluralism of religious movements?

Section I will deal with the history of the actual response. I suggest that it
has taken three basic forms: kerygmatic theology, history of salvation theology, and liberal theistic theology. I will describe these briefly. In Section II I
will engage in critical evaluation of the three positions. In Section III I will
present my own constructive ideas.

---

1. Jürgen Moltmann, *The Church in the Power of the Spirit,* trans. Margaret Kohl
(London: SCM Press, 1977), p. 155.

I. EXPOSITION

(1) The dominant Protestant response to the challenge of pluralism has been kerygmatic theology. Karl Barth stands as its uncontested leader. Through Hendrik Kraemer its implications for the relation of Christianity to other religious traditions won control of the ecumenical movement. This theology still determines the official formulations of the World Council of Churches.

Kerygmatic theology defines itself against apologetic theology. One main form of apologetic theology had been to display the universal character of religion and then to show that religion comes to its fruition and fulfillment in Christianity. This was the program of Ernst Troeltsch, the program which he finally abandoned.

Against this program Barth argued that the interest of Christian theology should not be in religion. Religion is a human phenomenon which may indeed be studied as any human phenomenon is studied. But theology witnesses to what God has done in Jesus Christ. This is not a human phenomenon. It cannot be studied by historians or sociologists. It cannot be argued for or proved. It can only be attested by those who have been led by God to believe. Christians are those who have been called by God to witness to God's saving act.

Barth does not deny that Christians also produce a religion. But this is their sin rather than an expression of faith. They attempt to act so as to attain salvation. Religion is this effort of human beings to save themselves or to gain salvation from God. Faith knows that this is wrong, since God has already done all that needs to be done. Faith frees us from religion and for the world.

The implication for other religious movements was clear. Since they lacked faith in Jesus Christ they could be nothing other than efforts at self-salvation. In this they were no better and no worse than Christians who did the same thing. Christianity as a religion is on exactly the same plane as all other religions. In this sense Barth was a religious pluralist.

The negative evaluation of religions that follows from Barth's position is not a negative evaluation of human beings who participate in one or another religious tradition. God became human for the salvation of all human beings. God's work in Christ has reconciled all. Ignorance of this work may limit some of its effects, but it does not block the reconciliation. God has already, once-for-all, reconciled all humanity to God. The Christian approaches the participant in another religion, not as one who because of erroneous religious affiliation is in need of salvation, but as one who has already been saved by God.

The net effect of this view is not so much to condemn religions as to ignore them. The real drama is between God and individual persons. The structures of religious life can be neglected.

Although the World Council of Churches never committed itself to Barth's tendency to universalism, its approach since Tambaram has largely reflected other aspects of his theology. It does not understand Christianity as one religion alongside others which must establish its superiority as a religion. Nor does it understand Christianity as the fulfillment of the religious quest. On the contrary, faith is directed to Jesus Christ, in whom God acted without regard for religion, for the salvation of all people.

This theology comes to expression as the World Council seeks to relate practically to other communities of belief. One way is by proclaiming the gospel, and this is continuously affirmed in World Council pronouncements. But there is also need for Christians to work together with others in God's world. To this end it is important to overcome mutual suspicions and misunderstandings, and for this purpose it has instituted a subunit on Dialogue with People of Living Faiths and Ideologies.

The title of this subunit is informative. First, the dialogue is to be with people, not with religious communities and their representatives. Second, the avoidance of the word *religions* is significant. We do not talk with people by virtue of their religion. The term *faith*, while problematic in many ways, avoids a positive appraisal of religion. Third, no distinction is made between people who think of themselves as religious believers and those who are committed to other types of movements. Marxism is on the same plane as Hinduism.

The central purpose of dialogue in the World Council view is not exchange of ideas about the meaning of life, ultimate reality, or salvation. The central purpose is to build human community among people who for whatever reason are fragmented into conflicting groups. If sharing deep commitments, even religious ones, is conducive to building human community, that is permitted. But insofar as World Council-sponsored dialogue has in fact become interreligious dialogue, that is in tension with its mandate.

Recently the most influential current proponent of kerygmatic theology, Jürgen Moltmann, has spoken out against the pejorative implications of kerygmatic theology for other world religions. He has pointed out that these religions were not what Barth had in view, that there is much in them that is valuable, and that Christians should enter into dialogue with them with the expectation of learning and being changed in the process. In all this he goes beyond what the World Council has thus far been willing to say. Moltmann believes that precisely because "Christ has come and was sacrificed for the reconciliation of the whole world,"[2] Christians should have unlimited interest in other religions and what can be learned from them. Hence he advocates from the perspective of kerygmatic theology a full-scale interreligious dialogue.

This does not change, however, the secondary character of religion in relation to Christian concerns. He writes:

> For Christianity the dialogue with the world religions is part of the wider framework of the liberation of the whole creation for the coming kingdom. It belongs within the same context as the conversation with Israel and the political and social passion for a freer, juster, and more habitable world. Christianity's dialogistic profile ought to be

---

2. Ibid., p. 153.

turned to the future of the liberating and redeeming kingdom in the potentialities and powers of the world religions. That is a profile which Christianity can only acquire in dialogue with others.[3]

(2) The movement of the Roman Catholic church into dialogue has been based on a very different response to the challenge of pluralism: history of salvation theology. Instead of accepting the pluralism of religions and locating what is supremely important outside of the religious frame, Vatican II and most Catholic theologians since then have understood that God works for salvation in and through the religious life and the religious communities of human beings. Salvation is, for Catholics, a religious matter. The evaluation of the plurality of religions is the evaluation of their success and value in the history of salvation.

Karl Rahner is the single most influential Catholic theologian of this century. His position is that God works salvifically everywhere. People can be saved whether or not they are related to the Catholic church or consciously accept Jesus Christ. People saved in this way he calls anonymous Christians. The religions of the world are used by God in this salvific work. Thus they are positive vehicles of salvation. But they are not on a par with the Christian church. Once the Christian church is fully established in a community there is no longer any need for other religions there. Their function in the history of salvation is superseded by that of the Christian church. But this does not mean that these other religious communities do not continue to contain anonymous Christians.

Hans Küng has not been satisfied with this view. It seems to him still too arrogant. God saves Hindus as Hindus, not as anonymous Christians. Also, each religion continues to function in God's providence until the end. Its role is not superseded by Christianity. In this view, the mission of the church is service to these other religions.

Küng's position is still quite controversial, but it is not far removed from significant tendencies in the church's leadership. Pope Paul VI called for a dialogue about salvation with other religions, implying that they have real knowledge of salvation. In preparing for dialogue with Muslims the Vatican Secretariat appeared to assume that Islam has a more than temporary role in the economy of salvation and that the role of Christians is to help Muslims fulfill that role.

Official Catholic theology is thus willing to go a long way in expressing respect for other religions and their role in the divine economy of salvation. But like the official position of the World Council of Churches it avoids explicitly indicating that the church has anything to learn from other religious traditions. The position seems to be that the church is already in possession of all needed knowledge. The dialogue is part of its mission for the sake of the world. It is not out of its own poverty that it seeks wisdom from others.

---

3. Ibid., p. 163.

Many Catholic scholars have protested this lingering arrogance in the church's attitude and the one-sidedness of the dialogues that must ensue if only the other religion is to learn. But the most successful opening up of the history of salvation approach to Christian learning from others is by the Protestant Wolfhart Pannenberg.

Like the Catholic theologians Pannenberg sees the history of salvation as largely identical with the history of religions.[4] He sees that religions have always competed with one another in terms of the convincing power of their gods. All have an inner tendency toward universality, and they fail or succeed in new situations according to their ability to become appropriately inclusive. Thus no religions in fact remain the same. Successful religions are successful by virtue of their ability to assimilate what is of value in others.

There is a tension between these historical facts about all religions and the tendency of religions to find their norms in past manifestations of deity. Since they define themselves in terms of faithfulness to their deity and define the deity by past manifestations, they claim to be unchanging when in fact they are changing. This often inhibits needed growth.

The great exception in Pannenberg's view is Israel. Israel knew God as the God of promise; hence it looked to the future as the locus of God's full manifestation. It could affirm the new historical occurrence as the revelation of the God whom it already knew. Nevertheless, in Israel this openness to the new was severely checked by commitments to past forms of God's appearance. It is only in Jesus that this bondage to the past is radically broken. For the Christian, God is the God of the future. Hence in principle the Christian is completely open to learning from other religions more about this yet to be fully manifested God. In the process Christian beliefs can be transformed. It is precisely this ability of Christianity to be changed by others, Pannenberg holds, which constitutes its superiority and its ability finally to supersede all others.

(3) Other thinkers, more at the periphery of theology, have objected that even the most open of these positions still falls short of genuine acceptance of pluralism. Moltmann can be completely pluralistic about religions, including Christianity, but only because of his Christian conviction that the whole world has been reconciled to God in Christ. This belief itself is not subject to revision through dialogue with those who do not agree. Pannenberg is ready to submit everything fully to historical examination and in this important sense reserves nothing from the dialogue. But his claim that Christianity is destined to supersede all other religions establishes, on the basis of historical study, the absoluteness which pluralism opposes. Of course, if it is true, then it must be admitted. But many prefer to enter the dialogue without such advance assumptions of superiority of one's own tradition, even when that superiority is measured by its greater ability to be changed through dialogue.

---

4. See Wolfhart Pannenberg, "Toward a Theology of the History of Religions," in *Basic Questions in Theology*, 2 vols., trans. George Kehm (Philadelphia: Fortress Press, 1970–71), 2:65–118.

This group of thinkers prefers to see dialogue as an exchange among people engaged in a common quest who seek to learn from one another without raising the question of the relative merits of the positions they bring into the dialogue. The participants recognize that they have been formed in diverse communities and that what they can contribute is informed by their experience in those communities. But ideally they make no special claims for the authority of what they say. Among Catholics, Hans Küng and Paul Knitter favor this approach. Among Protestants, Wilfred Cantwell Smith and John Hick exemplify it. I am calling their position liberal theism.

Since it is assumed in this approach that the dialogue partners are sharing in a common quest, the nature of that quest requires definition. It is ordinarily understood that all have experienced God and are seeking to know God and live appropriately to that knowledge. Theism is the common assumption. Religions are understood to express the human relationship to God, and it is for the sake of understanding God and God's relationship to the world that people from varied religious traditions engage in dialogue.

There are, of course, differences among the advocates. Wilfred Cantwell Smith prefers to avoid the term *religions*.[5] He sees that this term reifies existing communities of believers, whereas in fact there is a fluid history of the religious life of humanity in which communities and movements take ever-changing form. Dialogue should be among human beings whose religious life incidentally owes more to one or another temporary and provisional community or strand within the whole. It is the faith of human beings which is the basis of sharing. This faith is one reality wherever it is found. There is diversity in the forms and expressions of this one faith. There is no diversity of faiths. The task today is to develop a world theology based on the faith and experience of the whole of the human race rather than confessional theologies expressive of the experience of limited communities. Hence Christian theology should give way to world theology. The world theology developed by those who come to this task from Christianity will bear the marks of their Christian experience. But the ultimate purpose is to achieve full inclusiveness, not to preserve the accent of one tradition or another.

Although much of this is acceptable to John Hick, he has given chief attention to clarifying how one ultimate reality can be experienced so diversely.[6] He calls this ultimate reality *God* but cautions that this term must be freed of its particularistic connotations in order to serve as the name of that which has been known in such divergent ways in the different religions. He recognizes that this one reality has been experienced both as personal and as impersonal and that in different experiences different aspects of the one reality may be involved. But the reality in question is the ground of all

---

5. See Wilfred Cantwell Smith, *Toward a World Theology* (Philadelphia: Westminster Press, 1981).

6. See especially John Hick, "Towards a Philosophy of Religious Pluralism," *Neue Zeitschrift für Systematische Theologie* 22 (1980): 131–49.

existence. It is the noumenal cause of all our phenomenal religious experience. Hence no one experience or culturally informed strand of experiences will exhaust it, and all the religious traditions can contribute to more adequate understanding.

II. CRITIQUE

(1) I find something to agree with in all three of these positions, and partly for that reason I cannot accept any of them. The kerygmatic theology rightly shows that what God aims at in the world is far broader than religion. Moltmann is correct that the interreligious dialogue and all our concerns about religious pluralism are a "part of the wider framework of the liberation of the whole creation for the coming kingdom."[7] Religions, like other human movements, may contribute to that liberation. They may also hinder it. Christians have the same reason to engage in dialogue with Marxists as they do with Buddhists. The category of religion is not determinative of who we are as Christians or who our dialogue partners should be. The question is instead from whom we can learn most that will help us work for the liberation of the whole creation and whom it is most worthwhile for us to try to influence.

But kerygmatic theology has underestimated the importance of historical and cultural traditions, most of which have strong religious elements. The emphasis on dealing with human beings as human beings does not do justice to the profound differences among human beings as they are formed in these diverse contexts. We cannot understand human beings and work with them except as we see them as participants in such communities. This is facilitated when without embarrassment we engage in dialogue with representatives of these communities who can help us to understand not only themselves as individuals but many fellow participants in those communities. Also we should not hesitate to speak, as far as we can, for Christianity as a whole or for the segments of Christianity which we can effectively represent. In short, interreligious dialogue has an importance that the kerygmatic theologians are only barely beginning to acknowledge.

(2) The history of salvation approach has led the Catholic church to full appreciation of the importance of this dialogue. Also, while kerygmatic theology sees history only in terms of the one event of Jesus Christ and the secular movement for the realization of God's purposes in the world, those who follow the history of salvation approach can examine the complex ways in which God has accomplished salvific changes in human society throughout global history. This is much more adequate. The religions, their actual interaction, and their real historical effects can be examined. Strategies for Christian action can be shaped in terms of responsible judgments about the diverse religious movements, their past and present contributions to the whole work of salvation.

---

7. Moltmann, *Church in the Power of the Spirit*, p. 163.

The idea of the Christian mission as service to other religions takes on far more seriousness and critical force when viewed in this context than when something similar is said from the kerygmatic point of view. All of this is admirable.

In Catholic formulations thus far the openness to historical inquiry is checked with regard to the Catholic church itself by some dogmatic commitments. But this is not necessary to the history of salvation approach itself. It is quite possible, as Pannenberg shows, to appeal only to historical evidence and let the chips fall where they may—with respect to Christianity as much as to any other religion. And more clearly than any others in this school, Pannenberg shows that the eschatological thrust inherent in the history of salvation approach frees us for complete openness to others. We do not need to defend any past or present form of Christianity in faithfulness to Christ. On the contrary, faithfulness calls for openness, so that the truth may be served and incorporated.

I not only appreciate what has been done in the perspective of the history of salvation but also identify myself with this approach. However, I disagree with particular ideas that seem to be common to all of the major practitioners. For them the history of salvation is bound up with the history of religions. I see no reason for us to suppose that this is the case, or at least I see no reason to assume it. It is as easy to see salvific functions in secularization as in religion. If religion is defined, as is so often the case, as having to do with God, then we must raise the question as to whether Buddhism is a religion and, if not, whether that separates it from the history of salvation. I would prefer to assume that Buddhism has played and is playing an important salvific role along with Marxism and the movement for the liberation of women. To what extent these are religious does not seem to me to be of central importance. I assume that few important human movements are wholly lacking in religious elements, but many of them are not well named as religions, and many do not think of themselves as theistic. It is important that inquiry into the history of salvation take seriously the history of religion, but it is even more important that its subject matter be history as a whole and that the role of religion within saving history be a topic for investigation. In short, I favor a secularized history of salvation as the context for dealing with the religious pluralism of our time.

(3) I agree with the liberal theists in most of their criticisms of the existing forms of both kerygmatic and history of salvation theologies. They are right that some kind of Christian absolute appears in all the major formulations and that this inhibits total openness to other traditions and their claims. This is least true when, as with Pannenberg, the absolute is argued for from public evidence and is itself subject to testing. But I agree with the liberal theists that even in Pannenberg's case the quest for an absolute as a basis for understanding reflects the long tradition of Christian imperialism and triumphalism rather than the pluralistic spirit.

I agree also with the need for moving toward a world theology which Smith holds before us. An adequate theology for our time must be one which deals with the totality of the evidence, and the diverse religious experiences of the world are an important part of that evidence. But I find his proposal unsatisfactory on several accounts.

First, like the history of salvation theologians, he associates theology in too limited a way with religious experience or what he calls faith. Clarification of our knowledge of God is as dependent upon the social and natural sciences as upon the diverse expressions of faith. His world theology is built on too narrow a base. Second, while he recognizes that his own move to world theology expresses the influence of Christianity, he does not seem to recognize or celebrate how deep the urge in that direction is within Christianity or how specific are the reasons for it. That the world theology to which he points has a Christian character is for him more a limitation than an affirmation of faith. I would reverse this. I see the goal as, precisely, a *Christian* world theology. I would rejoice if there could also develop a Buddhist, a Hindu, a Muslim, a Jewish, and an animist "world theology." But I would expect these to be quite different one from the other. Perhaps some day they would converge. But the desire for them to do so soon shows lack of appreciation of pluralism. Third, his seeking a basis for mutual appreciation of people in the universality of faith impresses me as too provincial. He knows of course that faith is not a central term in all traditions, and that employing it does suggest the sort of favoring of the Christian tradition which he otherwise deplores. He counters that he is abstracting the idea of faith from its specifically Christian character and interpreting it in light of the diversity of religious experience. But I remain convinced that focusing on faith distorts the approach to the truly pluralistic situation. Instead of beginning with the assumption that we can identify what is common to all, it would be better to listen as speakers from each strand of human historical life tell us what they have found most important and how they describe it. I am convinced that in many instances, Zen Buddhism being a notable example, what is central would not be described as faith.

I am not asking merely for a more careful account of what is common to all religious people. My point is that we should give up the use of any language that first separates religion from other phenomena and then tries to identify what is normatively characteristic of all religion. Let us allow Buddhists to be Buddhists, whether that makes them religious or not. Let us allow Confucianists to be Confucianists, whether that makes them religious or not. Let us allow Marxists to be Marxists, whether that makes them religious or not. And let us allow Christians to be Christians, whether that makes us religious or not. Quite apart from any such categories as religion or faith, there is plenty of reason to see that these proper names point to diverse ways of living and experiencing that are important for both the past and the future of the world. Hence, we should take them all seriously, as far as possible on their own terms, and allow each to challenge our beliefs and assumptions. That is a better way to a world theology than the effort to determine what is common to all.

Much the same objection applies to Hick's effort to find a common focus in God. The choice of the term *God*, despite all disclaimers, has the same effect as Smith's choice of *faith*. It suggests lack of attentiveness to what Buddhists are trying to tell us. But shifting terminology to the transcendent or the absolute does not help. [Hick in fact has shifted from "God" to "the Real." His later position is criticized below, pp.147–48.] The problem is the quest for what is common. Truly to accept pluralism is to abandon that quest. If our liberal theists really wish to be open, they should simply be open. The openness is inhibited by the need to state in advance what we have in common. When commonalities emerge, they should be celebrated. But we should not assume that because we find something in common with one dialogue partner—Islam, for example—we should expect to find that in common with another dialogue partner—Buddhism, for example, or Marxism. Also, when differences emerge we should celebrate them too. Indeed, it is the most radical differences that stimulate the most fundamental reconsideration. It is the insistence of Zen Buddhists, for example, on going beyond faith and theism that makes conversation with them so stimulating for those who find faith and theism to be of ultimate importance.

III. PROPOSAL

In this concluding section I want to offer an overview of the meaning of pluralism for my own Christian self-understanding.

My starting point is with Pannenberg in the conviction that Christianity is one historical movement alongside others. Nothing about Christianity justifies its exemption from thoroughgoing historical-critical investigation. Our beliefs about it can only be shaped by such investigation. Nothing historical is absolute; so any tendency to absolutize any feature of Christianity is idolatry.

As a participant in that movement I understand its goal to be, in Dorothee Sölle's words, "the indivisible salvation of the whole world."[8] She understands that chiefly in political terms, and that dimension is extremely important. But salvation must include the whole of the created order, as Moltmann knows, and not only the human sphere. In addition, the salvation of the human involves dimensions that are not usually considered political: the attainment of a unified and adequate understanding of reality and of a mode of experience and action that is appropriate to that understanding.

I see other movements alongside Christianity, and I find it important to evaluate them. Some I judge evil or trivial. Others seem to be carriers of some good but apparently have nothing to offer that cannot be better offered in existing Christianity. Still others contribute to the indivisible salvation of the whole world in ways that Christianity as now constituted does not and can-

---

8. Dorothee Sölle, *Political Theology*, trans. John Shelley (Philadelphia: Fortress Press, 1971), p. 60.

not. These are of great interest. It is the recognition that there are such movements that constitutes me, in the first instance, as a pluralist.

These movements also vary greatly in value and importance. The contributions of some may be highly specialized and limited. Others offer entire ways of life and thought. Some of these are extremely different from Christianity and yet appear—to the Christian—to be of great value and importance.

If being a Christian meant maintaining Christianity in its now established form, then the results of the recognition of these parallel movements would be relativism. One would either cease to be a Christian or else accept Christianity as one possible way of organizing life among others—and leave it at that. Relativism is very difficult to reconcile with Christian faith, which calls for whole-hearted commitment. If other movements seek other ends than the Christian end, and yet have equal validity with Christianity, then how can one give whole-hearted commitment to the Christian goal? To do so would be idolatrous. But to give partial commitment to the goal would be lukewarmness. Idolatry and lukewarmness are the Scylla and Charybdis of contemporary Christianity.

But there is an alternative to relativism. If Christianity is a living movement, then it does not ask commitment to any form which it has taken in the past. It asks commitment to the task of enabling it to respond rightly in the ever-changing situation. In relation to other movements of the sort we are considering, that means learning from them. To believe that Christianity should be constantly changing and growing does not lead to relativism. The fullness of Christianity lies in the ever-receding future. One can be a whole-hearted participant in the present movement as long as one believes that the particular limitations to which one is now sensitive can be overcome.

Let me put the matter strongly. If being a Christian means unqualified affirmation of any form Christianity has ever taken, I cannot be a Christian. But in fact such an affirmation would not be Christian at all. It would be idolatrous and faithless. It would be absolutizing the relative and refusing to attend to the call of the living Christ. But to give complete devotion to the living Christ—as Christ calls us in each moment to be transformed by the new possibilities given by God for that moment—that is not idolatrous or faithless. That is what Christianity is all about.

In faithfulness to Christ I must be open to others. When I recognize in those others something of worth and importance that I have not derived from my own tradition, I must be ready to learn even if that threatens my present beliefs. I cannot predetermine what the content of that learning will be or preestablish categories within which to appropriate it. I cannot predetermine how radical the effects of that learning will be. I cannot predetermine that there are some beliefs or habits of mind which I will safeguard at all costs. I cannot even know that, when I have learned what I have to learn here and been transformed by it, I will still see faithfulness to Christ as my calling. I cannot predetermine that I will be a Christian at all. That is what I mean by full openness. In faithfulness to Christ I must be prepared to give up even faithfulness to Christ. If that is where I am led, to remain a Christian would be to become an idolater in the name of Christ. That would be blasphemy.

Openness to truth concretely entails openness to the particular truth embodied in another tradition. Such openness leads to the assimilation of that truth. Sometimes Christianity can appropriate what another tradition offers in such a way that that movement no longer has any reason to retain separate identity. Its function in the history of salvation is complete. It is in principle superseded. It may turn out some day that everything in Marxism that is of importance in the history of salvation can be appropriated within Christianity. If so, then Marxism would be in principle superseded by an enriched Christianity.

Pannenberg envisions that ultimately Christianity will supersede all other religions. But that expectation does not seem to take the depth of the diversity among the religions with sufficient seriousness, or to recognize them as complex wholes which lose something of their importance for the history of salvation when they are reduced to contributions which Christians can incorporate. As a Christian I am challenged to learn as much as I can, and to appropriate as richly as I can, from these other traditions, allowing myself thereby to be transformed. I must leave to the future the question of whether there are limits such that each religious tradition will maintain a separate contribution to the history of salvation until the end. The pluralistic attitude leaves those questions open. It does not thereby relativize Christianity in a way that reduces commitment to Christ.

My own scenario differs from Pannenberg's at this point. I believe that Christians are in the process of being transformed by other religious traditions. I will take Mahayana Buddhism as my example. I believe that in faithfulness to Christ Christianity will be Buddhized and that we can already discern some of what is involved. The Buddhization of Christianity will transform Christianity in the direction of a greater and deeper truth, a new and better quality of life, and a fuller ability to serve Christ in the political sphere as well. One need not be halfhearted in participating in this process in faithfulness to Christ.

If Buddhism remains static while Christianity allows itself to be Buddhized, then a scenario such as that proposed by Pannenberg makes sense. In the long run there would be no reason for Buddhists to remain Buddhists if their wisdom had been given a larger scope in an enriched Christianity. But it is unlikely that Buddhism will remain unchanged. While Christianity is Buddhized, Buddhism can be Christianized. Pannenberg may be correct that other religions including Buddhism have more tendency to find their norms in the past and to be unable to identify their fundamental principle in the process of transformation. But Buddhism has shown marvelous powers of transformation in China, Korea, Japan, and now the United States. Perhaps one feature of Christianizing Buddhism will be to enable it to recognize and affirm its historicity more fully than in the past. In any case, a self-transforming Christianized Buddhism appears to be a real possibility. If so, a Buddhized Christianity will confront a Christianized Buddhism. The plurality of movements that constitute the history of salvation will thus remain, though their number may be reduced.

My central thesis here is that for Christianity to be, and to remain to the end, one among others does not involve its relativization in the destructive sense in which this is now felt by so many. It does relativize every form taken by Christianity in time. It does not relativize the process of creative transformation by which it lives and which it knows as Christ.

At another level and in another sense, however, that too must be recognized as one principle by which one community lives alongside other principles by which other communities live. This is a fundamental theological problem for the Christian. As a Christian I believe that Christ is the way, the truth, and the life and that no one comes to know God except through Christ. Does that mean after all that I am rejecting pluralism? I do not think so.

I believe that what Christians understand by "the way, the truth, and the life" is bound up with creative transformation. I believe also that what Christians understand by *God* can be known only in this way. But for the most part this has not been the interest of Buddhists. Buddhists are concerned to gain freedom from suffering by realizing the reality which they already are, their Buddha-nature. They tell us that this can be done only by giving up all attachment, even the attachment to the realization of Buddha-nature. This is a quite different goal from coming to know the Christian God. I believe that they understand what they are doing and how to do it. If we want to realize our true nature in this sense, we must study their methods.

Gautama found freedom from suffering through radically overcoming all attachment. He thereby attained nirvana. Jesus incarnated the Word of God. These statements do not conflict with each other. I believe they are both true. Believing that Gautama attained nirvana and uniquely showed others how to do so does not conflict with believing that Jesus uniquely incarnated the Word and shows us the Christian God. Both statements are universal claims of vast importance in the history of salvation. The truth of one does not reduce the truth of the other. That there are others besides Jesus whose achievements are of universal importance does not reduce the universal importance of Jesus. It does not count against making radical and exclusive claims for either nirvana or the Word. It means only that we must state very carefully the relation of Jesus, the Word, and Christ. For my part I mean by *Christ* the effective presence of the Word in the world, a presence uniquely realized in Jesus. My exclusive claims for Christ need not conflict with exclusive Buddhist claims for the realization of Buddhahood of which Gautama is the paradigm instance. General comments to the effect either that Jesus is the only Savior or that there are a plurality of saviors do not help. We must always say, saved from what to what. Christians need not give up our exclusivist claims, but we should be very careful to state what it is that is exclusive and to examine our claims in relation to all others. We should strive to share what has been exclusive to Christianity as we appropriate what has been exclusive to other traditions. That is what a Christianized Buddhism and a Buddhized Christianity are all about.

This essay is written from within the Christian commitment. All the judgments I have made are Christian judgments. From the point of view of some people, that approach is already rendered obsolete by the pluralism of our situation. They believe that the task now is to stand outside of all the positive religions and to understand them objectively as scholars. Speaking as a Christian I can say that I am glad that some have done this. Historical, psychological, sociological, and phenomenological studies of religion have benefited all of us. But from the Christian point of view, more is lost than gained by shifting from identification with the Christian community to identification with the academic one. Prizing objectivity and learning is fine. But the academic community as such has no larger context of commitment within which to use these rather minor values. Accordingly it has lost the ability to discern importance and to define the university in terms of any humane purpose. To stand outside of all religious communities in order to appraise them impartially has modest value except as it has an effect within the communities. In any case that stance is not truly pluralistic. It has opted for one commitment against the commitments of the communities it evaluates, and it usually does not appreciate the way in which its own commitments are relativized by theirs. It too easily becomes absolutist in its attack on the tendencies to absolutism of those it studies.

From a Christian point of view the values that are present in the academic community are easily assumed within the Christian one. We, too, prize fairness and openness in the quest for truth and understanding. Indeed, in the modern West, these values were derived largely from Christianity in the first place. In the relation of Christianity to the academic community I see no basic problem with supersession. But of course for that to come about, the tendencies to idolatry which now beset Christianity will have to be overcome.

It has taken Christians a long time to recognize that there are other movements in the world that are bearers of authentic contributions to salvation that differ from our own. Indeed, even now the resistance to that acknowledgment is very strong. Many Christians fear that their faith will be undercut by such an admission. They want to believe that all that is needed for the indivisible salvation of the whole world is found in the past and specifically in the past of our own tradition. This is understandable, but it is also sin. It is not an expression of faith but of defensiveness, which is faithlessness.

What is most striking, however, is not the timorousness of Christians as we work out the meaning of pluralism for Christian self-understanding. What is more striking is the relative speed with which leading thinkers and leading institutions are moving toward an adequate statement. Both the World Council of Churches and the Vatican have come a long way in recent years. In comparison with the distance traveled, the further distance that is needed is relatively short. All that is required is an act of total trust in the living Christ.

3

Global Theology
in a Pluralistic Age

In this essay, Cobb confronts a reality that is often sidestepped by devotees of a new unity and dialogue among the religions. If one looks honestly at the history of humanity, one will have to admit that religions have been just as great a source (maybe greater) of division and conflict than of unity and peace. Religion does not have a very good track record as an agent of good will and friendly conversation. In fact, some would hold that to call the religions of the world to dialogue is as hopeful a task as calling for conversation between fighting cocks. Cobb is hopeful but realistically so. He believes that the track record can be changed. What's more, he holds that theology can make a contribution to bringing about this change.

But it has to be a realistic theology. Using a different lens than the one he used in the previous two essays, Cobb focuses on four types of theology that seek to foster new unity and dialogue among religions. Each urges a particular basis or framework for unity: one model proposes science as a source of truth that can bind together the differences of religions; another holds up a common goal for all religions based on a common essence in all of them; a third approach recognizes real differences among the religions but holds that each of them contains something special that can contribute to the general well-being of humanity; finally, there is the theology that entertains the vision of all the religions shedding their differences and blending into a new world religion.

Cobb finds all these theologies wanting, mainly because all of them, each in its particular way, abstracts from, or tries to manipulate, the distinctive identity, history, and vitality of each religion. So he formulates his proposal for "global confessional theologies." The plural noun is what distinguishes his model from the other four. He calls upon each religious tradition to look into its own confessional identity in order to find its own unique reason and

49

resources for reaching out to, talking to, and learning from others. Through such a process, the uniqueness of each religion will be preserved—but also changed, and made more global.

P.F.K.

This essay first appeared in Dharma World *14 (Nov.–Dec. 1987):31–37.*

NONE CAN DENY TODAY that this is a pluralistic age. Actually, every age has been a pluralistic age from a global point of view. But there have been times, sometimes long periods, when large portions of humanity were barely aware of religious traditions very different from their own. There have been other times, as in the late Roman Empire and today, when almost everyone is forced to come to terms with religious differences, even quite fundamental ones.

The use of the word "pluralism" can be simply descriptive, and I have been using it that way. But it is one of those descriptions that suggests an interpretation, namely, that the diversity is acceptable and that people should learn to live with it in mutual appreciation. A pluralistic age should be one in which most people agree to live and let live, to acknowledge one another as fellow citizens of the planet with the right to think and worship as one pleases as long as what pleases one does not threaten the well-being of others.

Most of us have thought in recent decades that we were moving into a pluralistic age in this sense too. Governments, on the whole, have written the toleration of religious diversity into their constitutions. And over a period of decades it seemed that most religious leaders insisted that they did not want to force their views on others. Indeed, in many places the dominant attitude of religious communities toward one another seemed to be one of increasing cordiality. It seemed that with the passing of time the dream of a thoroughly pluralistic world—in this richer sense—would be realized.

There is less reason today to be sanguine. Religious particularity is being reemphasized everywhere. Mutual suspicion among peoples seems to be growing, and the peoples in question often define themselves along religious lines. The resulting violence is extensive.

Some deny that these quarrels are really religious. In one sense the denial is clearly correct. What divide Roman Catholics and Protestants in Northern Ireland are not traditional theological disputes from the time of the Reformation. Verbal theological agreements between the Vatican and Calvinist theologians would not do much toward resolving the political issues.

But just this objection points to the real nature of religions as they function in our world. They are ways in which communities organize their collective lives. They thereby strengthen bonds among adherents but at the same time intensify the sense of the otherness of those who order their lives in different ways. As Paul Tillich said, religion is the soul of culture.

One might argue that even cultural differences between the contending forces are not crucial, that the quarrel is really economic. But just this objection shows how false it is to isolate factors in this way. Of course, the problems are economic. But the sense of homogeneity and of boundaries of each group is not initially and primarily a matter of economic classes. The economic oppression of Roman Catholics in Northern Ireland results from the fact that they are excluded from the dominant community. Economic differences are not the cause, although the class differences resulting from cultural discrimination intensify the cultural differences in a vicious circle. Religion does play a crucial role in dividing the people.

Even where there is no overt fighting, a general climate of authoritarian particularity is widely apparent. Most publicized are the Vatican's efforts to undo some of the results of Vatican II. There are only a few cases of actual discipline of those who have exercised their freedom to think for themselves. But these few cases have been enough to intimidate other theologians and leaders into greater caution.

In the largest Protestant denomination in the United States, the Southern Baptists, the takeover by fundamentalists with little interest in traditional Baptist principles is now almost complete. Those seminaries that have nurtured independent thinking are likely to experience faculty resignations if not official purges. Pejorative comments about Jews are less likely to be challenged from within the denomination than in the past.

Most other mainline denominations in America show a tendency to reactionary policies, although fortunately they are not so extreme. The Presbyterians have refused to accept my colleague, John Hick, as a Presbyterian minister because of the theological adjustments he has made for the sake of pluralism. The United Methodists are moving to demote the authority of tradition, reason, and experience so as to highlight the unique status of scripture. I believe similar trends could be documented worldwide.

At the same time that our religious institutions are tightening the reins, masses of people are simply losing interest. They have not necessarily lost interest in religious ideas and religious experience. But they do not find institutional expressions of their interests. If they are religious at all, they are so quite privately. That means that the gap between those within and those outside the churches is widening.

Most of us deplore these trends. We want to see a livelier interest in religion combined with mutual appreciation and a softening of boundaries. We need to ask, What went wrong? Why has the tide turned against us?

There are many reasons. I will focus on just one. We are historical beings. That means that the past is really part of us today. And the past that shapes us differs according to the traditions in which we stand. It contributes decisively to our identities.

When we are very sure of our identities, and when the world seems a hopeful arena in which to live, we can afford to turn attention outward and be open to one another. But when our identities are threatened, and the world appears threatening, we reemphasize our roots. To do so means to reemphasize our particularity, and usually, to do so in traditional religious terms. The very mobility and intermixing of peoples that produced the pluralistic situation in the first, descriptive sense, tends to undercut it in the normative sense.

In such a situation, why do we concern ourselves with explicit beliefs, with what I shall call theology? Have we not already seen that theology is not the issue in any of the great conflicts today? The real problem is to work through social conflict, and verbal agreements about doctrine do not contribute much to this task. In relation to the tightening authoritarianism in so many religious institutions, the need is to change the sociological conditions that lead in this direction. Discussion of doctrines seems superficial in comparison.

Despite the obvious truth in these comments, I continue to believe that theology does have an important role to play. First, without shared beliefs, no community can hold together for very long. One of the reasons for the current authoritarianism is to make sure that there are such shared beliefs and that they not be too seriously questioned or challenged. Theology has played a large role in the shaping of the several communities, and in the long run it plays a large role in directing them.

Second, theology plays a double role in most communities. On the one hand, it provides what Peter Berger calls a sacred canopy. It sanctions the practices of the community and shows that they are superior to those of other communities. It encourages obedience to authority and the tightening of the bonds within the community. But on the other hand, theology reminds believers of elements in the tradition that are in tension with practice. These elements may be ones that, if accented, will lead to persecutions and holy wars. That cannot be denied. But there are also neglected elements in most of our traditions that call for more open and human relations with others and for greater personal freedom. Theologians can champion these. Much depends in the shaping of a community as to which features of its tradition are accented by its effective leaders. And that means that theologians are important. We must be concerned about theology.

I do not mean by "theologians" here the professional teachers of theology. Although I do not exclude us altogether, we must recognize that often our role is very slight. I mean instead whoever is able to shape the beliefs of the community by drawing on aspects of its history and by reformulating tradition in the new context. It is the outcome of the struggle to shape the community in this way that is important for all of us, including theological professors.

Theology normally happens separately in the several communities. Most of it is little more than the ideology of a community of believers, the way it assures itself of its superior validity. Our subject here is not this kind of parochial theology, but global theology. We would like a theology that would transcend parochial differences and draw all people together. What could that be? On that question we are likely to diverge. In the remainder of this paper I shall sketch four answers that liberal religious people sometimes give to this question and indicate my dissatisfaction with them. I will then offer a fifth proposal and defend it.

THE SCIENTIFIC APPROACH

Many liberal people have called attention to the importance of science in our world. Whereas religions are diverse, science seems to have won its way everywhere. People of almost all religious persuasions accept its authority both because of its success in providing evidence for its contentions and also because of its ability to inspire technological marvels. In some way it seems desirable to bring religion into close relation with science.

There are various ways in which this can be thought of. At one extreme is the virtual substitution of science for religion. According to this view, natural science can gradually replace poorly founded religious beliefs with well-founded scientific ones. The social sciences can tell us how to organize our collective lives. Scholarly history can tell us what really happened in the past and thus dispel myths and legends. We can move in this direction by universal education. In the end, it is hoped, the divisiveness of religion will be outgrown and we will celebrate our common humanity.

In the West we associate this kind of thinking with the positivism that reached its zenith at the time of the French Revolution with the worship of Reason. For many, the events of that time and subsequent times have proved disillusioning, but the dream has not disappeared. Since we have no more reason to be disillusioned with this than with the positive religions that continue to play their roles, it should not be dismissed on that basis.

My critique is a theoretical one. I believe science cannot function for us in this way because it does not take us very far toward truth. It moves away from concrete reality into the realm of abstractions. People cannot live by abstractions, and a pattern of abstractions cannot tell us how to constitute ourselves in community.

I do not mean at all that the sciences can teach us nothing of importance. That would be absurd. Most of my own more assured beliefs are the result of scientific teaching. But scientific doctrines are necessarily abstract, and the more scientific our knowledge becomes, the more abstract it becomes. This is inherent in all academic disciplines. In the natural and social sciences the abstraction moves toward mathematics.

Consider this matter more closely. A science is not an open-ended inquiry into what-is. It is based on the selection of one segment or aspect of what-is. Among the natural sciences, physics, chemistry, and biology divide up concrete actuality among themselves and then subdivide it almost endlessly. Thus the subject matter of each is already an abstraction from nature. Then they adopt a method of inquiry that seems likely to yield results. This highlights those features of their abstracted subject matter that can be treated by this method. Those not amenable are largely ignored. Then there is the further pressure to quantify, which encourages one set of methods and discourages others, leading to still greater abstraction. The resulting mathematical formulae prove very powerful indeed, at least in some instances, but they are far removed from nature. This becomes most obvious if we human beings try to think of ourselves as we appear in terms of natural science. None of us would agree that the fullness of our personal being is expressed.

But one may object that what is missed by the natural sciences is picked up by the social and psychological sciences. Unfortunately, this is not the case. For the most part they model themselves on the natural sciences, seeking to quantify and mathematize as physics has done. The results are, again, selectively illuminating, but they carry us far from the concrete relationships among persons that are crucial to community.

The problem is particularly clear if we ask which science can give us guidance in facing the real issues of our time. Which science can guide us away from nuclear war or ecological destruction? The answer is that none is very helpful. But can we not solve that problem by bringing several sciences together? The answer is No. The addition of abstractions does not bring us very close to the actual world.

Most of us have never intended that science replace religion. But many have thought that the way ahead lies through the scientific study of religion. If religion is to be redirected away from its fratricidal roles, we need to understand it more accurately. Once believers understand it scientifically, it is hoped, they can overcome its parochial tendencies, free it from superstition, and move it toward global character.

The tendency in this approach is to reify religion, to think as if there were some reality to which that word points that underlies the various religious traditions in the world. But that is misleading. There may, indeed, be some kinds of activity, such as prayer, that appear independently in all traditions and are universally considered religious. Certainly it is good to know more about such phenomena. But what is most important about Buddhism or Christianity is not easily apprehended when we focus attention on religious aspects of behavior or feeling. There is an important sense in which neither Buddhism nor Christianity is a religion.

To illustrate, the sense of the holy has been taken as the essence of the religious. There is no doubt that both Buddhism and Christianity witness to the importance of this phenomenon. So something about Buddhism and about Christianity as religions can be learned by studying the holy. But the most important characteristics of both elude the student of religion as a universal phenomenon.

I am certainly not opposing the scientific study of religion. It has its place. But it is a smaller place than some of its proponents suppose. It cannot become the basis of a global theology in a pluralistic age.

A COMMON GOAL

A second approach sometimes recommended by liberals is to accent what is common to the beliefs and practices of all religious traditions. In the Middle Ages theologians spoke of "natural theology" as that part of theology that is accessible by reason alone. It is assumed that since all people are rational, all should be able to agree on the tenets of natural theology. If then we all recognize that what is peculiar to each tradition is less important than what unites us, the rancor of interreligious quarreling should decline. Also, since the important beliefs are ones that commend themselves to the free and untrammeled mind, religious authoritarianism is countered.

Few today would suppose that what Thomas Aquinas identified as natural theology meets all the requirements of our time. In his day the religious pluralism was Jewish-Christian-Muslim. And most of the best thinkers of all three traditions found Aristotle to be the greatest of philosophers. Hence it made sense to treat a position developed from that of Aristotle as the attainment of pure reason.

Much has happened in the course of thought since that time, and the science and mathematics on which Aristotle based his philosophy no longer stand. Although there are still many whose philosophies are deeply influenced by Aristotle, a "natural theology" offered by that tradition will not be expected to command assent among those who have been more influenced by other schools. In short, systems of thought supposedly built on reason alone have turned out to be as pluralistic as those based on revelation.

We might hope to escape this multiplicity of philosophers by seeking to limit our natural theology to science-based beliefs. But I have discussed already the problems inherent in the appeal to science. Meanwhile philosophers seeking to move toward agreement have generally abandoned synthetic or constructive thinking altogether. They have hoped to find common ground by limiting themselves to description and analysis. But what is attained in this way hardly suffices to constitute a natural theology.

Many who recognize that agreement on a natural theology is unobtainable still believe that all the great religious traditions have a common salvific goal. The image of many paths up the same mountain comes especially from India, but it has found resonance throughout the world. One may argue that despite differences in beliefs and practices, there is a common human condition, a common need, and a universal concern to meet this need. Although some paths may be better than others in general, or at least for persons of particular cultural and personal characteristics, argument about such matters is unimportant. Each should follow the path that appeals to her or to him. The destination is the same.

The first question to ask about such a proposal is: Is it true? If it is, it can certainly be helpful in setting the stage for interreligious tolerance and mutual appreciation. But if it is not, we must beware of its misleading implications.

Is there a common human condition? Surely, at some level, there is. But the pressure to find what is truly common presses us back to those features of our existence that are most fully determined biologically. It is far from clear that the needs to which religion responds are to be found at that level.

One could still argue that religion is common to all human beings, that though much about us is biologically determined we differ from other animals in the extent to which our lives are lived in transcendence of and tension with our biological condition. One could then identify the problem to which all religions respond with the tension between the biological basis of human existence and the cultural formation super-imposed upon it. However, this would not go far to establish a common need and a common goal. For the cultures are so diverse and the tensions they introduce so different that human needs are not readily discernible as identical.

When we look at the avowed goals of the several traditions, without imposing unity upon them, their diversities are apparent. Resurrection of the body to everlasting blessedness on a final day of judgment is not, on the surface, very similar to the extinguishing of personal existence. Of course, in order to make my point I have selected from among the many images available in both the Christian and the Buddhist traditions two that are in particularly marked contrast. The gulf could be narrowed. One could take the beatific vision and relate it to the realization of emptiness. Working with those images, one could find points of contact and, through special interpretations of each, bring them close together. This is the strategy of those who are deeply committed to the view of a common goal.

But this strategy has an unintended consequence. It turns out that what it presents as the true goal of both Christianity and Buddhism differs markedly from the actual goals hoped for by most participants in both traditions. It sometimes celebrates this difference by contrasting an esoteric tradition in all religions with the exoteric one and holding that only the former is valid. But precisely this strategy shows that what real human beings actually hope to attain is far removed from what the proponent of the common goal of all religions advocates. A unity that omits the real belief and interest of most people is not the unity we sought.

MUTUAL SUPPLEMENTATION

A third strategy for peace and unity among the religions can be offered based on the recognition of diversity. It is a strategy that recognizes that different religions perform different functions. In China, for example, over long periods Confucianism played the major role in ordering public and family life and relating the present generation to its ancestors. But those concerned with inner realization would seek this in Buddhist monasteries. Somewhat similar patterns can be discerned in the Mediterranean world during the time of the Roman Empire, where the public religion of the state could allow for mystery religions to flourish alongside it as long as they did not threaten the public order.

Similar patterns are reemerging today. There are those who look to Christianity for guidance in the moral and social spheres while practicing Buddhist meditation to meet some deeply existential needs. Might we not examine each of the religious traditions to see what particular contribution it can make to the whole range of human needs and then view the traditions as mutually supplementary?

This solution has its merits. But it abstracts features of religions from the religions as a whole. I noted earlier that it is the nature of religious traditions to constitute the soul of culture. They tend to be intimately involved in providing identity to adherents. Hence there is a difference between adoption of certain features of a religion and actually becoming an adherent.

Where religions are viewed as specialized means of making certain contributions to life and society, something else provides the unifying identity of the people. In China, this was being Chinese. Participation in Chinese peoplehood provided the fundamental ground of unity and personal orientation. Given this unity and identity, one could view the offerings of Confucianism, Taoism, and Buddhism with some detachment and select what one wanted. Problems sometimes arose with Buddhists who took their identity as Buddhists too seriously and allowed it to supersede their identity as Chinese. But the great majority of Buddhists were willing to allow their Buddhism to be secondary to their being as Chinese. We can say that being Chinese was the fundamental religion of the Chinese people.

The religions stemming from Israel are less amenable to accepting a subordinate role in identity formation. This was correctly understood in Japan and led to the bloody suppression of Christianity in the seventeenth century. Of course, Christians in overwhelming numbers do compromise with national loyalty. For many members of Christian churches in the United States, primary identity is national and church membership is chosen for certain more limited purposes. Where this is the case, then one may look to various other religious movements for other limited purposes. The point here is not that this situation cannot occur or even that it is rare, but that it cuts against central elements in the belief system. Serious Christians cannot accept for Christian faith a role that subordinates it to nationalism.

It would, of course, be possible for liberal religious leaders to advocate the pattern of specialized contributions that can view religious traditions as mutually supplementary. But the price is high. Since individuals and communities need some center from which to view the plurality, if this center is not provided by one of the traditional religions, it will be provided somewhere else. Almost always this will be by the tribe or nation. Mutual tolerance among the religions will be purchased at the price of removing the main checks against nationalism as the real religion of the modern world. And nationalism, severed from its connection with traditional religions, tends to be harsher and brasher.

THEOLOGICAL SYNTHESIS

A fourth option is syncretism, or synthesis. The recognition of diversity among religions can lead, not to seeking to limit emphasis to what is common among them or to giving each a specialized role in a whole that is determined from outside all of them, but to drawing the truth of all into a new creative unity. Such a unity would be, in effect, a new religion. However, this would not be a religion that sprang full-blown from a new revelation, but a religion that drew upon the insights and achievements of all traditional religions while freeing itself from the dross that affects them all.

Here we have for the first time an image that is clearly one of a global theology. It would be a theology for all people asking them to remain faithful to the best of their past traditions while appropriating the best of all others in a convincing synthesis. Such a religion would provide the comprehensive horizon of meaning within which all of life would be lived. It would also function as the soul of a truly global culture. While not denying an important place for national loyalty, it would supersede such loyalty as the deepest principle of identity in all who accepted it. Thus supreme loyalty and identity would move beyond its present parochial definition to a truly global one. Such a religion would certainly be a powerful force for understanding and peace.

There can be no question about the attractiveness of such a goal. Of course, it has its dangers even as a goal. The longing for unity tends to prejudice people against those who resist the proposed unifying beliefs. Every previous effort to attain unity has been accompanied by some form of persecution of those who refused to be unified. The persecution of the Jews in Christendom is an important example.

Even if we decided that unity is so important that we must risk the accompanying persecutions, we would be hard pressed to turn this dream into a program of action. When we gather to discuss what our unified beliefs and practices will be, immediately disunity appears. We may all agree in principle that we should include the truths of all traditions, but on the issue of what those truths are we disagree. Usually the traditions from which we come affect the judgments of what the contributions of others really are. Liberals are hardly closer to agreement than are conservatives.

CONFESSIONAL GLOBAL THEOLOGIES

I want now to propose a fifth response to the pluralistic situation. This response takes the particularities of the several religious traditions seriously and supports their role in giving identity to the lives of people. Rather than seeking to free people from their Buddhist or Christian identity, I believe we should encourage strengthening and deepening of that identity against the identity many gain from nationalism and some from their professional roles.

Of course, simply by itself this would seem to accept the status quo or even intensify its problems. But in my reading of the history of religions, most have a tension built into them. I have already commented on this. They do bind believers together against the rest of the world and thus accent the problems of mutual suspicion and misunderstanding. But most of them also, in the very core of their teaching, call for justice and love toward outsiders as well as toward insiders. Most of them call for a commitment to truth, even unpalatable truth. Most of them inspire hope for a world of peace.

Global theology in a pluralistic age need not cut its ties to the particularity of such religious traditions. Instead it can work within each religion to make the theology of that tradition more global. In the name of what is most sacred, even what is most particular, in each tradition, adherents can be called to more global religious thinking and practice.

My suggestion is that there is no global strategy for developing global theology in a pluralistic age. The strategy is pluralistic. It will be quite different for Muslims, for Hindus, for Sikhs, for Jains, for Buddhists, for Jews, and for Christians. An outsider can make some suggestions for what this will mean in any given tradition. But the work of globalization must be done by believers out of genuine conviction that in today's pluralistic world the deepest meaning of their own faith requires such globalization. Movement toward global theology in each tradition will include openness to other traditions and to learning from them. Hence the results will resemble those of the previous option. But they will also differ.

Christians moving toward a global theology will find in Christ the reason for openness to Buddhism and to learning from it. They will also find in Christ the reason for renewed appreciation of Judaism and its continuing living truth. They will be transformed in their understanding of their own faith by this reception of the truth of Buddhism and of Judaism. But they will not experience this as a break from Christianity or being cut off from their Christian identity. Instead, they will experience this as a deepening and purification of Christian identity.

I suggested earlier that a quest for a single global theology synthesizing the best in all the traditions in a higher unity would find that the particular standpoints from which the unity is sought would lead to a renewal of the diversity. That is, there would be diverse judgments as to what from each tradition should be preserved and what discarded. The quest for a global theology would produce several candidates among which disagreements would continue.

In making my own proposal for a pluralistic approach to global theology, I am simply accepting this human situation. I hope to turn it into an asset rather than an impediment. I propose that we celebrate our differences and deepen our commitment to our several traditions. There is a richness in diversity that we should not be in a hurry to discard. Also, the abandonment of the quest for one universal faith will discourage the tendency to condemnation of dissenters.

Nevertheless, if each tradition moves toward global theology through opening itself to what appears to it most attractive and positive in other traditions, there will be a movement toward greater resemblance. A Buddhism that has truly learned in its encounter with Christianity and a Christianity that has truly learned in its encounter with Buddhism will resemble each other more than Christianity and Buddhism now do. Perhaps some day they will cease to be two traditions but instead will merge into one. But perhaps not. That is not a question with which we need to concern ourselves.

Openness of religious traditions to one another does not mean only openness to ideas and practices. It is also openness to one another's histories. Our identities are constituted by our histories. It is because we read history from the point of view of Israel and Jesus and the Christian church that some of us are Christians. We need not suppose that the events that constitute our history are ones of which we should be proud in order to acknowledge them as describing what "we" have done and what had happened to "us." We *are* those who have done those things and suffered those things.

True openness to other traditions will require that we make their history our own. We Christians will view Muhammad as our prophet as well. We will see Gautama as the Enlightened One and the story of Buddhist missions as part of our heritage. The vast wealth of diversity of Hindu tradition will be ours as well.

That this will happen some day is not pure fantasy. Already many of our young people have studied the religions of South and East Asia and claim that heritage as their own. It is true that some of them, in the process, lose their rootedness in Israel and Christian history. They are converted from Christianity to Hinduism or Buddhism. But there are others for whom the appropriation of Indian and Chinese traditions does not displace the importance of their own. Their identity is thus expanded rather than shifted by the additional histories on which they draw in their self-understanding.

These pioneers often feel uncomfortable in the narrower climate of most Christian churches. That is understandable. The vanguard of a new reformation rarely feels comfortable in the unreformed community. There is often keen misunderstanding and lack of mutual appreciation. One side clings to the heritage from the past. The other calls for openness to others. The emergence of a true global theology depends on displaying the inner unity of these two moves. We must show that we are open to the other because we are truly faithful to our heritage. For Christians this means that because Christ is the center there can be no boundaries. Because we are faithful to Christ, we seek truth wherever it can be found. Because Christ is the principle of interpreting all history, all history is our story.

In a pluralistic age we need a plurality of theologies. Indeed, we have and will have such pluralism whatever we say or do about it. Let us not deplore that or seek to replace this plurality with any single approach or system.

But in a pluralistic age it is ever more important that the plurality of theologies become more and more global. There are trends in this direction at the same time that there are trends toward greater isolation and mutual suspicion. It is not a foregone conclusion which trends are going to shape the future. If we allow those who teach exclusivist doctrines control over the major symbols of the several faiths, we have reason to fear that social and religious power will be theirs. It is our task to contest this control, to display that the heart of each tradition is an impulse toward global vision and understanding, that mutual love expresses our deepest convictions better than mutual exclusion. This is our calling as liberal religious thinkers.

4

Beyond "Pluralism"

In this essay, written as a critical response to the call for a "pluralistic theology of religions" for the collection edited by John Hick and myself, entitled The Myth of Christian Uniqueness *(Maryknoll, N.Y.: Orbis Books, 1987) Cobb marks off his distance from the so-called pluralists. In a sense, this distance is found in the reason why he agrees with them: Cobb agrees with the pluralists that no one religion can claim to be absolutely or finally superior over all others—but* not *because, as the pluralists say, all religions have the same basic (or essential) task which each carries out with rough parity, but, rather, because all of the religions have* different *tasks and therefore you can't say that one carries out its own task better than another. As we have seen in the previous essays, Cobb wants to respect and preserve the real differences among the religions. He fears that the pluralists don't do this. He's really accusing the pluralists of not being pluralistic enough: in their talk of what the religions have in common, they lose sight of the differences.*

But in this essay, Cobb clearly recognizes a danger in his own more authentic pluralism; it can easily slide into what he calls "conceptual relativism." If all religions are so thoroughly different, the truth of a religion becomes whatever the religion says it is. There are no interreligious criteria for what is right or wrong.

So Cobb proposes in this essay a "relatively objective norm" that he thinks all religions engaged in dialogue can assent to: that there's more to truth than what they know in their own religion, and they can learn a little more of this "more" by opening themselves to and talking with other religions. Cobb ends his essay by suggesting that because of their commitment to Jesus Christ, Christians can full-heartedly embrace this norm—perhaps more enthusiastically than other religions can. But he would not be surprised, indeed he'd be delighted, if these other religions would prove him wrong about that "more enthusiastically."

Cobb, one might suspect, needs to say more about this "relatively objective norm"—not to clarify why all religions can embrace it, but how it works.

Just because I learn something from someone else that I didn't know before-hand, can I be sure that what I've learned is true?

P.F.K.

I

HOW ODD I FIND IT to be writing for a collection of essays in criticism of the-ologies espousing religious pluralism! Yet I have agreed to do so because of the very narrow way—indeed an erroneous way, I think—in which *pluralism* has come to be defined. By *that* definition of pluralism, I am against pluralism. But I am against pluralism for the sake of a fuller and more genuine pluralism. Let me explain.

I declined to write a paper for the conference that led to the publication of the book, *The Myth of Christian Uniqueness*, because I did not share in the consensus that conference was supposed to express and promote. In the minds of the organizers, that consensus was to be around the view that the several major religions are, for practical purposes, equally valid ways of embodying what religion is all about. The uniqueness that is rejected is any claim that Christianity achieves something fundamentally different from other religions. From my point of view, the assumptions underlying these formulations are mistaken and have misled those who have accepted them.

Probably the most basic assumption is that there is an essence of religion. This essence is thought to be both a common characteristic of all "religions" and their central or normative feature. Hence, once it is decided that Bud-dhism, Confucianism, or Christianity is a religion, one knows what it is all about and how it is to be evaluated. The next step is then the one about which the consensus was to be formed. Given the common essence, let us agree to acknowledge that it is realized and expressed more or less equally well in all the great religions. It is hoped in this way to lay to rest once and for all Christian arrogance and offensive efforts to proselytize. Christians could then contribute to that peace among religions that is an indispensable part of the peace the world so badly needs.

If, as in my case, one rejects this whole view of religion, then it is very dif-ficult to take part in the discussion as thus posed. I do believe there is a fam-ily of traits or characteristics that guides the use of the term *religion* for most people. But the term is used even when only some, not all, the traits are pres-ent. For example, most people in the sphere of dominance of the Abrahamic faiths think of worship of a Supreme Being or deity as a religious trait. Yet when they find this absent in most Buddhist traditions, they do not automat-ically deny that Buddhism is a religion. They notice that it is permeated by a spirit of deep reverence or piety, that it aims to transform the quality and char-acter of experience in a direction that appears saintly, that it manifests itself in such institutions as temples and monasteries in which there are ritual obser-vances, and so forth. The overlap of characteristics suffices for most people, so that Buddhism is almost always included among the world's religions.

If one turns to Confucianism one finds a different set of overlaps with Abrahamic assumptions about religion and a different set of discrepancies. By a certain stretch of terms one can find in it a worship of a Supreme Being, but the function this plays is far less central than in Judaism, Christianity, and Islam. There is great concern for the right ordering of human behavior, but much less interest in transforming the quality and character of experience. So is Confucianism a religion? This question divided Jesuits and their opponents in the seventeenth century, and the vacillation by Rome prevented what might otherwise have been the conversion of the Chinese court to Catholicism.

In the twentieth century the more acute issue is whether communism is a religion. Those who take their cue from the Abrahamic faiths notice at once the denial of God, but such denial does not exclude Buddhism. They notice also the evangelistic fervor, the selfless devotion evoked, the totalistic claims, the interest in the transformation of the human being, the confidence that a new age is coming. And in all this they see religious characteristics. One might judge that communism actually resembles Christianity, at least in its Protestant form, more closely than does Buddhism, yet the features it omits or rejects seem the most "religious" aspects of Christianity. A popular solution is to call communism a *quasi-religion*, whatever that may mean.

It would be possible to draw up a long list of characteristics that one person or another associates with the word *religion*. A list drawn up by a Buddhist would be likely to overlap with, but differ from, a list drawn up by a Muslim. Does that mean that one list would be more accurate than the other? That would imply that there is some objective reality with which the lists more or less correspond. But there is no Platonic ideal named "Religion" to which the use of the term *ought* to conform. The term means what it has come to mean through use in varied contexts. Each user should be at some pains to clarify his or her meaning. But arguments as to what religion truly is are pointless. There is no such thing as religion. There are only traditions, movements, communities, people, beliefs, and practices that have features that are associated by many people with what they mean by religion.

One meaning of religion derived from its Latin root deserves special attention here. *Religion* can mean "a binding together"; it can be thought of as a way of ordering the whole of life. All the great traditions *are*, or can be, religions in this sense. So is communism. All are, or can be, ways of being in the world. In most instances they designate themselves, or are readily designated, as Ways. If this were all that were meant by calling them religions, I would have no objection to designating them as such. But we would need to recognize that this use does not capture all the meanings of religion that are important to people. In fact, we do not cease thinking of these traditions as religious when they fail to function as the overarching ways of life for people who identify themselves with them. In the case of Buddhism in China, most people who identified themselves as Buddhists also identified themselves as Confucianists. Neither constituted an inclusive way of being in the world. For many people, being Chinese provided the comprehensive unity of meaning, the basic way of being, in the context of which they could adopt Buddhism for certain purposes and Confucianism for others. When religion is taken to mean the most foundational way of being in the world, then being Chinese is the religion of most of the Chinese people. This meaning of religion needs to be kept in mind along with others, but in most discourse it functions more as one of the characteristics that may or may not be present than as the decisive basis of use of the term.

If one views the situation in this way, as I do, the question, so important to the editors of *The Myth of Christian Uniqueness*, can still arise as to whether all the great traditions are of roughly equal value and validity. But the requisite approach to an answer to this question is then much more complex than it is for those who assume that all these traditions have a common essence or purpose just because they are religions. The issue, in my view, is not whether they all accomplish the same goal equally well—however the goal may be defined. It is first of all whether their diverse goals are equally well-realized.

Consider the case of Buddhism and Confucianism in China. What of their relative value and validity? They coexisted there through many centuries, not primarily as alternate routes to the same goal, but as complementary. In crude oversimplification, Confucianism took care of public affairs, while Buddhism dealt with the inner life. Perhaps one might go on to say that they were about equally successful in fulfilling their respective roles, but that statement would be hard to support and does not seem especially important.

Questions about the relative value of the great religious traditions can all be asked, and asked with less confusion, if the category "religion" is dropped. Both Buddhism and Confucianism are traditions that are correctly characterized in a variety of ways. By most, but not all, definitions of "religious," both can be characterized as religious. But to move from the fact that they are, among other things, "religious," to calling them religions is misleading and has in fact misdirected most of the discussion. It is for this reason that I am belaboring what appears to me an all-too-obvious point. The horse I am beating is not dead. It is alive as an assumption of the editors of *The Myth of Christian Uniqueness*. The assumption is so strong that, so far as I can discover, no argument is given in its support, and arguments against it, such as mine, are systematically ignored rather than debated.

I oppose the "pluralism" of the editors of (and some of the contributors to) *The Myth of Christian Uniqueness*, not for the sake of claiming that only in Christianity is the end of all religion realized, but for the sake of affirming a much more fundamental pluralism. Confucianism, Buddhism, Hinduism, Islam, Judaism, and Christianity, among others, are religious traditions, but they are also many other things. Further, of the family of characteristics suggested by "religious," they do not all embody the same ones.

Few of the supporters of either "pluralism" or "anti-pluralism" deny the fact of diversity. Our differences is that they discern within and behind the diversity some self-identical element, perhaps an a priori, that they call religion.

It is this that interests them and that functions normatively for them. The issue among the Christians who espouse this view is whether Christians should claim superiority.

What strikes the observer of this discussion is that among those who assume that religion has an essence there is no consensus as to what the essence may be. Even individual scholars often change their mind. The variation is still greater when the scholars represent diverse religious traditions. Yet among many of them the assumption that there *is* an essence continues unshaken in the midst of uncertainty as to what that essence is.

I see no a priori reason to assume that religion has an essence or that the great religious traditions are well understood as religions, that is, as traditions for which being religious is the central goal. I certainly see no empirical evidence in favor of this view. I see only scholarly habit and the power of language to mislead. I call for a pluralism that allows each religious tradition to define its own nature and purposes and the role of religious elements within it.

II

If we give up the notion of an essence of religion, there remain two modes of evaluation of individual religious traditions: internal and external. I will consider these in that order.

If a religious tradition claims to provide a way of life that leads to a just, peaceable, and stable social order, then we can ask whether, when its precepts have been most faithfully followed, the result has been a just, peaceable, and stable social order. If a religious tradition claims to provide a way to attain personal serenity and compassion toward all, then we can ask whether, when its precepts are most fully followed, the result has been personal serenity and compassion toward all.

These evaluations are not easy, but they can be made with some reasonable justification. On the other hand, when goals are stated in less factual ways, the evaluation becomes more difficult or even impossible. For example, if it is claimed that dramatic historical changes would occur if for one day all members of a community perfectly observed all the precepts, and if such perfect observance has never occurred and is highly unlikely ever to occur, evaluation cannot be empirical. Even more clearly, when the results of following the precepts are located in another world and another life, no evaluation is possible. Nevertheless, most religious traditions make *some* claims that are realistically examinable.

My own judgment is that no religious tradition would long survive if it failed to accomplish in the course of history and personal lives some measure of its goal. Hence, on the whole, religious traditions fare relatively well based on the norms to which they themselves are committed. Generally, by its own norms, each succeeds better than do any of the others. No doubt some do better than others even measured by their own norms, and within all of them there are massive failures as well as successes. Whether rough equality is a useful generalization is hard to say, but as people from different traditions meet, it is a good assumption with which to begin.

The second form of evaluation is external. These external judgments can be based on the norms of other religious traditions or secular communities. Here, of course, chaos ensues. Each does well by some norms and badly by others. The more important question is whether any of these norms have validity outside the communities that are committed to them. Is there any way in which one or another norm can claim validity of a universal sort?

This is where the essentialist view is so handy, and it may be one reason why it is clung to with such persistence. If religion has an essence, and if embodying that essence well is the primary goal of every religious tradition, then it becomes objectively meaningful to evaluate all religions by this normative essence. Since I have rejected that, I have no ready access to any universal norm. It seems that pluralists of my stripe are condemned to a pluralism of norms such that each tradition is best by its own norm and there is no normative critique of norms. This is the doctrine of conceptual relativism. It seems to do justice to each tradition, but in fact it vitiates the claims of all, since all claim at least some elements of universality.

Are we forced to choose between an essentialist view of religion, on the one hand, and conceptual relativism, on the other? I think not. The actual course of dialogue does not support either theory. One enters dialogue both as a believer convinced of the claims of one religious tradition and as a human being open to the possibility that one has something to learn from representatives of another religious tradition. Furthermore, this duality of attitudes is often united. In many instances, precisely *as* a believer one is open to learn from others, believing that the fullness of wisdom goes beyond what any tradition already possesses.

The belief that there is more to truth and wisdom than one's own tradition has thus far attained is the basis for overcoming the alternatives of essentialism and conceptual relativism. It entails belief that while one's own tradition has grasped important aspects of reality, reality in its entirety is always more. This means also that the ultimately true norm for life, and therefore also for religious traditions, lies beyond any extant formulation. As dialogue proceeds, glimpses of aspects of reality heretofore unnoticed are vouchsafed the participants. This is not felt as a threat to the religious traditions from which the participants come but as an opportunity for enrichment and even positive transformation.

The problem with conceptual relativism is not that it sees a circularity between beliefs and the norms by which they are judged. This is the human condition. The weakness is that it pictures this as a static, self-enclosed system, whereas the great religious traditions can be open and dynamic. This does not justify someone claiming to stand outside all the relative positions and to be able to establish a neutral, objective norm over all. But it does mean that normative thinking within each tradition can be expanded and extended through openness to the normative thinking of others. For example, in dialogue with Buddhists, Christians can come to appreciate the normative value of the realization of Emptiness, and can expand the way they have thought of the purpose and meaning of life. The norm by which they then judge both Christianity and Buddhism is thereby expanded. Similarly, in dialogue with Christians, Buddhists may come to appreciate the normative value of certain forms of historical consciousness, and the resultant norm by which they judge both Buddhism and Christianity is changed.

Of course, the enlarged norms of the Christians and the Buddhists that result from this dialogue are not universal and objective. When a Buddhist who has gained from dialogue with Christians enters dialogue with Hindus, quite different issues arise. If the dialogue is successful, there will be further expansions in the apprehensions of norms. But again, such expansion, however far it goes, does not detach itself from its historical conditions. It becomes more inclusive and more appropriate to use over a broader range. It does not become ultimate and absolute.

There is one relatively objective norm that can be abstracted from this process. It is relatively objective in that it follows from features that characterize all the traditions to the extent that they acknowledge the pluralistic situation in which all are plunged today. I will summarize these.

First, all the great religious traditions make some claim to the universal value of their particular insights and affirmations. This makes unacceptable a sheer conceptual relativism.

Second, most of the great religious traditions teach a certain humility with regard to human understanding of reality in its depth and fullness. Hence, they discourage the tendency, present in all, to identify ideas that are now possessed and controlled with final expression of all important truth.

Third, as the great religious traditions become more aware of one another, there is a tendency for some mutual appreciation to develop among them. They acknowledge that they learn something from mutual contact. They may claim that what they learn is to value neglected aspects of their own traditions, for in this way they can maintain the tendency to claim the perfection of their own sacred sources. But in fact the understanding that emerges is not the one that obtains when only their own tradition is studied. Some adherents are willing to acknowledge this.

Fourth, as they are in fact transformed by interaction, the norms by which they judge both themselves and others are enlarged. The universal relevance of their own insights is vindicated as other traditions acknowledge their value. The comprehensiveness and human adequacy of their traditions is enlarged as they assimilate the insights of others.

It is important to reemphasize that the points above are drawn from the actual experience of dialogue. They do not characterize those sections of each of the traditions that are unwilling to engage in dialogue at all. The pluralistic situation can lead to fundamentalist self-isolation in all the traditions. What I am seeking in this essay is a way of thinking about the situation appropriate for those who are committed to dialogue. Fortunately, there are many of these in all the traditions, and it is among them that new ways of understanding the relations among the traditions can arise. It is to this understanding that the editors of *The Myth of Christian Uniqueness* want to contribute. My intention is to offer a different proposal.

The implication of this summary of what happens in dialogue, then, is that one norm that can be applied with relative objectivity to the great religious traditions has to do with their ability, in faithfulness to their heritage, to expand their understanding of reality and its normative implications. A tradition that cannot do this is torn between several unsatisfactory options in this pluralistic world. One option is to claim that despite all appearances, it already possesses the fullness of truth so that all who disagree or make different points are to that extent simply wrong. A second option is to accept its own relativization after the fashion of conceptual relativism, asserting that its message is truth for its believers but irrelevant to others. A third option is to detach itself from its own heritage in part, acknowledging that this heritage absolutizes itself in a way that is not acceptable in a pluralistic world, and then to operate at two levels—one, of acceptance of the heritage, the other, of relativizing it. The distaste most persons who engage in dialogue feel for all three of these options is the basis for claiming relative objectivity for the proposed norm.

It may be that judged by this norm, all the great religious traditions are roughly equal. On the other hand, it may be that some are more favorably situated than others to benefit from the radically pluralistic situation in which we are now immersed. Certainly the readiness for dialogue and learning depends in all of the great religious traditions on the subtraditions in which people stand. All traditions have fundamentalist subtraditions that reject all new learning, insisting on the total adequacy and accuracy of what has been received from the past. Even participants in those other subtraditions that are most ready and eager to take advantage of the new pluralistic situation are not equally open to everything. The traditional understanding they bring to bear has a great effect on what they can receive through interaction. There are profound differences in the way the several traditions prepare their participants to hear what others are really saying. Whether they do this equally well is a question to be discussed and examined rather than set aside out of false courtesy.

III

In the first section I expounded my view that there is a radical pluralism of religious traditions. In the second section I argued that this view need not lead to relativism, because most traditions are open to being influenced by the truth and wisdom contained in others. In this third section I will consider first some ways in which Chinese and Indian religious traditions open themselves to others. I will then describe the way in which Abrahamic traditions approach this matter and argue for the peculiar capacity of Christianity to become increasingly inclusive in its understanding.

In the previous sections I noted how in China different religious traditions could function in a complementary fashion, in a context that was determined by a more inclusive horizon, that of being Chinese. This is one strategy for dealing with religious pluralism. Being Chinese opens one to learning whatever can be incorporated into that culture and way of being in the world. Confucianism springs out of that culture, and the fit is excellent. Buddhism has improved and adjusted itself so that it too could play a large role, but one subordinate to the Chinese ethos. Of course, its presence also changed that ethos. The Abrahamic faiths have been much more difficult to assimilate into a fundamentally Chinese ethos.

The method of the Indian religious traditions is somewhat different. Hinduism means little more than the traditional religions of the Indian people, but it does suggest a way of allowing this multiplicity of faiths and attitudes to co-exist. They are all viewed as ways in which people respond to the ultimate reality of Brahman. Hindus in general celebrate the diversity of approaches to Brahman, with some subtraditions worshipping various deities taken to be manifestations of Brahman and others seeking to realize oneness with Brahman through strenuous spiritual disciplines. The image of many paths up the same mountain expresses the way in which Hindus of many subtraditions have been able to accept and affirm one another with a remarkable degree of tolerance. As Hindus have met other religious traditions, they have typically been prepared to extend this same accepting attitude toward them. They are willing to listen and learn about other paths up the mountain.

Hindus such as Radhakrishnan, who have given thought to the world religions, are convinced that Hinduism already has the embracing vision that is needed for all the religions to live with one another and to learn from one another. Unfortunately, this approach has not worked well in relation to the Abrahamic faiths. Hindus are prepared to accept these if they will understand themselves as paths up the mountain already well known to Hindus. But on the whole, representatives of the Abrahamic faiths cannot understand themselves in this way. They often express their refusal in exclusivistic terms, arguing that they alone have the way of salvation, so that Hinduism is a false guide. But even those representatives of Islam and Christianity who are not so arrogantly exclusivist resist being viewed as offering only another way to the goal already fully realized by the profoundest Hindu saints and mystics. This seems to entail viewing the God of Abraham, Isaac, and Jacob as only one among many manifestations of that one absolute reality known so much more fully and adequately by Hindus.

Buddhists can also think of many paths up the same mountain, but another image may be more illuminating for them. Buddhism has only one commitment, namely, to enlightenment. Enlightenment may occur in various traditions in various ways. One need not be a Buddhist in order to be enlightened. Indeed, enlightenment liberates one from all identification with historical or cultural movements. These are all superficial. Masao Abe characterizes the enlightened perspective as the "positionless position."[1] From this perspective one can be open to whatever truth and wisdom is discoverable in any tradition. Thus there is complete openness to learning through dialogue with others. At every level except the ultimate level there is willingness to change or be transformed through the dialogue. But all of this must be for the sake of an enlightenment that relativizes everything else.

It is because it relativizes Buddhism itself that the Buddhist can be so free. The question is whether others can accept that relativization of their insights and wisdom. In the case of the Abrahamic faiths, this does not seem to be possible. They can accept relativization of every specific formulation. But their faith in God cannot be subordinated to something else without abandoning the heritage.

My point in the above is simply to note a limitation in the forms of openness that characterize the Indian religious traditions. They can be open to a great deal, but it does not seem they can be open to the ultimate claims of the Abrahamic traditions about faith in God. The question is now whether the openness that is possible from the side of the Abrahamic faiths can deal any better with the wisdom of India.

If we quickly scan the history of these faiths, the answer seems to be that their record is much worse than that of the Indian traditions. Belief in one God and in that God's unique revelation has led these traditions to exclusivism and intolerance. Of the three, Judaism has been most willing to live and let live, but its core teaching is not inherently so tolerant. The tolerance comes from its preoccupation with the people Israel, such that the destiny of others is of less concern. When, as in both Christianity and Islam, the core teaching about a God who is revealed in specific historical ways and calls for obedience to that revelation is separated from the ethnocentric features of Judaism, the zeal to bring the message to all has led both to heroic self-sacrifice and to brutal intolerance.

Yet there are features of this belief in God that have also led to openness to learning from others. It is generally believed that the God who is revealed in quite specific ways has also been present and active in the world always and everywhere. The believer can expect to see some signs of that activity throughout creation and especially among human beings. When members of the Abrahamic faiths have encountered what seemed good and true in other traditions, they have typically held that this, too, was the work of God. For example, all three traditions borrowed extensively from Greek philosophy. Especially in the case of Christianity and Islam, this borrowing involved, for good and ill, a profound transformation. In the case of Christianity it can be argued that its ultimate victory over Neo-Platonism for the commitment of the intelligentsia of the late Roman Empire was due to its ability to assimilate the wisdom of Neo-Platonism, while the Neo-Platonic philosophers

---

1. J. Hick and H. Askari, eds., *The Experience of Religious Diversity* (Vermont: Gower Publishing Co., 1985), p. 172.

were not equally able to assimilate the wisdom of the Hebrew and Christian scriptures.

One way of viewing the Christian advantage in this case is that Christians believed in a God who acted in history. For this reason they could believe that new developments expressed God's intention and purpose. It is more difficult to give religious meaning to current events when the ultimate is conceived as related in one and the same unchanging way with all events in the world. Then the truth is static and the way of coming to that truth is not through the changing course of events but through pure thought or religious experience.

The openness to being led into new truth in the course of events is accentuated in the Abrahamic traditions, and especially in Christianity, by the focus on the future. Christians know that they now see dimly, that the fullness of light is yet to come. The truth is what will be known, not what is already grasped. Of course, even in Chistianity this future-orientation is always in tension with affirmations about the fullness of the revelation that is already given in Jesus Christ. Centering on Jesus or on Christ often functions as a form of closure, as an insistence that nothing more needs to be learned. Christians at times have wanted to purify the church from everything that was assimilated from the Greeks and Romans so as to be more purely biblical. The deeper question is whether centering ourselves on Jesus or on Christ truly has this effect of closure or whether this is itself a misunderstanding of the meaning of Christocentrism.

It is my conviction that Christocentrism provides the deepest and fullest reason for openness to others. I have argued that thesis at some length elsewhere,[2] and it would not be appropriate to repeat the arguments here. I will only make a few simple points. It is hard to see how one can be truly centered on the historical Jesus if one does not share his hope for the coming realm of God. To claim to be Jesus-centered without sharing his future-orientation is, at least, paradoxical. This does not mean that we ignore everything about Jesus except for his future orientation. In his own ministry the coming realm is already manifest. Hence we know something of the character of the future for which we hope, and we order our lives now to realize that character as best we can. That character is, above all, love, not only of those like ourselves, but of those we are prone to count as opponents as well. Surely that includes love of adherents of other religious traditions, and surely also that love expresses itself both in sharing the Good News with which we are entrusted and in sensitive listening to what they have to say.

If we shift our focus to Christ, understood as the divine reality as incarnate, foremost in Jesus, but also in some measure in the church and the world, then the focus on the actual course of historical events and the presence of Christ in those events seems necessary. The question is then what

---

2. John B. Cobb, Jr., *Christ in a Pluralistic Age* (Philadelphia: Westminster, 1975). See also, chapter 5 below, "Toward a Christocentric Catholic Theology."

Christ is doing in the world today. It is not hard to think of that work as reminding us of our finitude and breaking our tendency to think that our own opinions are final and adequate. It is easy to think of that work as calling us to listen to the truth and wisdom of others. Many Christians certainly feel more faithful when they listen in love and respect to what others have to say than when they insist only on restating the ideas that they bring from the past. To learn from others whatever truth they have to offer and to integrate that with the insights and wisdom we have learned from our Christian heritage appears to be faithful to Christ.

The test is whether in fact one *can* integrate the wisdom of alien traditions into one's Christian vision. This is not easy and there is no simple recipe. St. Augustine's Neo-Platonic Christianity was a major intellectual achievement that required personal genius and disciplined work. To do equally well today in relationship to Hindu and Buddhist wisdom will take equal daring and sustained effort. My point is not that it is easy. It is only that it is faithful to Christ and precedented in our history. I have attempted myself to make some contributions to describing what a Christianity deeply informed by Buddhism may be like.[3] A number of others are working on this project. I am convinced that it is a task whose time has come and that Christian faith offers us unique motivation and unique resources for the task.

IV

So am I affirming Christian uniqueness? Certainly and emphatically so! But I am affirming the uniqueness also of Confucianism, Buddhism, Hinduism, Islam, and Judaism. With the assumption of radical pluralism, nothing else is possible. Further, the uniqueness of each includes a unique superiority, namely, the ability to achieve what by its own historic norms is most important.

The question is whether there are any norms that transcend this diversity, norms that are appropriately applied to all. I have argued that the contemporary situation of pluralism does generate one such norm for those who are committed to dialogue—one that in this situation has relative objectivity. This is the ability of a tradition in faithfulness to its past to be enriched and transformed in its interaction with the other traditions.

I have qualified my claim about this norm by saying that it is relevant only to those who are committed to dialogue. But I have implied that interest in dialogue is characteristic of important segments of all the great religious traditions today. Indeed, it is my view that the dynamic subtraditions in the religious world today are finding it increasingly difficult to maintain a stance of indifference toward the presence of other religious traditions or even one of mere opposition. Hence I find it easy to move from a norm relevant to those involved in dialogue to one with broad implications for the religious world today.

---

3. John B. Cobb, Jr., *Beyond Dialogue: Toward a Mutual Transformation of Christianity and Buddhism* (Philadelphia: Fortress, 1982).

I may be claiming too much. Some traditions may understand their primary task to be maintaining the separateness of their people from others or keeping their inherited wisdom intact and unaffected. For them the ability to be enriched and transformed is not a norm at all. It is only insofar as a tradition claims universal relevance that its exclusion of the insights of others is problematic in terms of its own norms. Of course, the claim for universal validity can continue to be made while ignoring the similar claims of others. But in this form it remains a mere claim. To demonstrate the validity of the claim requires that the claims of others also be understood and the relation among them explained. The ability, in faithfulness to one's heritage, to display the universal relevance of the wisdom of all traditions in a coherent way has a certain relative advantage once the aim at universal relevance is thought through in a pluralistic context.

The argument of the previous section is that Christianity is well equipped to move forward to the fuller universality I believe to be desirable. I have not said enough to establish that no other tradition is equally well equipped for this task. Negative argumentation of this sort is an ungracious work. I hope that other traditions will compete vigorously with Christianity. Whereas much past competition among the traditions has been mutually destructive, competition in learning from one another and being transformed by what is learned will prove constructive. I hope that the Christian advantage in this competition is less than I have supposed.

I am making a claim to Christian superiority. It is not a claim that Christians are better people than others, or that Christian history has made a more positive contribution to the planet than have other traditions, or that Christian institutions are superior. The claim is only that a tradition in which Jesus Christ is the center has in principle no need for exclusive boundaries, that it can be open to transformation by what it learns from others, that it can move forward to become a community of faith that is informed by the whole of human history, that its theology can become truly global.

I have avoided in the foregoing the issue of conflicting truth claims. This is because I do not find this the most productive approach. Of course, there are such conflicts. There are conflicting views of the natural world, of human nature, and of God. It is not possible that everything that has been said on these topics can correspond with reality, and for this reason many thinkers regard the sorting out of these claims and adjudication among them as crucial for religious thought.

My view is that none of the central claims made by any of the traditions are likely to be literally and exactly correct. Indeed, in many traditions there is an internal emphasis on the difficulty, if not the impossibility, of grasping the truth and expressing it in language. Laying out the conflicting doctrines and developing arguments for and against each is a questionable preoccupation. Instead, it is best to listen to the deep, even ultimate, concerns that are being expressed in these diverse statements. Here I am at one with those in opposition to whom this essay is written. They, too, seek to go beyond what is said to something deeper. We differ only in that what they find is something common to all the traditions, whereas I believe that what we find is diverse. My goal is to transform contradictory statements into different but not contradictory ones. My assumption is that what is positively intended by those who have lived, thought, and felt deeply is likely to be true, whereas their formulations are likely to exclude other truths that should not be excluded.

I will illustrate what I mean by the clearly contradictory statements:"God exists." and "No God exists." If we approach these statements with the assumption that the words *God* and *exists* have clear and exact meanings that are identical in the two statements, we have no choice but to say that at least one of them is wrong. But surely we are past this point in our reflections about religious discourse. We have to ask who is speaking and what concerns are being expressed. When a Buddhist says that no God exists, the main point is that there is nothing in reality to which one should be attached. When a Christian says that God exists, the meaning may be that there is that in reality that is worthy of trust and worship. *If* those translations are correct, at least in a particular instance, then it is not impossible that both be correct. Of course, the Buddhist is likely to believe that the Christian is wrong, and the Christian is likely to see no problem with attachment to God. There are then real disagreements between them. But the Buddhist could in principle acknowledge the reality of something worthy of trust and worship without abandoning the central insight that attachment blocks the way to enlightenment. And the Christian could come to see that real trust is not attachment in the Buddhist sense. Both would thereby have learned what is most important to the other without abandoning their central concerns.

Of course, there are many grossly erroneous statements that have been affirmed with great seriousness by adherents of the great religious traditions. It is not true that the world is flat. There is no point in seeking some deeper meaning behind such statements, since we know how they arose from a literalistic reading of certain passages of scripture. There are similar ideas in all the traditions. There are also far more damaging ideas, such as misogynist ones, in most of the religious traditions. These, too, should be condemned as false. But my assumption is that alongside all the errors and distortions that can be found in all our traditions there are insights arising from profound thought and experience that are diverse modes of apprehending diverse aspects of the totality of reality. They are true, and their truth can become more apparent and better formulated as they are positively related to one another.

Whether Christian thinkers as a whole will open themselves to learning from others in this way remains to be seen. Faith in Jesus Christ is often, perhaps usually, expressed in idolatrous forms, such that the relative is absolutized, the partial is treated as a whole. For the sake of Jesus Christ, people make their own beliefs normative for all and close themselves to criticism and new insight. In the name of Jesus Christ people have gone to war with the "infidel," slaughtered Jews, and tortured Christians whose opinions differed. There is no assurance that all this is at an end. Christians know that the power of sin is peculiarly manifest in the expression of lofty ideals and commitments.

My claim is simply that all this is not truly faithful to Jesus Christ, and that the true meaning of faith *has* expressed itself, imperfectly but authentically, in other features of our past history. I believe it is expressing itself today in movements of liberation and also in enthusiastic efforts to encounter other religious traditions at a deep level. Roman Catholics have appropriated many of the meditational methods of the East, and the experience generated by these methods cannot but be transforming. Both Catholics and Protestants are struggling with new ideas and ways of thinking. The Christianity that emerges will be different from anything we have known before, but that does not mean that it will be less Christian. On the contrary, it will be one more step toward that fullness that is represented by the coming of the Realm of God.

Christianity, like all traditions, is unique. Its role in history has been unique for good and ill. Its response to our pluralistic situation is unique. Its potential for becoming more inclusive is unique. Let us celebrate Christian uniqueness.

5

Toward a Christocentric Catholic Theology

This essay is another example of how a critical response can become the occasion for a constructive contribution. Once again, Cobb warns against what we might call a free-floating universalism—in this case, a "universal theology of religion" that would float above all the individual religions in order to view and interpret and connect them all. Cobb warns that such a bird's-eye view may exist for birds but not for humans. To try to stand above it all, outside of history, in order to view it all, ends up distorting what one is trying to understand; the universal perspective that one thinks one has is really a particular view that ends up distorting other particulars in order to include them in its "universal" embrace.

So rather than start with fabricated universals meant to include everything, Cobb suggests we begin with our given particulars and see how far they can be stretched to include what is beyond themselves. He starts with his own particular: Jesus the Christ. And in doing so, he develops more extensively what in previous essays he merely mentioned: a Christological foundation for a Christian theology of religions. Basing himself on a Logos—or better, Wisdom—Christology that sees Jesus as an historical expression of the universal, life-fostering Presence of the Divine, Cobb shows how "Christocentric" must lead to "catholic"—that is, how the particular must reach out to that which is not itself, in order to be itself! Thus, there is a dynamic tension between the particular and the universal; but it starts with the particular, and the tension must be lived out, explored, followed; it's not pre-established.

With such a "catholic Christocentrism," Cobb turns exclusivist interpretations of Jesus on their heads. Jesus is indeed the very well defined, locatable center of the Christians' circle; but the circumference of that circle cannot be defined as narrowly as Christians often have thought; indeed, one might say that according to Cobb, the limits of that circumference are not definable. Thus, when John has Jesus define himself as "the Way, the Truth, and the Life," outside of which no one comes to the Father, Cobb reminds us that Jesus is not talking about himself as an historical individual but about the Wisdom that he embodies. Cobb borders on what is "scandalous to pious ears" when he goes so far as to state that though the particular Jesus is essential to Christian life, fidelity to that Jesus requires one to be ready to give him up in order to pursue the Wisdom he reveals. The particular that orients us toward the universe of diversities may sometimes lead us to move beyond that particular! Cobb merely states, but does not unpack, this paradoxical possibility.

But he does give clear, and unsettling, indication of just how diverse that universe of diversities can be. First he suggests that not just the notion but the reality of what Christians call salvation may be really different in different religions (e.g., salvation and mokṣa are not different indicators pointing in the same direction, but two totally different directions). He goes further and suggests that the hypothesis that there is no one absolute behind all religions is more promising than the hypothesis that there is. When Christians talk about God and Buddhists about Emptiness, they're talking about two fundamentally different realities. That's how diverse the religions might well be!

But such differences, he remarks peripherally, need to be brought into some kind of creative synthesis. We should not leave them to languish in their diversities. That's a relief. But again, Cobb needs to say much more about just how this might be done. Where do we start in our efforts to link the diversities?

P. F. K.

This essay first appeared in Leonard Swidler, ed., Toward a Universal Theology of Religion *(Maryknoll, N.Y.: Orbis Books, 1987), pp. 86–100.*

I AM DEEPLY SYMPATHETIC with the concerns and purposes of those who are pursuing a "Universal Theology of Religion." Nevertheless, I do not like the way they name their project. I am not myself seeking a "universal theology of religion." My rejection of this language is no doubt partly a terminological matter of a relatively unimportant sort. But it also expresses basic commitments that may be appropriate for further discussion.

I will order my remarks as follows. In the first section, I state my objections to the goal of a universal theology of religion. The remainder of the chapter will attempt to show how a Christocentric catholic theology can better address the concerns of those seeking a universal theology of religion. The second section considers how the internal history of Christocentric thinkers can become inclusive or catholic. The next section briefly notes the importance of catholicity of subject matter as well. And the final section presents a more detailed discussion of how traditional Christian convictions are to be so formulated as to show that they are complementary to the deepest convictions of other traditions rather than in outright conflict.

My first objection to the project for a universal theology of religion is its focus on "religion." The World Council of Churches has avoided the term "religion" and has advocated dialogue with persons of other faiths and ideologies. I prefer this. To call Christianity, Judaism, Islam, Confucianism, Hinduism, Buddhism, and the primal traditions all "religions" focuses attention on aspects of their total life that are not, in most instances, the most important. That all these traditions have encouraged religious practices is beyond doubt, but that as a whole they are well categorized in light of this feature is very doubtful indeed.

If the word "religious" means nothing more than ways of binding together—that is, ways of organizing and directing life and thought—then I would withdraw my objection. But then there would be no need to add "ideologies," for ideologies too would be religions. In fact the word "religion" almost always highlights to the Western ear cultic practices and especially those associated with belief in divine being(s). It is this that renders it a poor choice as the primary category for many of the great traditions.

But does the WCC shift to "faiths" help? Wilfred Cantwell Smith has objected that we should speak of various ways in which faith is expressed rather than of a plurality of faiths. He makes a good point. I would add that I do not see faith as the center of all traditions. It belongs to the theistic traditions primarily, so that the use of this term places other traditions in an unsuitable category. Further, it is only by virtue of its theistic connotations that "faiths" requires supplementation by "ideologies."

The only positive suggestion I can make as to how we can speak of the great traditions of humankind is that we call them "ways." By "ways" I mean not only ways to live but also ways to understand life and the total context of life. I suspect that no *way* that has guided the life of large communities over any extended period of time is devoid of strong religious elements. But these are not always primary. Marxism has been a very important way in our time, but it deemphasizes or even denies its tendencies to divinize historical processes and heroes, and to evolve its own cultic patterns. And there are forms of Judaism, Christianity, Confucianism, and Buddhism for which cult and divinities are not central. Nevertheless, they are all comprehensive ways of life and thought.

Now it might well be said that what is meant by "religion" is what I mean by "way," so that my quarrel might be a rather petty one. Let us assume that. In that case, what about a theology of religion understood in this sense? Would a theology of religion then be reflection about the great ways of humankind? Would these ways of life and thought become themselves the subject matter of theological inquiry? Surely it is theologically appropriate to reflect about these traditions. And there have been important theologians who have taken human experience, activity, and thought as their topic. But for my own part, I believe this to be a mistake. I believe that theology should concern itself primarily with that with which these ways have concerned themselves, not with the ways as such.

I suspect here again that I am not in real disagreement with those seeking a theology of religion. Their emphasis is interreligious dialogue, not history of religions as an academic discipline. The latter tends to make the ways and their religious practices its topic, whereas dialogue usually focuses on what the participants see as most important. Hence I will assume that theology of religion, when religion is understood as I have proposed, deals with that to which the great ways of humankind point, and I will not raise further objections to this.

But what of a "universal theology"? Here I am genuinely uncertain as to the intention. But I fear that the meaning conveyed is that theology can begin with a perspective shaped neutrally by all the ways rather than by any one of them in particular. This means that a universal theology will replace specifically Christian theology, which is viewed as being inherently parochial.

If that is the meaning, then I protest in the name both of realism and of Christian faith. In the name of realism I protest that the pretense to stand beyond all traditions and build neutrally out of all of them is a delusion. In the name of Christian faith I protest against the implicit relativization and even negation of basic Christian commitments.

I propose as an alternative that what we Christians need is a truly catholic theology. Inasmuch as I am a Protestant you will understand that I do not mean by "catholic" something specifically bound up with the Roman Catholic Church. Yet as a Protestant I do recognize that the impulse to true catholicity may be stronger in the Roman Catholic Church than in the Protestant denominations, despite the sectarian tendencies that afflict it too.

I propose, secondly, that the impulse to catholicity is specifically christological and that it is Christocentrism that requires of the Christian the rejection of all arrogance, exclusivism, and dogmatism in relation to other ways. I believe a truly christocentric theology must be catholic, and that a truly catholic theology will satisfy much of what is sought by those who propose a universal theology of religion. The remainder of this chapter is devoted to clarifying and developing this claim.

First, who is the Christ in whom Christian theology is properly centered? Throughout the history of Christianity there has been a duality of focus that is essential to the idea of incarnation itself. There is, first, the one who becomes incarnate and there is, secondly, the one who is the incarnation. The Word became a human being in Jesus. I myself wish that the Johannine prologue had spoken of *Sophia* instead of *Logos*, and I propose that, despite the predominance of "Word" in the tradition, we speak today of "Wisdom."

Christocentrism means both that we should place our faith in the divine Wisdom, which is very God of very God, and that the embodiment of that Wisdom in Jesus provides us with the center of our history. These two aspects of Christocentrism are indissolubly connected for us. We trust the everlasting Wisdom because of what happened in Jesus. We affirm Jesus as the center of our history because in him we find the everlasting Wisdom.

The Wisdom we find incarnate in Jesus is present everywhere and at all times. Specifically, it is that by virtue of which there is life wherever there is any living thing, and it is that apart from which there is no human understanding at all. Hence the affirmation that this Wisdom is incarnate in Jesus cannot mean that Jesus is the only channel through which God is present in the world. On the contrary, the Wisdom we meet in Jesus is precisely the Wisdom that is already known by all. Exclusivism implicitly denies that this Wisdom is truly God, and thus opposes the Christian understanding of the incarnation, which, in turn, is the basis of Christocentrism.

Even those who acknowledge that God is somehow known to all sometimes argue that Jesus, and Jesus alone, has introduced an understanding of God adequate to all human needs. The words, "I am the way, the truth, and the life," which in their Johannine context apply to the divine Word or Wisdom, are wrongly taken to refer exclusively to a particular human being. Thereby the exclusivism banished by one aspect of Christocentrism makes its reappearance through a particular form of the other aspect. Because the problem lies in wrong affirmations about Jesus and, especially, in false conclusions from the doctrine of incarnation, I want to describe a form of incarnational theology for which Jesus is the center of history, and which leads away from exclusivism to true catholicity.

I should acknowledge, before proceeding, my indebtedness to one book of H. Richard Niebuhr. Reading *The Meaning of Revelation* as a seminary student was for me a revelatory experience. It permanently affected my understanding of the theological task. What I have to say today is indebted to that book.

Niebuhr helps us understand that we all live by our private and communal memories or internal histories. If you want to know who I am, I can provide some categories in which to place me: citizen of the United States, member of the United Methodist Church, male, white, seminary professor, and so forth. But if you really want to know who I am, you will have to let me share my story with you. Similarly you can define Christianity in terms of certain categories to which it belongs or certain of its official teachings or widespread practices. But if you want to know what it really means to be a Christian, you will have to study the history of Christianity and specifically how that history is now understood and appropriated by believers. It is in that way that you will discover that Jesus is the center of history for Christians.

Of course, to be the center of history is not to be the whole of history. The conventional story begins with Genesis and remembers the history of the Jews down to the time of Jesus. It includes the way the early Christians responded to Jesus and then follows the history of the expansion of Christianity and the specific ancestry of our present several communities. As Christians, most of us live out of some such story.

Now the problem with that story is not, as some suppose, that Jesus is at the center, but that the circumference is far too narrow. For most of us it does not even include the whole story of Christianity. In our Western church histories we are likely to neglect the Orthodox East after the credal controversies are ended. We Protestants learn very little of Catholic history after the Council of Trent. The ecumenical movement among Christians is doing much to heal this foreshortened memory and to enable us all to claim the whole of the Christian story as our story. This is a gain, and there is little doubt that we achieve this precisely through our joint acknowledgment of the centrality of Jesus to all of our Christian stories.

But this is obviously insufficient. If Christian ecumenism were to be won at the price of intensified exclusivism in relation to others, the price would be too high. Especially the emphasis on the centrality of Jesus in Christian ecumenism is in danger of intensifying the destructive wall that separates us from Judaism.

The story we Christians learn begins with that of the ancient Jews. But this story culminates in the fierce attack on the Jews placed on the lips of Jesus in the Gospel of John and in the struggle with the Jews recorded in the book of Acts. The story of those from whom we Christians separated with much bitterness is most of us something alien. It is indeed the story of those we reviled and persecuted, and it is not pleasant to recall it. Nevertheless, Christians are today attempting to learn that story. We must learn it first as *their* story, but we must also move beyond that. It must become part of *our* story as Christians-and-Jews.

Now whence comes for us as Christians the impulse to learn this story and to redefine what we mean by "we" to include both Christians and Jews? It comes from Wisdom. But I am trying here to focus on the particularities of history. Historical sources are difficult to prove, but I have no doubt that it comes from the story whose center is the Jewish Jesus. When we seriously take Jesus as the center of our history, we cannot be satisfied with the partisan rejection of Jesus' people that has characterized our gentile Christianity through the centuries. We look forward with Paul to the time when our gentile misappropriation of Jesus will not compel Jews to disown him. We believe that our destiny as Christians is bound up with the destiny of the Jews in one destiny of Jews-and-Christians. Indeed we understand that we are all Jews whether we are the natural or the engrafted branches.

My point is a simple one. The broadening of our internal history to include Judaism does not—for us Christians—displace Jesus from the center of our history. On the contrary, it is because Jesus is the center that we are moved toward the more inclusive history.

What about that other great offshoot of Judaism, Islam? Can Muslim history also become part of our internal history? We are much further from Muslims. It will take decades of study and dialogue before we can integrate their historical experience with ours. But already we recognize that the God whom Jesus called Father is also the one they call Allāh. We cannot feel ourselves wholly alien to those who do the will of that God, and we cannot but recognize the seriousness with which Muslims undertake that task. As long as Jesus is the center of the history by which we live, there will be a strong impulse for us to expand that history to include that of Islam as well.

To live by a remembered history is not to sentimentalize that history or to minimize the evil that plays so large a role within it. Concealing the evil and highlighting the good in our personal and communal stories is a temptation to which all succumb. But the Jewish scriptures are remarkable in the extent to which they evade this temptation. The heroes are also sinners. The Jews know themselves as a people often faithless to God. In the Gospels also the disciples appear as foolish and weak. Unfortunately a tendency to adulation of Christian heroes begins in the Acts of the Apostles and has infected much of the Christian story ever since. But to learn that our story is one of exclusivism, anti-Judaism, sexism, racism, corruption by power, corruption by wealth, corruption by piety, corruption by nationalism, and a host of other sins does not keep it from being our story. Because Jesus is its center we can understand this evil for what it is and repent.

Similarly, as we appropriate the stories of Jews and Muslims as part of our enlarged new story, we do not do so uncritically. We find many ways in which, in the light of Jesus, they are to be commended for avoiding sins to which we succumbed. But we will also inevitably evaluate their stories as well, and in the light of Jesus we will see ways in which they have much to gain by appropriating him more fully into their internal histories.

The expansion of our internal history is proceeding in another direction as well. Our critical study of the scriptures was long directed toward isolating the pure Jewish and Christian strain from the many other influences that gain expression there. We celebrated our history largely by contrasting it with paganism. That is now changing. We continue to celebrate the creativity of the Jewish people in weaving together the many strands of influence into a creative and dynamic faith in one God, but we no longer view the strands that are woven together as something to be despised. Our Jewish heritage leads us to reclaim our Egyptian, Canaanite, Mesopotamian, Persian, and Greek heritage as well. Our internal history expands. But it does not become simply the sum total of all those histories told in any way and from any perspective. On the contrary, we appropriate all into an enlarging history whose center remains, for us, Jesus. It is the nature of that center to allow and demand the expansion of the circumference.

Thus far, in a very schematic way I have indicated what I mean by expanding our internal history to encompass a larger part of human history, not in spite of Christocentricity but because of it. But even this is not enough. There are other histories, those of India and China and Korea as well as Africa and the indigenous peoples of the New World, that cannot be brought into our internal history simply through the historical expansion of the story we tell ourselves. In order to include these stories, too, is it necessary to give up the centrality of Jesus and seek some other principle of organization or revelation for the larger whole? Should I, after all, give up my Christocentric catholic project in favor of the universal theology of religion?

The answer to this question requires honest self-examination. I do find myself desirous of incorporating into my internal history a wider one than that historically connected with Jesus. Why? What draws me in that direction? Why am I not satisfied to identify myself strongly with one portion of humanity and to view others simply as others? What pulls against the we-they dualism that also afflicts me? As far as I can tell, there is a double answer corresponding to the dual elements in Christocentrism. First, whenever I draw the line between "us" and "them" I seem to discern wisdom on both sides of the line, and I cannot be satisfied consciously to reject or ignore what I, at the same time, recognize to be wise. That I understand that wisdom to be the divine Wisdom, present in the other, focuses and intensifies this need to overcome the barriers that separate.

I have also learned that a besetting temptation to which I and others are continually succumbing is to identify that bit of understanding already possessed with the whole of wisdom, or with what is really important in it. I have learned that this is arrogance and that nothing cuts us off from God more surely than this idolatry of what we already possess. I have learned that coldness or indifference to others in the concreteness of their being, which includes their understanding, is the rejection of God's love for us as well as the refusal to love God. I have learned that my destiny is bound up with that of the whole globe.

The question now is, Where have I learned these things? There are many answers: home, school, church, books, friends. But when I press the question more deeply, I must come back to the fact that it is from the Christian story that I have learned them, primarily from the Bible. And when I ask how in fact I understand the Bible, I must confess that I read it in terms of a center that is Jesus. My impulse to live out of a story larger than the one that is historically interconnected with Jesus comes from Jesus.

That, of course, is only a beginning of the answer to the larger question. Suppose we Christians are impelled to include Gautama Buddha within our internal histories. Granted, the impulse comes from Jesus. Will the result be simply an expansion of the history from which we live so that the center remains Jesus? Or will Gautama introduce a new center—one that displaces Jesus from centrality?

Such displacement of Jesus is not to be rejected a priori in the name of Christian faith. On the contrary, faith expresses itself in action whose consequences we cannot anticipate. If faithfulness to Jesus leads to the displacement of Jesus from centrality, then such displacement is itself faithful.

There are certainly those who, consciously or unconsciously impelled by Jesus, have turned to Gautama and found there a new center that displaced the old. My argument is that this is not the necessary result, and that when Jesus is removed from the position of center of all history by the appropriation of Gautama, much that could be included in the history of which Jesus is the center can no longer be included. I do not mean here to judge the question of the value of a fully Buddhist way in comparison with a Christian way. My comment is of a different order. So far as we now can see, much that is of value from the Christian perspective—that is, much that the way centered in

Jesus seeks to include—is neither valued nor included in the Buddhist way. Hence, from the Christian perspective, there are reasons to try to include Gautama within the circle centered in Jesus so that the rest of what is included in that circle can be retained.

In dealing with the other expansions of the Christian circle I have spoken chiefly of additions. This is one-sided; every addition involves some transformation of that to which the addition is made. This feature is greatly intensified in relation to Buddhism. One cannot add Gautama to a basically unchanged complex. To bring him in is to transform everything. The historical consciousness, the quest for meaning in history, cannot remain unchanged when the internal history in question includes Gautama's radical critique and denial of historical meaning.

I have written elsewhere, in *Beyond Dialogue* especially, about a crossing over to Mahayana Buddhism and a coming back to Christianity and how the Christianity in question is thereby transformed. I will not repeat that here. My point is only that the expansion of the internal history from which we live to include the Buddhist achievement as well need not displace the centrality of Jesus, although it will transform all that is known from that center.

The task of dialogue and going beyond dialogue in relation to each of the great ways of humankind is a vast one. We have barely begun to deal with the fundamental changes that must be effected within our Christian faith. The changes that come about through one dialogue may make the next dialogue still more difficult. After each new transformation, the work that was done earlier will have to be done again. But a truly Christocentric faith must seek catholicity in this way.

How is this Christocentric catholic theology to be compared to a universal theology of religion? It is not less universal in the sense of omitting some segment of human experience and wisdom from its purview. But it does not pretend to a neutral or impartial perspective on the whole. Does this render it biased or arrogant? I do not think so. It would be arrogant to assert that the project of catholicity is one that all should pursue, and it would be biased to assert that the only way catholicity can be attained is by Christocentrism. But it is not arrogant to explain that we as Christians are impelled toward catholicity, and to acknowledge that what impels us is our Christocentrism.

Indeed, one of my concerns about the promotion of the project of a universal theology by Christians is that it is difficult to avoid giving the impression that Jews and others should join us in this project. It can be, in relation to Jews, another way of placing them on the defensive if they decline to surrender their identity as Jews to join the quest of universal theology of religion. There are, I think, impulses within Judaism toward a catholic theology, but it is not for Christians to evaluate the importance of those impulses in Judaism in comparison with those toward the preservation of Jewish distinctiveness, or to determine how these are rightly related to one another. It seems more honest and more open to others to explain where we stand as Christians rather than to claim to place our project beyond confessional diversity. My thesis is that a catholic theology can gain the advantages of a universal theology without the arrogance entailed in claiming to attain such universality.

Thus far I have been considering the catholicity of theology in terms of the internal history that shapes the Christian. My understanding is that Christian theology is thinking that is consciously expressive of a perspective shaped by the shared history of Christians. Christian thinking remains parochial as long as that history is parochial. It becomes catholic to whatever extent that history is inclusive. Ultimately the only history adequate to its center in Jesus will be the history of life on this planet.

Christian theology should become catholic in another way as well, and, indeed, becoming catholic in the first way will tend to make it catholic in the other as well. Sometimes it is supposed that Christian theology deals properly only with ideas that are reflected in a particular segment of history, such as the Bible. The topics of theology are narrowly defined in terms of the tradition. Indeed, in the attempt to establish theology as a "science" (*Wissenschaft*), some Protestant theologians of the previous generation carefully explained its task as the interpretation of specific texts, those on which sermons are to be preached. Most of the topics dealt with by St. Augustine or St. Thomas fall outside the purview of theology so conceived. Indeed, most of the issues of life and death with which society now struggles turn out not to be appropriate topics for theological discourse!

In contrast, a truly catholic theology must be catholic in its concerns. Of course it will be selective. It does have a special need to understand the history that has shaped it and the center that governs the understanding of that history. But chiefly its principle of selection will be its sense, coming from that history, of what is most important today. To questions of peace, justice, personal wholeness, ecological health, racism, sexism, hunger, and freedom, as well as those of God, the church, salvation, and eschatology, it will bring the resources and the perspective shaped by the most catholic history it can internally realize. I do not think this project is likely to be called forth by a theology of religion.

I would make another point in agreement with Wilfred Cantwell Smith. Through dialogue we should be able to learn the ways in which our customary affirmations growing out of our own histories are heard by others as denials of their deepest convictions. We should, then, undertake to reformulate our beliefs so that this negation of others will be reduced and finally overcome.

The underlying assumption here is that the aspects of reality that persons come to see through different communal histories differ profoundly, but these aspects are not in flat contradiction. This assumption is based on still deeper ones. First, reality is extremely complex but not self-contradictory. Secondly, what persons really see is there to be seen. The problem, illustrated again and again in all sorts of dialogues, is that our account of what we see is usually inaccurate and exaggerated, and that we quickly move from affirmation of what grasps us to denial of what grasps others. In appreciative listening to others we can come to reformulations of our own convictions that are more accurate and more limited, leaving space for the accurate and limited formulations of the convictions of others.

Examples are numerous. We can take the familiar and central one about salvation. Having experienced personal salvation through faith in Jesus Christ, many Christians have taught that no salvation is possible in any other way. But obviously such sweeping negations follow neither from the Christian experience of salvation, nor from convictions about Jesus Christ's saving power that are appropriate to the experience. A more accurate analysis of the role of Jesus and of the divine Wisdom in effecting our salvation is needed. Also we need to clarify just what we mean by salvation or just what type of salvation is effected for the Christian believer. It is quite likely that the precise salvific experience brought about through faith in Jesus Christ occurs in no other way. But the Christian should listen carefully to the Hindu account of *mokṣa* or the Zen Buddhist account of *satori*, recognizing that these are just as authentic as the Christian experience. Whether we shall stretch the meaning of salvation to include such other experiences and then distinguish diverse modes of salvation, or limit the use of "salvation" to the Christian experience while retaining *mokṣa* and *satori* to refer to the others, is an important decision, but in either case it will be possible to continue to make Christian claims for the dependence on Jesus Christ of what Christians have most prized without entailing any pejorative implications about Hindu and Buddhist experience.

I have gone to great lengths earlier to indicate that we should go beyond merely clarifying our diversity in ways that allow a genuine pluralism. For the Christian it is important not only to understand the experience of others in their difference but to find ways to incorporate these diverse experiences in a transformed Christianity. But even this will not do away with a continuing pluralism. We must continue our care to affirm even our most catholic convictions in such a way that they do not deny the always continuing divergent convictions of others.

Of course, it is unlikely that this project can be completed any more than can the others. Those coming from other traditions may insist on formulations of their convictions that we cannot accept without denying what is centrally important to us. However careful we are, others will hear our affirmations as pejorative, especially because we cannot give up all the language that has been used during centuries in which Christian doctrines did constitute negations of what others affirmed. For example, no matter how carefully we explain what we mean by asserting that Jesus is the Christ, many Jews will continue to hear our affirmation as a contradiction of their insistence that the Messiah has not come. But the abandonment of the word "Christ" on our part is not the appropriate response. Instead we must work together repeatedly to clarify the difference between what Jews mean by "Messiah" and what Christians legit-imately mean by "Christ." We need to join the Jews in their longing for the coming of the Messiah and the messianic age.

Many persons who agree that there are differences among the Christian experience of the forgiveness of sins, the Hindu experience of *mokṣa*, and the Zen experience of *satori*, such that no conflict is involved in acknowledging the authenticity and importance of each, believe that there is another level at which this type of solution cannot apply. This is the level of "ultimate real-ity." Of course, most will agree that "ultimate reality" is beyond our finite conceptualities. Hence we would expect that approaching it from diverse per-spectives will lead to diverse affirmations about it, none of which are finally exhaustive. But whereas the forgiveness of sins, *mokṣa*, and *satori* may be acknowledged, quite simply, as different experiences, many suppose that what is approached as "ultimate reality" must be one and the same, however diversely it is apprehended and conceptualized.

This conviction about the self-identity of "ultimate reality" is strength-ened by dialogue among Jews, Christians, and Muslims. All three agree that the One they worship is one and the same. They may argue about what this One is like, how it has acted, what is its will, what more is to be expected from it in the future. But they are sure that their diverse languages and images have a common reference transcendent of all that any of them can think or say. For example, the One of whom they speak is the reality that created and creates all that is.

But what happens when believers in the One Creator of all enter into dia-logue with representatives of traditions that do not affirm a creation or a cre-ator? Zen Buddhism will serve as the example. Historically some Christians have simply refused dialogue on the grounds that Zen Buddhists are the worst of all reprobates—atheists. But most Christians have seen too much of power and validity in Zen Buddhism to dismiss it in this offhand way. Two alternatives remain.

The first has dominated the dialogue to date. Christians have thought that "Creator" was but one way to understand the One who has been worshiped by the Jewish family of religions. This One is most fundamentally "ultimate reality." Hence the question is not whether Zen Buddhists affirm a Creator but rather how they approach "ultimate reality." The fact that their approach to, and what they say about, "ultimate reality" differ so profoundly from our approach and doctrine only reinforces the awareness that "ultimate reality" is far beyond all that any of us can say or think.

Lest anyone should miss the distinction between this way of avoiding con-tradiction among the convictions of the several great ways and the former one, allow me to recapitulate. With respect to salvation it would theoretically be possible to say that there is but one experience of salvation, which is variously described as the forgiveness of sins, *mokṣa*, and *satori*. But careful study ren-ders such a judgment implausible. If one looks in Christianity for an experi-ence more like that of *mokṣa* or *satori*, one will turn to the mystics who do not describe their culminating experiences as the forgiveness of sins. Almost everyone recognizes that there are many different types of experience even within a single religious tradition, and that there is no reason to suppose that the diverse accounts of religious experiences are all efforts to describe one and the same type of experience.

With respect to what is experienced, however, the situation differs. Here the dominant approach is to assume that that which forgives sins is also the reality that is realized in *mokṣa* and *satori*. In this approach, the difference of experience is understood to be the reason that the reality is spoken of in quite diverse ways. But difference in image and concept is not taken to mean that there is a difference in the reality itself.

This approach to dialogue is compatible with what I said earlier about the vast complexity of reality on the one hand and the noncontradictory character of the diverse experiences of it on the other. Nevertheless, it contains an assumption that I find unwarranted. This is the assumption that there is a one-to-one correspondence between what is thought of as "ultimate reality" in our Western tradition and that with which all "religious" traditions concern themselves. One advocate of this position, Paul Knitter, acknowledges that indeed this is an unproven assumption, and he recommends that it be treated as a hypothesis. Nevertheless, he asserts that just this hypothesis should be held by those who seek dialogue.

My belief is that there is no need to encumber the dialogue with this hypothesis. Indeed, I believe that the dialogue becomes more fruitful when we are fully open to the opposite hypothesis. For example, we should consider that what the Zen Buddhist names "Emptiness" or "Emptying" may not be the same as what the Christian names "God." Of course, if I am correct about this difference, we are left with the task of formulating a creative synthesis in which the relationship between Emptying and God can be understood in ways that neither Buddhists nor Christians have adequately articulated in the past. But what is wrong with that?

What is wrong, I am told repeatedly, is that there can be only one "ultimate reality." I am left with the impression that those who affirm this doctrine regard it as self-evident and suppose a pluralistic metaphysics to be nonsensical. They may, of course, be correct. But is this supposition itself not subject to dialogue? Is it absolutely self-evident, for example, that the ground of form and the ground of matter are identical? Is Plato's cosmology in the *Timaeus* self-evidently absurd?

My suggestion is that it is best to enter each dialogue with both hypotheses in view. It may be that what my dialogue partners will speak of is their experience of that same reality that I know in Jesus Christ as God. If so, fine; I have much to learn from them. But it may be that they will speak of something else, something of which I am even less well informed. If so, I must listen all the more intently. I will have all the more homework to do afterward in integrating what I learn with what I thought I knew. I will need to revise not only my theology but, perchance, my metaphysics. But surely that is nothing against this approach. Surely Christians must be as open to revising metaphysics as to revising theology!

This brings us full circle to my anxiety about the formulation of the project for a universal theology of religion. I fear that this project is the easy way out of our present problems. Consciously or unconsciously we are likely to hold to the metaphysical concomitants of our respective ways and relativize only the historical and theological concomitants.

Let me be more concrete. Many Christian theologians are convinced that underlying the totality of the reality that we can approach through our ordinary modes of inquiry there is another that eludes us. It is the One, the "ultimate reality," that contrasts with everything finite. Schleiermacher tells us it is that on which everything else is absolutely dependent. Tillich calls it Being Itself and declares that it is our ultimate concern.

Those who hold to this metaphysics are likely to suppose that, because everyone is in fact related to this one "ultimate reality," and because this is finally the most important of all relationships, all the great traditions of the world give expression to how this relationship is apprehended. Hence these theologians advocate dialogue and expect through dialogue to become aware of more about how this relationship functions in human life. But what the *relata* of this relationship are, they already know. Through dialogue, it is presumed, we can overcome some of the parochial features of our own historical relationship to "ultimate reality" experienced as the God of the Bible.

Given these assumptions it is not surprising that the hypothesis is favored that Buddhist Emptying, also, is this one "ultimate reality" underlying all finite things. Commitment to the hypothesis is strengthened by the fact that Buddhists also expect that all truly concerned persons are dealing with one and the same reality, the one they call Emptying. From both sides there is agreement that Christians name "God" the same reality that Buddhists name "Emptying."

Yet when these Christians and Zen Buddhists clarify their fundamental metaphysical assumptions about reality, the assumed identity becomes acutely problematic. Christians speak of the *underlying* reality, the reality that somehow is the cause of the finite or the phenomenal world. Zen Buddhists point to the reality *of* that finite world itself. It turns out that the assumption common to both dialogue partners—that their reference is identical—leads to the contradictions both wish to avoid. Each claims the other is referring to something that the other repudiates as its reference.

One can, of course, appeal again to the fact that both Zen Buddhists and Christians insist that the reality with which they have to do vastly exceeds all that they can say or think. Both can affirm, for example, that what they point to transcends the antithesis of the personal and the impersonal. But does that help to overcome the difference between them? I think not. The basic difference is between the true nature of finite reality on the one hand and the ground of finite reality on the other. Perhaps both transcend the distinction of personal and impersonal. But that does not overcome the difference.

It is interesting to observe what happens in those instances in which the impasse appears to be broken through. Inasmuch as the Zen Buddhist account is inextricably bound up with Zen Buddhist experience, there can be no movement from that side. The Buddhist effort is to help Christians surrender their clinging to something that transcends or grounds the actual, finite world. Because Christian experience is far less directly bound to the metaphysics of Christians, some Christians modify their formulations, redefining transcendence in terms of the depth of finite reality and abandoning the distinction between ground and what is grounded. They find in Christian mysticism points of contact with Buddhist experience. They give up the imagery of Creator in favor of the creativity that constitutes the finite world itself. In short, they treat biblical modes of thought as cultural expressions that they can outgrow. Their ties to the history of their own community become attenuated. They maintain these ties only by emphasizing the exceptional strain of apophatic mysticism which is found within their tradition.

I suggest that this is not a happy outcome of dialogue. I do not wish to preclude the abandonment of Christocentricity on the part of Christians who engage in dialogue, or even their conversion to the other tradition, but changes that largely uproot one from one's own tradition impoverish at the same time that they enrich. It is time to recognize that the metaphysics of universal ground is in fact an abstract expression of the biblical understanding of creation and hence not a neutral basis for dialogue among all the great traditions. It is time to recognize also that it is not the one metaphysics everlastingly appropriate to the Christian faith. There are other ways of translating the biblical experience of a Creator into metaphysical language that may contribute more fruitfully to dialogue with Zen Buddhists.

I will not try here to spell out alternative metaphysical approaches. If I use the term "metaphysical" very broadly—as I have done—then I can suggest that both Heidegger and Wittgenstein provide metaphysical bases for dialogue with Zen Buddhists that do not entail the problems I have noted. Elsewhere I have tried to show the fruitfulness of a Whiteheadian approach. But my task in this chapter is theological, not metaphysical. As a Christian theologian I commend all efforts to break Christianity out of its parochial limits and especially out of its implicitly or explicitly negative relationship to the other great ways of humankind. But I am troubled by the dominant proposals for carrying out this task. I do not believe these proposals will commend themselves to the most sensitive and committed representatives of some of the other great ways. I do not believe they commend themselves to Christians. Hence I am calling for a different approach—for Christians, a Christocentric catholic one.

It is my hope that the followers of the other great ways will also find within their own traditions reasons and means for analogous openness to learning from one another and being transformed by what is learned. If this leads some day to a merging of all the great ways into one that is at the same time Jewish, Christian, Muslim, Hindu, Buddhist, Confucian, primal, and so forth, so be it. If that merged way is fully and authentically Christian, I as a Christian see nothing to fear from that. But if all the great ways continue to the last day distinct from one another, each open to all, enriched by all, and transformed by all, I as a Christian see nothing lacking in that. My belief is not that all human beings should join Christian churches but that Jesus Christ has something of greatest importance to contribute to all. To the end we will continue to witness to that. If Jews appropriate Jesus while remaining Jews, and Buddhists, while remaining Buddhists, I, as a Christian, see nothing lacking in that.

We do not now need to decide between an ultimate goal of merging all the great traditions into one and the alternative of their living side by side in mutual openness to the end. We do now need to decide what theological contribution we can now make to moving toward either of these ends. My proposal is that for Christians the finest contribution will be a Christocentric catholic theology.

PART II

Beyond Relativism

Toward World Transformation

6

Responses to Relativism

Common Ground, Deconstruction, and Reconstruction

With this essay which first appeared in Soundings, *Cobb signals, even more clearly than in the previous essays, his uneasiness about the dangers of the path he has chosen for exploring interreligious dialogue: his path is one which starts with, and constantly respects, the real diversity of religions. But as he looks around his academic community, he witnesses how such respect for the differences of the many can become a prison locking each of them into separation from each other. Whereas up till now, he has been committed to "relativizing the several religious traditions" and "breaking the shackles of absolutist thinking," now he finds himself concerned about eliciting and communicating the "positive values and passions" of each of the religions. If previously Cobb wanted to move "beyond absolutism," now he wants to move beyond "relativism."*

What brought about this shift in his concerns and thinking? In candid biographical asides, in which Cobb reveals his feelings of "alienation," "guilt," "helplessness and wellnigh homelessness," he states clearly what has so shaken and redirected him: the "global crises" of human and environmental devastation and suffering. Because all religions (and scholars of religions) "collectively face real problems of utmost urgency," they must not only relativize and recognize the limitations of their individual claims; they must also search together for a "wide consensus as to . . . [the] nature and importance [of these problems] and how they can be resolved." Now Cobb is calling the religions to move beyond an isolating relativism toward a mutual effort to transform and save this world.

But how? Where find this "consensus" regarding the nature of, and solutions for, our global problems? Cobb rejects "the quest for common ground"—both George Lindbeck's curtailing of common ground to that

which one finds in one's own linguistic backyard, and John Hick's univer-
salizing of common ground as something deep within each of the religions.
Lindbeck's quest leads to a breakdown of communication between the dif-
ferent languages, while Hick's quest ends up in a subtle imperialism in which
what one announces as common to all is really one's own reading of it. But
Cobb is equally dissatisfied with what he calls the deconstructionist response
to relativism; it seems that every time a consensus seems to be forming, the
deconstructionists dissolve it into its differing linguistic (or socially con-
structed) pieces. They can't seem to put the differing linguistic pieces into a
shared plan of action or commitment.

So Cobb proposes a model of reconstruction. *As I read it, his model con-*
tains two central ingredients: 1) that adherents and scholars of the religions
share an "ultimate concern that we leave to our descendants a habitable
planet," and 2) that each religious community recognize that it offers some-
thing both valuable *and* limited *to rendering our planet more habitable. In*
this way, the religions will both share a common passion for a common con-
cern, and at the same time they will be able to listen to and learn from each
other. Whatever common ground there is between them will not be
"posited" beforehand, but "found" in the process of shared passion and lis-
tening. Just how much real common ground might be found between the reli-
gions, Cobb doesn't say.

P.F.K.

This chapter was first published in Soundings 73 *(Winter 1990):595–616.*

To ENTITLE A CHAPTER "responses to relativism" implies that relativism
requires a response, and to list some responses implies that those are the most
important. That *is* how I was thinking when I submitted the title. Later I
thought I should have added another response: acceptance. Perhaps relativism should simply be affirmed. In that case there would be no need to go
further.

Indeed, I have often called myself a relativist. I have often understood relativism to be the affirmation that every event, every assertion, every belief is
conditioned by a multitude of factors: physical, social, historical, psychological, biographical, and so forth. This is almost self-evidently true. I have
understood relativism to mean further that I need to recognize and acknowledge that my own assertions and beliefs, including all those expressed in this
essay, are conditioned, and I take this to be no more than the correct existential implication of the general statement. Of course, I can then be charged
with making absolute statements about universal relativity, but that ploy does
not seem very important. *Of course* my statement that all human assertions
and beliefs are conditioned is itself conditioned. We can discuss the history
of thought about thought that has led to the wide acceptance of this belief
today. But to recognize that it is conditioned need not mean to abandon it.

I do not reluctantly acknowledge relativity of this sort. I affirm it emphatically as one of my deepest convictions. I find it liberating. For me it is good news. It can free us *from* the quest for certainty and *for* a far less inhibited, more imaginative search for insight and understanding. In this sense I enthusiastically endorse relativism.

Then why evaluate the other responses listed in my title? Why not just declare them unnecessary?

The answer is, of course, that the situation of universal relativity and the conditionedness of all thought are often interpreted in ways whose consequences are disturbing. Instead of liberating people to think imaginatively and creatively, these interpretations lead to narrowing the range of thought and restricting it to defined channels. Instead of eliciting strong convictions, they encourage disengagement from all commitment. Instead of stimulating effective action in a relativistic world, they direct energy to endless and fruitless discussion. It is those interpretations of our relativistic condition which have these debilitating results that I am calling relativism in the remainder of this chapter.

The fundamental divide between the relativism I affirm and the relativism I oppose lies in the conclusions drawn from the conditionedness of all thought. I interpret this to mean that all apprehension of the world is perspectival, fragmentary, and in some measure distorted. To me this means that the first step in the improvement of thinking is awareness of these limitations, the examination of some of the conditions shaping thought, and attention to what others see from different standpoints. This makes possible revision of the initial apprehension. Of course, the revising is also conditioned. There is no overcoming of conditionedness, but there is a movement toward less fragmentary and less distorted perceptions.

The other interpretation of this situation emphasizes that not only does each way of apprehending the world express the given conditions, but every reason that can be provided in favor of one or another apprehension presupposes the standpoint of that apprehension. The result can be called "conceptual relativism." For the conceptual relativist, reflection necessarily occurs *within* a given frame of reference, and there is no way to bridge the chasms that lie between alternative systems of concepts.

Such a view can have some positive effects. It works against cultural arrogance and imperialism, encouraging instead mutual tolerance. It allows followers of various schools of thought within the university to live and let live. Further, some find it possible to acknowledge the ultimate arbitrariness without thereby weakening their own convictions.

Nevertheless, the belief that there is finally no justification for one's ideas tends to weaken the hold of those ideas and to inhibit acting upon them when such action is costly. The belief that those who oppose the direction one favors are equally justified and unjustified in their opposition, that there is no court of appeal beyond the sheer difference, reduces one's incentive to press for public action expressive of one's views. Or if one continues to press ahead, one must do so in terms of pure power politics, since persuasion has become irrelevant.

The tendency in teaching that follows from conceptual relativism is to move from the position of advocacy of one or another of the relativized positions to that of objective expositor of the plurality of views. This effort to expound alternative positions as neutrally as possible rather than avowed advocacy of particular positions dominates the university. For example, a "philosopher" today is more often defined as one who has scholarly mastery of some range of philosophical literature than as one who thinks philosophically about the world and develops and defends a philosophical position. The position that is thereby in fact advocated and communicated to students is a somewhat detached interest in what others have thought.

The disciplinary organization of knowledge also institutionalizes a form of relativism. It would not *have* to do so. It would be possible to view the several disciplines as cultivating diverse perspectives on a shared reality and as together helping the student to a richer view of the world. But in the university there is no place for correlating or integrating the contributions of the several disciplines. Further, the question of a common reality on which they all throw light is dismissed as "metaphysical." Accordingly, the disciplines become diverse language games, each to be played by its own rules.

What can be seen as the same topic may appear in various games, but even then the several treatments are not supposed to inform or even complement one another. For example, several disciplines study how knowledge is acquired—in particular, physiology, psychology, sociology, and philosophy. But if one is engaged in the study of epistemology as a branch of philosophy, it is considered a "category mistake" to introduce considerations from the physical or social sciences. This relativity of questions and answers to academic disciplines works against the relevance of the university to the understanding of real-life problems.

Relativism can be more drastic than either of these forms. Taken to its most consistent and extreme limit, it leads to solipsism. That is, if one believes that each person's reality is a function of that person's situation and that there is no way to talk about a common world, then in principle there is no escape from solipsism. Of course, there are in fact no solipsists, or, at least, no participants in public discussion are solipsists. Nevertheless, arguments against the convictions of others are often formulated in ways that, if pursued consistently, would lead to solipsism. Although no one is that consistent, the relativistic climate of the university encourages modesty in claims to know reality rather than boldness of exploration.

I have pointed to these three ways in which relativism pervades the climate of the university to indicate that my central concern is not about abstract theories defended here and there. Of course, such theories are defended, and they deserve serious response individually on their own terms. But I do not here undertake to engage in that detailed debate. Instead, I am acknowledging distress about the dominant intellectual climate of the contemporary world in general and its institutionalization in the university in particular. It is this climate to which I seek responses.

Before I proceed to such responses, however, I feel the need to explain *why* I am so agitated. Thus far I have only indicated that the relativistic climate encourages detachment rather than advocacy, that the university has institutionalized disciplines as self-referential language games, and that the powerful critical arguments of late modernity discourage imaginative inquiry and speculation. If you have been well socialized into the modern university, you may agree with these characterizations and still ask: What is wrong with that?

I

To explain why I am disturbed by this situation, I need to describe what has shaped my perceptions and concerns, in short, to relativize my own stance by identifying a few of the factors that condition the thinking expressed in this chapter. I will limit myself to biographical factors, that is, to personal experiences. But among my personal experiences I am selecting some in which I suspect many others also participated in the latter part of the seventh decade of this century.

I refer to experiences of alienation. First, I became alienated from my national identity. I was not one of the first to see what was transpiring in Vietnam for what it was. Indeed, I can remember hesitantly defending U.S. policy while on sabbatical in Germany in 1965-66. This reluctance to oppose my nation's actions stemmed from two factors. First, my identity as a citizen of the United States and my pride in my country were all the deeper for having grown up in another country. No doubt I had a strong need to believe in the fundamental virtue of the United States as an actor on the international stage. Second, my enthusiastic assimilation of Niebuhrian realism enabled me to tolerate considerable doses of evil in national actions without disowning those actions. But my gradual realization that United States policy in Vietnam was fundamentally wrong, and that this wrongness was in continuity with much of the role my country had played and was playing in the world, transformed my identity as a citizen from a source of pride into a source of guilt. That change has been reinforced in the eighties.

Second, I became alienated from my identity as a citizen of the modern world. I had not particularly thought of myself in those terms. I only began to realize how deep that identity was in the process of alienation. Without thinking about it, I had assumed as gain or progress the rise of modern natural science and the social sciences, the emergence of modern historical consciousness, the organization of knowledge in the modern university, the improved technology and increased productivity of modern industry, and the modern heightening of individuality with its accompanying emphases on democracy, universal education, and human rights. I supported the development programs that were designed to transfer technology to underdeveloped countries in Latin America, Africa, and Asia, and to extend to them the achievements of modernity in the North Atlantic nations. Taking all this for granted, I accepted as my own vocation the understanding of the Christian faith within this context.

In 1969 my eyes were opened to the fact that the modern world was destroying the earth, that it was, and is, fundamentally anti-life. I could not, of course, deny my identity as a citizen of that modern world and a participant in it. But since 1969 that participation has ceased to be a source of satisfaction and has become a source of guilt. I know now that when I ride in an automobile or a plane, I am both exhausting resources the future will need and polluting the world it will inherit as well as contributing to horrendous changes in global climate that will inflict enormous suffering especially on the poor. I know that when I eat beef I am contributing to the torture of animals, the destruction of tropical forests, and the dispossession of Latin American peasant farmers and hunting and gathering peoples. Even if I became a vegetarian, I would still participate in a system of modern agriculture that has led to the unsettling of rural America, the growth of urban slums, the erosion, impaction, salinization, and killing of the soil, the rendering of hundreds of millions of once independent people around the world unable to feed themselves.

I will not go on to say what I am supporting when I pay my taxes or buy the products of modern industry. I feel helpless and often wellnigh homeless. Even before my experience of alienation I knew that no human being can live without immersion in sin, but the depth of the sin and its permeation of all of life had not been clear to me. Whitehead had taught me, if I needed teaching, that all life is robbery and that the robber requires justification. But I had thought a human life could justify this unavoidable robbery. I had supposed that with all life's ambiguities it was possible to make one's life count for good. Since 1969, as I have realized how many are robbed by my daily life, it has been hard to be sure that my life could be justified. I have come to appreciate in new ways the meaning of the old language that we are justified by grace and not by works. Yet that does not make works unimportant. We can still try to rob less rather than more, and we can try to move toward ways of living that would rob less still.

I hope that these autobiographical reflections will enable you to understand what motivates me to write this. In 1982 Gordon Kaufman in his presidential address to the American Academy of Religion urged us to recognize that our situation is too critical to allow us to go on with business-as-usual. That meeting of the AAR included more attention to the global crisis than have others. I want to add my voice—belated as I am—to his. Business-as-usual is participation in both the assumptions and the practices of that modern world that is destroying life. The earth cannot afford an intellectual religious leadership that promotes such destructive values.

I have acknowledged one form of relativity—the autobiographical. This acknowledgment could lead to relativism. One could judge that everything I say is part of a circle of ideas determined by particular experiences and hence has no value or validity for those who have not shared just those experiences. But I do not draw this conclusion. The relativity of all thinking to the standpoint from which it is done and the relativity of all standpoints to the particularities of the biography of the thinker do not entail what I am calling relativism.

Allow me to make this point with an example. When a liberated woman tells me what she has come to perceive and understand through a process of consciousness-raising, I do not discount her conclusions because she came to them through particular experiences, ones that I have not had. Her insights are relative to her experience, but she can share with me what she has come to see in such a way that I recognize that it is there to be seen. Sometimes I can be led to see it myself despite the very different perspective I bring as a male. Of course, she is not infallible: the scales have not completely fallen from her eyes, and her present perceptions are not free from distortion. Indeed, she may even be partly blinded by the rage that quite naturally accompanies the new awareness. But none of this means that what she now sees is so bound to her particular perspective as to be real only for her or only for those who have shared her experiences of consciousness-raising. The pattern of relationships she now notices was there before she noticed it, and it is still embodied in the behavior of many who continue to be oblivious to it. Even though as a man I cannot share her experience, that pattern of relationships is there in my world too, and I am seeing my world more accurately when I acknowledge it than when I remain blind to it.

It is my belief that my own experiences of alienation have also led me to see features of public reality. That I came to see the interconnections of food consumption, animal suffering, agribusiness, expropriation of peasant land, destruction of tropical forests, species extinction, and changes in global weather only through particular experiences does not mean that these interconnections exist only in my private world. They affect also those people who do not recognize them. The relativity of insight to experience does not affect the reality of the structures that are seen.

My conviction is that such things as the reduction of the ozone layer and the changes of global climate will affect everyone regardless of the conceptual schemes with which they operate. Because I think that these matters and others I have mentioned are both important and difficult to deal with, I covet the commitment and attention of many people. I especially covet the aid of those who have been set aside by society to reflect and do research. Hence I am disturbed to find that the ethos of the university discourages commitment to solving collective human problems and to redirecting study and research in ways relevant to them. I locate a central reason for this in the implicit and explicit relativism of the late modern mind and its institutionalization in academia.

My argument thus far is that the climate of relativism works against an adequate response to the crises that face humanity. Such a response requires some community of persons passionately sharing a consensus both about what is happening and about the importance of responding and then order-ing their work in ways that are appropriate to this need. My complaint against us, meaning by "us" the academic community, is that on the whole we do more to encourage and exemplify a debilitating relativism than to pre-cipitate a process of creative response.

There are respects in which this charge may be less applicable to those of us who are teaching about religion than to many others. At least at some point in our lives religion has seemed personally or culturally important to most of us. But in other respects we may be peculiarly responsible. Consider the role we play.

One of the normative interests that has motivated many of us to become teachers in the field of religion has been the desire to overcome the parochial and doctrinaire attitudes that pervasively affect the climate of most religious communities. Our passion has been to open the minds of religious people to the values of other traditions, and thus to relativize their own beliefs and practices. We emphasize the relativity of those beliefs and practices to his-torical and cultural experience, hoping to break the shackles of absolutist thinking and feeling.

From my point of view this is extremely important. In itself it is quite the opposite of relativism. To the true relativist, bigotry and closed-mindedness are no worse than any other stance, whereas for those of us who believe in uni-versal relativity they cut against the fabric of the world and block the attitudes and actions so urgently needed for creative response to the world's crisis.

Unfortunately, as a community of scholars we have been far less success-ful in transmitting the positive values and passions of religious communities than in relativizing the several religious traditions. Our academic disciplines support us in displaying the socio-historical conditioning of religious belief and practice. They do not support us in calling forth deep commitment to the creative possibilities for the several traditions to which recognition of this relativity gives rise. As we faithfully transmit and advance our academic and intellectual traditions, we engender and strengthen tendencies toward debil-itating relativism rather than passionate involvement in new religious forms or public response to the degradation of the earth and the oppression of the powerless.

Our collective effect on the public religious scene in this country, at least on the Christian part of that scene, has been destructive. Many of those who have listened to us have left the churches without finding or forming new reli-gious communities. Those who have remained in the liberal denominations have little guidance from us as to the message and mission of the church. Accordingly, liberal Christianity has too often come to mean either tradi-tional beliefs minus the most problematic ones or convictionless churchian-ity. Its adherents know they are not Fundamentalists, but this largely exhausts their shared ability to define themselves. The declining old-line denominations are now trying to reclaim lost ground by reemphasizing the traditional beliefs they retain in ways that separate them further from what goes on in university departments of religion. The question has become, Why be Christian at all if one is not a Fundamentalist? Obviously, in this situation it is the religious right, the group that has systematically ignored or rejected all that we have to say, that prospers and comes to dominance. That form of progressive Christianity that even now tries to give some leadership in responding to the global crisis—more at least than does the university—has been wounded and weakened by our work.

My assumption here is that we collectively face real problems of utmost urgency that can be dealt with adequately only on the basis of wide consensus as to their nature and importance and as to how they can be resolved. My argument thus far is that we academics in general make the attainment of such consensus more difficult by our direct and indirect support of relativism. My question is, How can we cease to play this destructive social role? I shall consider three types of response: (1) the quest for common ground, (2) deconstruction, and (3) reconstruction.

II

(1) *The quest for common ground.* The quest for common ground has been one factor leading to the linguistic turn so widely characteristic of recent thought. It is held that the locus of common meaning lies in the shared language of a people. This language orders reality for those who use it.

George Lindbeck has attracted attention and support for his view that a religion is like a cultural-linguistic system. To be a participant in the religion is to be socialized into the correct use of religious symbols and thus to have one's reality ordered by them. In this way rules are established for discourse within the community of faith.

Although one can see how during long ages the users of a particular language gained unquestioned meaning from it, the appeal to language for common ground is more ambiguous today; linguistic groupings are not always identical with cultural and national ones. To give language preference may or may not be a wise strategy in particular instances. Further, we have discovered that within a single language such as English many "language games" are possible. Although "ordinary language" has a certain primacy, the specialized languages of the academic disciplines, of the professions, of the arts, of youth culture, and of ethnic and religious groups cannot be discounted. The "common ground" provided by language appears to be shrinking.

Another difficulty with this "common ground" is that it is necessarily divisive among cultural-linguistic communities. After long attempts to minimize cultural-linguistic differences on the ground of a supposed common human nature, the emphasis on the importance of these differences in constituting our "nature" is a healthy reaction. But emphasizing this absence of common ground returns us to a dangerous parochialism.

The problem for religious traditions is clear in Lindbeck's work. He rightly sees the urgency of recovering a depth of distinctive meaning in Christian community. He proposes that this requires the cessation of adaptation to the views and values of the surrounding society. In particular the adjustment of beliefs to what can be made plausible or convincing outside the community should be abandoned. This requires that we not ask whether our beliefs are true in the sense of corresponding to a reality that can also be approached by historians, scientists, metaphysicians, or members of other religious communities. Instead we should find the norms for theology internal to the cultural-linguistic system that is Christianity, especially its deep grammar.

But just by doing this we seem to make undesirable, or perhaps impossible, significant dialogue between Christian theologians and representatives of other religious traditions. Since Christian beliefs would have their meaning only in relation to other aspects of the Christian symbolic system—and presumably Hindu beliefs would have the same character—even comparison of elements in the two systems seems precluded. The rich experience of learning from one another and rethinking our own traditions in light of what we learn seems to be invalidated or denied.

In the actual practice of "interfaith" dialogue, the quest for common ground is widespread. Here the common ground can rarely be cultural-linguistic. Yet some commonality can be found between any two communities. For example, in Roman Catholicism and Mahayana Buddhism there are monastic movements that are remarkably similar. Between Christianity and Islam there are extensive overlaps in the affirmation of monotheism and in the appeal to the history of Israel. In this way "common ground" can usually be found for dialogue.

However, many who are interested in encounter among representatives of diverse religious traditions seek common ground in a deeper sense. Some believe that "religion" has an essence that is manifested in diverse ways in several traditions. This essence is commonly conceived in one of two ways or in both together.

First, the essence may be some type of experience. Rudolf Otto's identification of the holy as characterizing distinctively religious experience is the most familiar example. Aldous Huxley, in his *Perennial Philosophy*, highlighted the experience of unitive mysticism. William Ernest Hocking saw the essence of religion as a passion for the spread of righteousness conceived as a cosmic demand. Wilfred Cantwell Smith sees faith as what is common to all. Masao Abe, coming from the Buddhist East, identifies the essence of all authentic religion as the attainment of emptiness or Sunyata.

Second, the essence may be sought in terms of that which is attended to or experienced rather than the experience itself. In the West this is often called God, and there is an initial tendency to assume that all religions attend to God. As the problematic surrounding the word "God" becomes clearer, there is sometimes a shift to what is supposed to be more neutral language, such as Being Itself or Ultimate Reality. But it turns out that none of these terms is genuinely neutral, that understanding of that to which the religious traditions attend varies as much as the experiences they most prize.

This move from the fact that any pair of the great ways have commonalities to the affirmation of a single common ground of all of them is not supported by evidence. It expresses instead a deep need on the part of many people to believe that "religion" has an essence such that all religious people can be seen to be engaged in a common enterprise. This is believed by many to be the only way to overcome mutual hostility. But practical reasons of this sort, however laudable the motivation, do not suffice to justify the assumption of a universal common ground.

Furthermore, in fact each proposal of common ground is incipiently paternalistic, informing members of some religious traditions that the heart of their experience or the object of their attention is not what they have thought but rather something else. The procedure designed to place all traditions on an equal footing by defining what that footing is from the point of view of one of the traditions is in fact a new form of imperialism.

John Hick recognizes this problem and seeks neutrality by adopting a position different from all the received traditions. Jews, Christians, and Muslims are told that their God is a phenomenal manifestation of a more ultimate reality, a noumenon that lacks or transcends all the characteristics they have found in their phenomenal deity. Hindus and Buddhists are told that Nirguna Brahman and the Dharmakaya viewed by Hindus and Buddhists, respectively, as the characterless ultimate are in fact only phenomena. Apparently only the modern philosopher, standing aloof from all religious traditions, can point to the noumenal ground of these manifestations! For my part I fail to see the gain involved in offending everyone for the sake of an elusive neutrality. Are not philosophies, in any case, as much caught up in relativity as are religious traditions?

I have opposed the effort to find the common essence of all religious traditions but have affirmed that there are common elements in any pair of these ways. Even this affirmation requires careful qualification. Whether these common elements are to be found in what is central to each is a separate question to be settled by factual examination rather than by a priori assumptions. Some of these common elements no doubt facilitate dialogue and cooperation. But often what is most valuable and interesting in the two communities is not what they have in common but what they can offer to each other as new.

Turning to the need for consensus in order to redirect the course of history away from degradation and oppression, I come to the same conclusion. To build consensus requires networking on the basis of elements of common ground actually experienced and affirmed among many divergent groups. Wherever agreements can be found that are supportive of effective action, these should be celebrated and built upon. But it is unwise to assume that underlying all our apparent diversities there already exists a common ground sufficient to support an adequate program of action. Commonalities are to be found, not posited. Furthermore, some of the existing common ground may reflect little more than shared participation in assumptions whose outworking is destroying our earth.

(2) *Deconstruction*. This brings us to a second strategy or response: deconstruction. There is no question of its importance and value. Most of the institutions and habits of mind we have inherited are implicated in the degradation and oppression we need to counter. I have already indicated my conviction that this is true of the organization of knowledge in general. This entails also the concrete expression of that organization in most of our academic disciplines and in the departmental structure of the university. There is no more important place to engage in deconstruction than where most of us earn our living.

All of the great inherited religious traditions play their role in sanctioning beliefs, attitudes, and actions that contribute to degradation and oppression. The way this happens is quite different in the theistic traditions and in the non-theistic ones, but all need to be deconstructed. Fortunately, this deconstruction has been in process for two hundred years and is far advanced in academic and intellectual circles. What is now more needed is the deconstruction of the new absolutes of method or anti-method, of worldview or anti-worldview, that have arisen in the process of secularization.

I am aware that my use of the word "deconstruction" is influenced by a major contemporary movement that is sometimes called by that name. But my use of the term may not correspond exactly with that of any of the leaders of this movement. This is true especially because I view deconstruction as an essential element in a response to global crisis, but not by itself a sufficient response.

The contemporary movement of deconstruction participates in the linguistic turn, so important in the twentieth century's intellectual history. It has been particularly effective in exposing the mystification and obfuscation of which language is capable. Feminists especially have used deconstructive techniques to show how pervasive are patriarchal motifs in our languages, and how language both furthers and masks the universal oppression of women. To a lesser extent deep ecologists have shown how pervasive in our language is anthropocentrism and how this has obscured the degradation of the biosphere. This process of deconstruction is capturing attention and enlisting the support of many of our finest minds. The deconstruction of inherited assumptions may help also to expose and overcome the deep-seated homophobia that engenders so much suffering in a large segment of humanity. The urgency of such deconstruction can hardly be exaggerated.

It may not be evident that this deconstruction is a response to what I am calling relativism, but I believe it is. To whatever extent the interpretive overlay covering the natural and social world is removed, the structures actually present in that world become more manifest. Recognition of those structures is not a common ground from which one begins; it is a shared conclusion toward which inquiries and analyses starting from diverse places may move. One can observe the kind of confidence and passion aroused in persons who have participated in this program, whether it is called deconstruction, or consciousness-raising, or conscientization. They often become free from the debilitating relativism of so much of the intellectual community derived from the dominant heritage of late modernity. Indeed, if there is a problem, it is that some lose the humility that comes with a clear sense of the relativity of all perspectives.

Nevertheless, when deconstruction is viewed not as a powerful and essential element in the needed response to relativism but as a comprehensive program excluding all other approaches, it ceases to function as a great aid and becomes a part of the threat. This happens when the linguistic turn, with all its fruitfulness, is absolutized into the doctrine that language is the comprehensive horizon of our existence, that the elements of language refer only to other elements of language, that texts should be interpreted exhaustively by reference to other texts.

When this happens, then deconstruction ceases to be for the sake of seeing natural and social reality more clearly and promotes, instead, the relativizing view that there is no reality to be seen. In this case, there ceases to be any reason to prefer one linguistic formulation to another, and the deconstructive process itself has no justification other than the pleasure it may afford practitioners.

The problem with deconstruction as an encompassing program is much the same as the problem that arises when any one method is privileged. This has happened from time to time with the empirical method, the sociohistorical method, the phenomenological method, linguistic analysis, and praxis, to name only a few. All these methods can be used in the service of life, but when they are turned into our masters, they bring death. Today, just because deconstruction is proving the most enlivening to those who *use* it, it is deconstruction against whose domination we must most carefully guard ourselves.

I hope I have made it clear that my criticism is not directed to deconstruction as a powerful method or tool. It is directed against allowing any method to become our master. Similarly, my criticism is not directed against the linguistic turn as a focus on an exceedingly important feature of reality. It is directed toward the solipsism of language to which it too often gives rise. This solipsism works against the recognition of the universal relativity of events and absolutizes one segment of the world, treating it as if it could be understood in separation from the others. I do not personally believe that anyone can actually live as if language were the encompassing reality, but one can pursue an academic discipline as if this were the case. Thus the affirmation of the doctrine can have, and has had, an effect on the course of events. It is proclaimed not by deconstructionists alone but by many others who have taken the linguistic turn, and it has encouraged ways of thinking that direct attention away from natural and social events. Today we cannot afford to have many of our finest minds preoccupied with language alone. It is urgent that attention be directed to events in the natural and social worlds: to what is happening to land and air and water, to the suffering inflicted on individual animals, to the destruction of species, to what we are doing to tribal peoples, peasant farmers, and to the unemployed and underemployed masses of the Third World, as well as to the threat to life involved in our huge stockpiles of nuclear weapons.

It is not my intention here to evaluate the work of individual deconstructionist thinkers. I am not qualified to do so. Like all movements of such importance it contains within itself disparate tendencies. I am welcoming and celebrating its power in liberating us from inherited interpretations that distort our vision and support our continued wasting of the planet and exploitation of the politically and economically weak. But I deplore the tendency to imply that there is no natural or social reality to be seen and thereby to continue and intensify the debilitating relativism of late modernism. If deconstructionists tell us that when we see degradation and oppression and the ways they are interconnected, we are just as much captives of artificial interpretations as when we complacently accept the dominant ideology that obscures these realities, then they join in reducing any possibility of consensus for change.

My own reflection about deconstruction has been stimulated chiefly by my encounter with Buddhism rather than with the contemporary French school. For twenty-five centuries Buddhists have been engaged in the deconstruction of conceptual thought. There is no question in their case but that the deconstruction serves a positive function. It is for the sake of seeing things as they are. There is no question also but that Buddhist techniques are effective, that they do enable people to see more clearly.

The primary focus of Buddhism has been on individuals. It has provided psychological, existential, and religious transformation. Its fruits in saintly life are often impressive.

Nevertheless, I believe that a price has been paid for the exclusive focus on deconstruction. Once the deconstructive breakthrough is achieved, there is little effort to reconstruct the world that has been deconstructed. Indeed, the continuing polemic against concepts as such works against reconstruction. Those who are freed from bondage to conventional thought continue to use the conventional language, now fully aware of its limitations. They do not try to find a less distorting way to think or communicate. As a result, Buddhist deconstruction can become a tool used to many ends. Samurai practiced Zen to become better samurai. Business executives today practice Zen to become better business executives. There is nothing wrong with this, but it does suggest that this deconstruction alone does not necessarily redirect thought and behavior. Hence, for one who believes the salvation of the world requires such redirection, this deconstruction does not suffice.

(3) *Reconstruction*. Although Buddhism in general has majored in deconstruction, the needed redirection can also be found among Buddhists. I am particularly impressed by the work of the neo-Gandhian leader in Sri Lanka, Sri Ariyaratne. Buddhist deconstruction has opened his eyes to what is really happening in Sri Lanka and also to what can happen. He is actively engaged, against great odds, in the conceptualization and actualization of reconstruc-

tion at the societal level. My point, therefore, is not to criticize Buddhist deconstruction but rather to point to its potential fruitfulness and relevance to our global needs when it is supplemented by reconstruction.

Similarly, French deconstruction has been used for positive purposes by many feminists. Even though the work of deconstructing patriarchy is so vast that it can fruitfully occupy a lifetime, for a true feminist this is in the interest of a different social order, one that is not patriarchal. The various elements of deconstruction are accompanied by indications of alternative ways to order society and structure institutions. Deconstruction and reconstruction go together in intimate connection.

In the world today there are numerous probes toward reconstruction. I have mentioned Sri Lankan Buddhism and Western feminism. Western environmentalists are also making their contribution, as are Latin American liberationists, ethnic groups in this country, Africa, and Asia, and gay and lesbian liberationists. There are also scattered voices in many fields: agriculture, architecture, economics, psychotherapy, to name only a few. There are encouraging movements of reconstruction in Judaism, Christianity, Islam, Hinduism, and Marxism, as well as in Buddhism. There are now stirrings in philosophy and the natural sciences. The SUNY series on Constructive Post-Modern Thought gives expression to the convergence of some of these developments. Occasionally moves for redirection are dramatically expressed institutionally, as at Medéllin. But collectively, all of these writers and groups comprise a tiny and often discouraged minority in the wider scene, and in any case they are fragmented, suspicious of one another, and often at cross purposes.

If humanity is to slow down the degradation of the earth and the worsening of human misery—and finally reverse it—then those who grasp this need, however fragmentarily and with whatever tunnel vision, will have to work together. Jesse Jackson has given us a glimpse of the kind of leadership we need in his Rainbow Coalition. His efforts deserve from us academics something more than detached criticism or benign neglect. They embody a vision we have failed to articulate.

An earlier model may be even clearer. In the 1970s there were three major liberationist communities: the Latin American, the African American, and the North American feminist. Despite some commonality in their directions, they were severely critical of one another—even mutually hostile. Latin Americans were convinced that class analysis is the key; Blacks, that racism is fundamental; and feminists, that sexism is the deepest and most pervasive problem. The Maryknoll Order organized a succession of conferences on "The Theology of the Americas" at which representatives of these groups met to interact. At the outset of the meetings the interaction of these groups did not center on the common ground they shared. Instead they confronted one another in terms of their differences, expressing their anger. But in the end they attained a consensus. Each accepted the central point of the other: All agreed that class, race, and gender are all critical factors in understanding oppression and working for liberation. It is this consensus arising out of the sharing of new insights that constitutes the kind of reconstruction we need.

Clearly all of these liberation movements have been involved in deconstruction. Hence I will not reiterate the importance of the deconstructive moment in the response to debilitating relativism. Also, the three groups would not have come together at all had they not recognized some commonality of interest. All agreed that the existing order is oppressive of some. All agreed that changes are needed. Hence common ground played a positive role.

But here I am stressing the third element of response: reconstruction. The common ground they could identify among themselves plus the several patterns of deconstruction in which they entered did not suffice to direct common action among them. That required an emergent consensus possible only as each listened to the others and learned from them what was not already a part of its own vision and commitment.

My conviction is that there is little hope for the future without this stage of reconstruction. It requires that there be some measure of mutual respect so that all are willing to acknowledge that where others have attained keen insight there is in truth something to be seen. That means that all acknowledge that their own positions do not exhaust truth and reality, that they can be corrected and enriched by hearing what others have learned. Indeed, it means that each enters the encounter with the other ready in principle to revise what one brings.

The consensus that emerged from the Theology of the Americas conferences did not put an end to disagreements. On the whole, each group continues to attach special importance to its distinctive principle of analysis. But the joint recognition of the truth of the other two principles changes the whole approach. Nothing remains the same. Learning from others at this deep level is not simply adding new information or insights. It is a form of growth that, following Henry Nelson Wieman, I have called creative transformation.

My personal conviction is that the multiple creative transformations that are needed can occur more easily as we abandon what Dewey called the quest for certainty. Today a quite similar point is made by rejecting foundationalism. As long as people are affirming some ground or foundation that is beyond doubt and necessarily common to all, it is unlikely that they can be fully open and free to learn from others who do not acknowledge that ground or foundation. Hence I identify myself with anti-foundationalism, unless that position is taken to deny that there *is* any given natural or social world at all. That judgment can lead anti-foundationalists to just the debilitating relativism I oppose.

Whereas the full recognition of the relative character of all our thought is one requirement of a healthy reconstruction, a second is belief that in this radically conditioned way a shared natural and social world *is* apprehended. On the one hand, there is no uninterpreted apprehension of a natural or social world, and all interpretation is conditioned by language, culture, history, physiology, personal biography, and so forth. On the other hand, there is no experience that is *totally* illusory. If we could share these two assumptions, then at least in principle we would be open to one another's insights and ready to revise our own. The process of creative transformation could work among us toward a consensus sufficient to direct action.

The view that I am here advocating is often called relativism. I stated at the outset that if "relativism" is taken to mean only the recognition of the conditionedness of all thinking, I embrace relativism enthusiastically. Relativism in this sense is compatible with strong convictions while encouraging the hope for the attainment of more nearly adequate ways of thinking. But in this chapter I have meant by relativism something different—a position that cuts against strong conviction, denies the possibility of attaining more nearly adequate and accurate ways of thinking, and discourages the quest for the consensus needed for action, thereby justifying the continuation of socially irrelevant activities in a time of crisis.

It is obvious that the two beliefs that support the sort of reconstruction for which I call are themselves vulnerable to critique from supporters both of what I have called absolutism or foundationalism and of what I have called relativism. On the one side, those who seek certainty and claim to build on firm foundations believe that the abandonment of this quest results from failure to have attended with sufficient care to the force of their arguments. On the other hand, much sophisticated analysis has been designed to persuade us that we have no access to any reality beyond our own immediate experience or beyond language. In that case, we have nothing to learn from one another, at least about the destruction of nature or the social structures of oppression.

An equally fundamental relativistic criticism can be directed to the judgments of value and importance that underlie the whole proposal. I find it a matter of almost ultimate concern that we leave to our descendants a habitable planet in which society can so structure itself as to make life at least tolerable for most of its members. The relativist can rightly point out that many do not care about these matters and that I can provide no proof that they should. From the relativistic perspective I am limited to appealing only to those who, for whatever chance reasons, share my biases, my conceptual scheme, or my cultural situation. From my perspective, on the other hand, there are deeper levels of our being that, when allowed to surface, do involve awareness that our shared destiny is important for all of us.

I am concerned at the right place and time to carry on theoretical discussions with thoroughgoing foundationalists and relativists. We academicians have encouraged a self-defeating idea that only after theoretical questions are settled can we move to action. We thus lend support to those who resist change as threatening to their power or wealth. We must learn to support action in a real world in which action can never await definitive theoretical solutions.

I tried out an earlier version of this chapter on a group in Claremont. I was heard by a number of those present as calling for academicians to become more active in social programs or even to leave academia to devote themselves to urgent causes. This hearing no doubt resulted from my own unclarity. But it is also indicative of how deeply entrenched is the assumption that academic work as such is irrelevant to the issues I have emphasized.

This is not a call to leave the university. It is a call for reform in academia itself, for us to reorient our fields of study in light of growing oppression and suffering and of threatening catastrophe. Intellectual leadership in the field of religion has never been more badly needed. My complaint is that the disciplinary organization of knowledge inhibits our offering the needed leadership. I believe that a different ethos in academia based on a realistic commitment to both deconstruction and reconstruction could go a long way toward encouraging work that would meet that need.

7

Order Out of Chaos

A Philosophical Model
of Interreligious Dialogue

At first reading, this essay, with its philosophical lens and language, seems to be utterly different from the preceding essay. Yet it is not. Both have a common concern: relativism. The preceding essay dealt with relativism as an impediment to the religious communities acting together to create a "habitable planet"; this one takes on relativism as an obstacle to the religions communicating with each other about the depths of their religious experiences. In both cases, Cobb continues his efforts to move beyond relativism to some form of life-giving relating among the religions.

But he warns us that the temptation to relativism is salutary: every perception of reality is conditioned and therefore relative; thus, there can be no absolute or final perceptions. And yet, each perception is not just socially constructed; it is also reality-constructed—that is, the real world, independent of our social conditionedness, is also giving shape to our perceptions. We may see only a part, but we are seeing something real. So if the limitations or relativity of all our knowledge is "bad news" for some, Cobb announces the "good news" that we can overcome the limitations of our own perceptions by learning from the limited perceptions of others. Our differing limitations, by connecting and conversing, can transcend themselves. For Cobb and his process-philosophical perspectives, reality is so complex and eventful and changing that the only way to overcome the limitations of our grasp of it is to learn from the limitations of others. In this way, we move beyond relativism and draw "order out of chaos."

Cobb boldly takes up the "chaos" of the religious world. Suggesting that religious experience enables us to become aware of aspects of reality that "the selectivity of experience normally blocks out," he recognizes three very different interpretations of those deeper or greater aspects of reality: religious experience as cosmic, acosmic, or theistic; or, ultimacy found in the interrelatedness of this world, as a depth beyond this world, or as a personal reality intimately related to the world. Cobb insists that we should not look at these three interpretations of religious reality as merely three different aspects of one Ultimate Reality. He urges us, rather, to consider that these different interpretations represent differences "both in the experience and in what is experienced" and that therefore "they are ontologically quite distinct." In other words, such different religious experiences represent not only really different ways of looking at what we might call the Ultimate, but really different ways in which Ultimacy is (Cobb is tempted to speak of differing but related Ultimates). But again, he urges us to rejoice in these ontological differences, for they can speak to and learn from each other. The acosmic Advaitin of Hinduism and the theistic Christian have something to say to, and learn from, each other.

But as this swarm of really—even ontologically—different ways of experiencing and interpreting religious reality come together to talk and overcome their individual limitations, are there any criteria by which they can evaluate their differences? Criteria that they can share? Cobb finds some help from philosophy, but it's very limited help. In the end, he makes a suggestion that harkens back to the previous essay: shared criteria, if they can be found, have yet to be fashioned through a joint effort of the religious communities; and perhaps the best place to start are the crises and challenges of making this a habitable planet. "Several traditions, perhaps all, may at some point accept identical criteria as relevant to them. For example, as the threat to human survival grows, some criteria may emerge that make sense to almost everyone." Cobb, it seems, wants to foster that emergence.

P. F. K.

This essay first appeared in J. Kellenberger, ed., Inter-Religious Models and Criteria *(New York: St. Martin's Press, 1993), pp. 71–86.*

I

IN THIS CHAPTER I would like to reflect philosophically on models and criteria dealing with the multiplicity of religions. There is now a rather large theological literature on interreligious dialogue, especially from the Christian perspective. However, there is much less reflection of a purely philosophical sort. In my own case, my philosophical beliefs are intertwined with my Christian ones, and my contributions to the theological discussion are deeply affected by my philosophy. But because I have been writing as a Christian, I have cut short the articulation of the philosophical assumptions. Here I would like to give them free rein.

That does not mean that my philosophy is based on pure reason unaffected by my Christian faith. One key element in my philosophy is the view that everything is interrelated, and that includes my beliefs. Also, all thinking is perspectival, arising in a particular set of circumstances and profoundly conditioned by them. At the same time, if it is thinking at all, it cannot be simply determined by the circumstances of its origin. Thinking is inherently an exercise in freedom, however circumscribed that freedom may be.

Not only is all thinking perspectival; so also is all experience. The fact that experience is perspectival and, hence, conditioned does not mean that it is illusory. From every perspective, whatever the determinative set of conditions, something is seen. Even in the extreme case of hallucination, *something* is experienced, however confused one may be as to what it is. The nature of experience is to be an experience of something.

This means that there is a world of entities just as real as I am, and that my experience arises in my relation to them. What is experienced may be events in my own brain that falsely lead me to suppose that there are other events of a certain kind in the world outside my body, but usually the experience of events in my brain does give useful clues about events outside my body as well.

The use of the word "event" in the foregoing paragraph expresses another central feature of my philosophy. I am myself a congeries of events and everything to which I relate has event character. Each of these events comes into being out of an inexhaustibly complex world, and each is itself inexhaustibly complex. Nothing actual can ever be exhaustively described. Nor can the patterns of relations among events ever be exhaustively known.

We live then in a world of innumerable events succeeding one another with unimaginable rapidity, each of which is inexhaustibly complex in its relationships with others. For an event to be totally open to this chaos would render it incapable of attaining any definiteness. And without definiteness there is nothing at all. To be an event, therefore, is to be selective, radically so.

Every event of human experience is based on extreme limitation with respect to the events that constitute its total world or environment. The world we experience is an exceedingly narrow selection from this one. This is especially true of conscious experience, but even unconscious experience must exclude most of what is there to be experienced.

This does not mean that our conscious experience fails to give us reliable knowledge of our environment. The evolutionary process has brought into being organisms so ordered that just that information most important for survival is highlighted. We have no awareness of the events in our brain and little of those in the remainder of the central nervous system. We have no awareness of the subatomic events that surround us or even of the molecular ones. What our sense organs have evolved to tell us is about large and fairly stable groupings of these physical events. Especially for such groupings in close proximity to us, our experience provides remarkably precise information with respect to their location relative to us. The importance of all this for obtaining food, avoiding danger, and caring for children is obvious.

Much of the selectivity and emphasis that makes significant experience possible seems to be physiologically determined. Much of it is probably the same for healthy human organisms around the world. But much more of the selective organization of experience is determined culturally and linguistically, and, beyond that, still more is determined by the peculiarities of individual biography. The boundaries between these types of determination are not sharp, and the details are not important for this chapter. What is important is that what we call ordinary experience, the experience that is largely determined physiologically, is reliable for the practical purposes for which it evolved, but not for others. It gives us true and important information about features of our environment that are practically important to us, but not about the individual events that collectively constitute the apparently solid and stable objects that it presents to us. The appeal to common sense is useful as long as we are asking common sense questions. It is not very useful when we are asking scientific or religious ones.

Tradition and language shape our perceptions far beyond what is physiologically determined. This is made clear in any cross-cultural analysis. Each tradition and culture highlights different patterns of relationship among the events that make us up and that interact with us.

An interesting example is the understanding of the human body in diverse cultures. The Chinese had traced quite different patterns of relations among bodily events than those that had been noticed by Western physiology. The initial tendency in the West was skepticism. But this was wrong. The empirical evidence, from acupuncture, for example, demonstrates that what the Chinese had noticed is there and that we can notice it too. This in no way invalidates the reality of the patterns to which the West had given its concentrated attention. Still different patterns have been attended to in the Indian yogic tradition.

The complexity of the human body will not be exhaustively understood when we have integrated what the Chinese and Indians have learned with what we already knew. Yet the resulting picture will be richer than what could be found in any one of the traditions by itself. It will come closer to corresponding with more of the patterns that actually characterize the body.

Some beliefs about the body in some traditions may be simply erroneous. People have simply projected relationships that are not present in the events at all. Indeed, we in the West know that some beliefs about what is curative, widely held until fairly recently, had few redeeming features. Furthermore, even the most reliable information is likely to be articulated in exaggerated and distorted form. The theories of Western physiology, for example, are still formulated in ways that leave little place for the truths that have been learned in China and India. The conceptuality employed is still substantialist. It is not really consistent with contemporary physics. Thus it distorts in many ways. We can reasonably expect that Chinese and Indian views of the body are also distorted.

Nevertheless, we should begin with the assumption that any tradition that has survived for some time is likely to be oriented rightly to some aspects of its world. What it has noticed may be quite different from what we have noticed, and it may have interpreted what it noticed in ways that are misleading even to itself. But the likelihood of total error is small.

I believe that what I see from my perspective is there to be seen. I believe that what persons in other traditions see from their perspectives is also there to be seen. That does not mean that either of us can provide infallible information about what we have seen. But it does mean that I should try to learn from the others' experience, perhaps learn to see what the others have seen.

Further, when we are dealing with sophisticated traditions that have long engaged in testing theory in practice and critically reflecting on the results, we have reason to expect that not only the experience, but also the interpretation, will have veridical elements in it. Again, that is not to attribute inerrancy to anyone's account of anything. All human experience remains an extreme simplification, and all interpretation involves distortion, but the extreme simplifications and the distortions from which we live can be checked somewhat as we interact with those who live by different simplifications and distortions. Even simplifications that are interpreted in distorted ways still tell something about the inexhaustibly complex world in which we live.

II

"Religion" means many different things, and one of the distortions that affects our communications is the tendency to think that it really *is* something or other. In the immense complexity of human experience and the many ways in which this experience simplifies and interprets its world, there are numerous types of experience that can be called religious. These experiences are highly diverse features of the human and nonhuman world.

One kind of experience that is sometimes called religious is that which opens us to features of the world that the selectivity of experience normally blocks out. Our physiology causes our sense experience to objectify our world in terms of stable objects. But occasionally people report experiences in which they feel themselves to be part of a dynamic field of energy events or sense the subjectivity of the organic or even inorganic surroundings. These types of experiences probably serve no important evolutionary function, but they are often greatly prized all the same. This prizing is both for the immediate enjoyment of the experience and because it is felt to be a source of a deeper truth about the world. It suggests a kind of belonging to the cosmos or kinship with other creatures, about which ordinary objectifying experience does not inform us. It sometimes leads to a sense of communion with the world about us.

In other cultures there are few breakthroughs in this direction, but there is great emphasis on experiencing other people as subjects like ourselves. Since they too are objectified in ordinary, physiologically determined, sensory experience, this, also, involves heightening aspects of experience that are ordinarily very dim. Because this is widely characteristic in our culture, where intersubjective relations are stressed, we often do not appreciate the special-ness of such experience.

Other cultures concentrate on the inward journey. This, too, can take a variety of forms. In some contexts it means to become attentive to motives and hidden purposes that affect action in the world. In other contexts it is to bring the nuances of the emotional life to full consciousness. In others it is to discover a "depth" that is free from all the particularities of ordinary experience. In still others it is to remove all culturally and existentially determined barriers to openness to what is as it is.

My assumption is that in general these many voyages of discovery all lead to knowledge. Again, what is learned is a tiny fragment of the inexhaustible whole, and it is likely to give rise to interpretations that are both distorting and exclusive of other views arising from other specialized experiences. But what has been experienced is real all the same, and the experience gives rise to elements of knowledge.

I am not particularly concerned whether one chooses to call any or all of these experiences "religious." With the possible exception of the "depth" that is free from all particularities, one is not likely to speak of what is experienced as "ultimate reality" or "the transcendent." These are words that bring some order into our reflection about the vast varieties of things, an order that, like so many that we impose, illumines some things at a high cost in obscuring others.

There are other experiences that Christianity has taught us to think of as theistic. There is the experience of a presence as of a Person or Spirit. There is the experience of release from guilt. There is the experience of communion with the Whole felt as personal. There is the experience of empowerment to act in unwonted ways. There is the experience of providential guidance. There is the experience of the ability genuinely to love another. There is a joy and peace that comes as a gift. The experiences are authentic. They inform us of something about reality. Whether the theistic interpretation, or an interpretation in terms of Ultimate Reality, illumines more than it distorts is subject to endless dispute.

I have listed experiences that are likely to come unsought. There are other experiences, which we more often call mystical, that are more likely to be the result of long and disciplined quests. Their authenticity, too, I do not doubt. But their interpretation, also, is endlessly questionable. It is some of these experiences that are most likely to suggest interpretations in terms of the "transcendent" or the "wholly other."

There are many other experiences that appear in some traditions more than in others. I have said nothing of the awe inspired by the starry heavens above or the moral law within. I have not spoken of worship in all its many forms or of the way it can inspire or transport the worshipper. I have not talked of prayer, whether petition or praise, or of the effects of practicing the presence of God or repeating over and over a simple pious phrase. I have said nothing of numinous feelings, of ecstatic speech, of prophecy, of communications with the dead, or of miraculous powers. Yet all of these have had great importance in various traditions and are readily understood as "religious."

My point here is not to offer an exhaustive account of anything. It is only to emphasize that there are many, many experiences that are felt as valuable in themselves and as sources of truths that are not provided in the ordinary objectifying sense experience of our environment. There is, I believe, no reason to be skeptical about these experiences, their value or truth, although there is a great deal of reason to be skeptical of the full accuracy of some of the interpretations offered and of some of the claims made for them.

What I have offered is already a vast simplification. Every instance I have mentioned is a rubric that brings together numerous and quite diverse experiences. Experiences do not come packaged. The labels we employ impose an organization upon them. In some instances the organization corresponds to one that the experiencers themselves employ; in some instances it does not. But in fact no two experiences are the same, and some element of choice is involved in any conceptual grouping.

I am not asking that we cease to employ labels and to organize our world. For various purposes some of these orderings are extremely useful and responsibly informative. Further, the fact that there is an arbitrary element in all does not lead to sheer relativism about them. Some orderings are misleading and worthy only of rejection. Ideas are not only more or less useful, they are even more or less true in the sense of ordering our thought according to patterns that have particular importance in the world that is ordered. Their truth is weakened when they are so formulated as to exclude other truths based on other patterns that also have importance in the world that is ordered. In short, the same events can be truthfully classified in many ways, and the choice among these true classifications should depend on the purpose at hand. At the same time, there are also classifications that simply mislead and misrepresent, and are, therefore, false.

III

One of the ways we order our world is with the names of the great religious traditions. I would defend the use of these labels as long as we remember that these traditions in fact exist only in and through a multitude of events. Traditions are not substances with attributes but movements with fluid boundaries and changing characteristics, and they contain great variety within themselves.

A tradition is the canalization of certain patterns of thought, activity, and feeling, as well as social ordering. Hence, despite its internal diversity there are some recurrent patterns that are felt, even by those who do not fully participate in them, to be somehow normative. To identify some of those patterns that are distinctively prominent in that tradition is a valid and useful way to describe it in its similarities and differences from other traditions. It is meaningful and important to ask what kinds of experiences those who most fully identify themselves with that tradition are likely to cultivate. It is about what is experienced in that way that others will have most to learn from that tradition.

From this philosophical point of view, the emphasis must be on letting representatives of each tradition define themselves in their own terms. If reality has the complexity I have attributed to it, then we will be unwise to start out with assumptions about what feature of reality, what patterns of relationship, have played the largest role in the experience of its devotees. They may have dealt with an aspect of reality of which we have not been aware. To approach them as if we knew in advance the alternative possibilities within which their insights are to be categorized is the kind of imperialism of which we are all guilty and all need to repent. It has characterized philosophers and historians of religion no less than representatives of religious traditions.

But after we have listened, we must, in order to learn, relate what we have heard to other parts of our experience and understanding. We need not subsume the new under categories we already possess. We may require new categories. But understanding requires connecting these new categories to those we have previously used even if this entails considerable revision of the latter. This ordering activity is necessary to our growth in knowledge and understanding.

Further, over time we may discover family resemblances at some deep level among differing traditions. These may derive from a common origin, or they may not. Certain patterns, of a sufficiently abstract sort, can emerge in a variety of contexts. We should keep checking our tendency to interpret others to fit our preexisting categories, making sure that we are listening as carefully as possible and imposing as little as possible, but when we have done that, we may impose a pattern at this level too. Such a pattern can have its truth, corresponding to patterns that are really present with special emphasis in the experiences of devotees despite the concrete differences in each instance.

Writers of textbooks on world religions have the choice of simply presenting each tradition in its own terms or of providing an order. Some years ago Jack Hutchison offered an ordering in his *Paths of Faith* that I have found illuminating. He distinguished three types of religions. He called them theistic, cosmic, and acosmic.

Despite my emphasis that interpretation of experience is distorting, my bias is to suppose that if, over a long period of time, certain patterns of experience have encouraged certain types of interpretation, that interpretation should be taken seriously. For example, if major traditions have understood what they experienced as acosmic, then we should hesitate to say that there is in fact nothing acosmic to be experienced, that they have in fact experienced the cosmic or the theistic and consistently misconstrued it. Of course, that *may* be the case. But to start out with that bias is to place greater confidence in one's own experience and its interpretation than my view of reality warrants. Only as a last resort should we come to the conclusion that a great tradition is fundamentally deluded.

This starting point in credulity does not entail supposing that the standard interpretations of the acosmic are reliable. Further, it may be that the term Hutchison has chosen will prove misleading. What I do find probable is that what is experienced by those whose interpretations suggest the term "acosmic" to Hutchison is not identical with what is experienced by those whose interpretations suggest the term "cosmic." I further anticipate that the different interpretations do express, however imperfectly, a difference both in the experiences and in what is experienced.

I have begun with the cosmic/acosmic distinction, because in both cases interpretation is close to experience. The situation is different with respect to the theistic. There the interpretive element is larger, and the interpreted experiences more diverse and in general more culturally conditioned. Nevertheless, I follow the same principle. Those experiences and that interpretation have been mutually reinforcing for a long time with many sensitive, perceptive, and thoughtful people. We should not start out supposing that we know that they have all been fundamentally deluded.

On the other hand, the large role of interpretation is obvious from the great diversity of interpretations that appeal to some of the same experiences. An examination of reasoning and argumentation becomes more important here than in the two other cases. One *must* reject many of the doctrines of God since they contradict one another. Even so, one should begin with openness, believing that there is likely to be some connection between what people have thought they were experiencing and what they have in fact been experiencing.

One element giving some support to the initial credulity is the fact that, at this high level of abstraction, more than one of these types can be discerned in most of the great traditions. In Hinduism, for example, where the acosmic note is struck most strongly in Advaita Vedanta, a theistic vision was strongly supported by the great Ramanuja. There is a theistic mysticism in India alongside the acosmic one. There are even mystics such as Sri Aurobindo who have had both theistic and acosmic experiences and have carefully described their differences. Aurobindo shows that reality can be such that both experiences are valid windows into diverse aspects. Aurobindo also had experiences that can best be characterized as cosmic.

Aurobindo is of particular interest because he not only had varied mystical experiences supportive of all three types of religious tradition, but also sought to understand how this was possible in a coherent way. It is not my intention here to spell out his religious cosmology. It *is* my intention to say that his is a valid undertaking, and that his at least partial success can assure us that it need not be nonsensical to suppose that one immeasurably complex reality contains theistic, cosmic, and acosmic features that can be related to in some separation one from the other.

Of course, for one with my philosophical predilections, these diverse features of the totality can not be unrelated to one another. Although they are distinct, they are not in fact separable from one another. I would propose that without a cosmic reality there can be no acosmic one, and that without God there can be neither. Similarly, without both the cosmic and acosmic features of reality there can be no God.

From this point of view, one could speak of a plurality of "ultimate realities," but this is misleading. It gives the impression that the three have analogous ontological status. But that is not the testimony of experience nourished in the three traditions. They are ontologically quite distinct. Cosmic reality has the status of multiplicity; acosmic, of unity. The old discussion of the many and the one comes into play. In most philosophies that have wrestled with that problem, the one is not just one more of the many nor ontologically of the same order. It is the unity of the many, that which the many have or are in common, their common ground or source. There is no one without the many, nor any many without the one. Nevertheless, they cannot be identified. In Tillich's vision the one is the being of all the beings. To use his language, the experience of one's identity with Being Itself, as Advaita Vedanta proclaims, is quite different from the experience of becoming completely open to the many just as they are.

I do not mean that this account does justice to all acosmic and cosmic experiences. It does not account for the blissful consciousness enjoyed by the Hindu mystic in unity with Brahman. Reality must be far richer and more complex than we have dreamed! I have intended only, schematically, to argue that there is nothing absurd in supposing that there is a distinction between acosmic and cosmic reality even though they are inseparable from one another. Both are real, but their ontological status is quite distinct.

But can a theistic reality fit into such a vision? Certainly we cannot simply add to the cosmic and acosmic reality the God of classical theism. *That* God already contains many of the features of acosmic reality in inner tension with the theistic ones. But without any commitment to the final truth or adequacy of the theory, consider the possiblity of a worldsoul, that is, of a unity of experience that contains all the multiplicity of events and interacts with them. Would such a reality conflict with either the cosmic or the acosmic one?

I think not. From one point of view it would be another expression or embodiment of the acosmic reality, that is, in the language used above, another being. But as the being that includes all beings it would not be, in Tillich's pejorative phrase, one being alongside other beings. The experience of this Being "in whom we live and move and have our being" would be fundamentally different from our experience of those beings that exist alongside and outside of us. This Being would be nearer to us than our hands and feet, yet radically transcend all that we could think or imagine. It would have no hands but our hands, no feet but our feet, yet it might play a crucial constitutive role in our moral and religious experience.

Again, my interest here is not to demonstrate the existence of something like a worldsoul. My interest is in clarifying how it is possible to think, even rather simply, of different real features of the totality as giving rise to quite divergent experiences. In a religious world in which the reality of what is known in one tradition is so often taken to exclude the possibility that what is related to in another tradition can have the character claimed for it, it is important to show that this need not be the case, that all may be correct in their fundamental positive beliefs, even if they are often wrong in their nega-tions of others.

My experience has been that talk of "the absolute," of "ultimate reality," or even of "the Real" obscures or negates this possibility. Built into such lan-guage is the assumption of the identity of that with which the great religious traditions are ultimately concerned. The diversity is located at a subordinate level. If we refrain from imposing such a unifying concept, if we allow the lan-guage of the several traditions to stand, then the possibility emerges that that with which each is ultimately concerned is real and important but not onto-logically identical with that with which the others are ultimately concerned.

I suppose that my suggestion corresponds in part to the widely used story of the blind men and the elephant. That, too, suggests that different traditions relate to different aspects of reality and tend to suppose that what they expe-rience is the one appropriate object of religious interest. However, I have hes-itated to associate myself with that story too closely. It is usually told by those who believe that there is indeed just one reality, the one elephant, experienced in diverse ways. For me to use the story I would have to emphasize that what the men really experienced was not the elephant in a particular way but just the trunk, the leg, or the flank. I would then have to go on to argue that these represent three ontologically diverse features of an incomprehensibly complex reality. I doubt that the story can be made to bear such a burden.

IV

In the previous section I have tried to show that the complexity of reality is such as to include theistic, cosmic, and acosmic features. Cultural differ-ences deeply influence which features are attended to, but the resultant rela-tivism does not invalidate the diverse experiences. Each of the great types of experience can be seen to be veridical.

I have belabored this point, perhaps excessively, because I have found again and again that it is met with incredulity. The ultimate self-identity of the religious object is an axiom not easily to be overthrown. It is asserted in each of the traditions, most clearly in the theistic and acosmic ones, and it resonates with the bias of most philosophers. Its denial seems to many both absurd and sacrilegious.

If I were asserting several unrelated or competing ultimates, the charge of absurdity would make sense. But it is not absurd to say that the many can-not be reduced to the one or the one to the many. There may be a widespread bias in favor of the primacy of the one, but if the one exists only in the many, the opposite bias is equally legitimate and illegitimate. It is not absurd to affirm both without bias in favor of either. I have also tried to show that the affirmation of God need not conflict with either.

If I were asserting that the cosmic and acosmic objects of ultimate concern existed alongside the God of theism, like other gods, then from the point of view of theists I would indeed be blasphemous. The God of theism cannot be one God among many. But the existence of God does not preclude that of the cosmos as distinct from God. Nor do I see that it precludes the reality of Being Itself as an acosmic principle. To say that the Nothingness or Emptying realized by Buddhists is different from the God of whom the Bible speaks is not sacrilege.

One major source of difficulty in gaining a hearing for my views is that the idea of God in the Western tradition has developed quite far from its biblical roots. In particular it has incorporated acosmic elements from its Neo-Platonic sources. This incorporation has been an enrichment, but also a confusion. Since Thomas the mainstream of philosophical theology has thought of God both in theistic terms and in acosmic ones, in Tillich's terms, both as the Supreme Being and as Being Itself. Heidegger, Tillich, Macquarrie, and others have seen the conceptual impossibility of holding these two together. But meanwhile we have developed a church in which there is both theistic and acosmic religious experience. The dilemma is serious and is one cause of the confusion and lack of confidence in all of our talk of God.

Furthermore, we must not take the categories imposed on the complexity of the world too seriously. There is no reason that every experience must conform to one or another of these categories. On the contrary, there is no reason for there not to be experiences that unite elements of the theistic and acosmic. Particularly in a culture in which conceptually this mixture has occurred, we would expect to find an effect on experience itself.

Furthermore, from the perspective of the philosophy to which I subscribe, the joint presence of the theistic and the acosmic in one experience is not something odd. On the contrary, in ordinary experience both are having their effect. What has happened in different religious cultures is the concentration on particular features of experience to the exclusion of others. In the purest forms of acosmic experience, the theistic aspects of experience are suppressed or abstracted from, and vice versa. But there is no reason that both cannot be allowed at once. Often the religious experience of Western mystics seems to be at once of theistic and of acosmic reality—one might say that it is of the theistic as embodying the acosmic reality, or of the acosmic as qualified by the theistic reality.

Indeed, in this combined intellectual and experiential process, for many people the meaning of the word "God" is no longer purely or even primarily theistic. I do not refer only to those who, like Tillich, frankly separate God from theism, rejecting the latter. I refer also to the dominant tradition of orthodoxy in which it is at least as important to assert of God the attributes of acosmic reality as the theistic ones.

In the long run it will be necessary to deal with the conceptual tensions. It will not be necessary to reject the authentic experience associated with it. Perhaps that experience can even be strengthened when the conceptualization is clearer. It will then also be easier to acknowledge diverse legitimate uses of the word "God," as the theistic reality pure and simple, as that reality as embodying the acosmic, or as the acosmic as qualified by the theistic.

At the same time, we can recognize that there is a purely acosmic reality to which the name "God" can now be applied only at the cost of considerable confusion.

V

Are there criteria for appraising the several traditions? Certainly there are in principle some criteria on which representatives of all of them could agree. If someone tried to establish a new religion by clearly fraudulent and deceptive means, this would count against it. If the teaching of a religion encouraged behavior that was clearly destructive of its own members or of others, that too would count against it.

These criteria are not entirely irrelevant in the appraisal of the great traditions. Looking back at our history as Christians we can discern both deception and destructive teaching. Some of our teachings have been destructive both for ourselves and for others. Persons in other traditions can discern similar problems. The relative freedom from egregious evils of this sort can count as a quite objective plus in the evaluation of the great traditions.

But for most purposes it is more useful to evaluate the traditions at their best than at their worst. Are there bases for such comparative evaluation? Is such evaluation always circular? That is, do the criteria employed in the evaluation arise out of some traditions but not out of others? If so, can they be philosophically defended anyway? Or can a philosophy provide its own criteria independently of the support of the traditions?

These are complex questions and could be the basis of another essay. But in this concluding section I will offer some comments.

I do not believe that philosophy provides an unconditioned perspective from which to generate norms and criteria more objective than those that arise out of the great traditions. The values of philosophers are just as perspectival and conditioned as those of other people—with one qualification. The free act of thinking involves some small measure of transcendence over the conditioning power of circumstance. And it may be that philosophers on the whole exercise this freedom more than do the intellectual leaders of most religious traditions. If so, they have a distinct contribution to make to the discussion of criteria.

My factual judgment is that indeed philosophers do cultivate critical thinking more than do the intellectual leaders of most religious traditions. Unfortunately, this strength is counterbalanced by a weakness. Philosophers are more likely than leaders of most religious traditions to exaggerate the degree of their freedom from determination by their culture and history.

From these comments I will propose some criteria for evaluation of the great traditions. How accurately do their leaders understand the basis of their own thinking, its confessional character and also its freedom? How strongly do they develop the possibility of free critical thought and encourage others in it? How open does this make them to learning from others?

I shall essay an additional criterion. How valid are the insights nourished in the tradition, and how accurate are the interpretations that are offered?

Before proceeding to other criteria, it is important to comment on these. They are not neutral or objective. Rather, they express the typical bias of the philosopher. Further, they reflect a particular philosophical tradition, one that affirms both the conditioning of all thought and its transcendence of conditioning, both the relativity of all thinking and the reality of the world that is thought about. They presuppose that some kind of correspondence is possible between thought and thing. In other words, these are criteria that are important to me because of my particular philosophical convictions. Incidentally, they are convictions that fit well with my Christian faith and have no doubt been nurtured by it. But they are philosophical in the sense that I am prepared to present them and argue for them without reference to their source.

My philosophical perspective suggests other criteria as well. For example, it emphasizes the interconnectedness of all things, with the implication that the decay of some patterns is likely to have an adverse effect on others. When one looks at the actual world from this point of view, one finds that indeed the decay of the biosphere is threatening the future of humanity as well. This seems so important that one looks around at the several traditions that command loyalty and influence human behavior to ask, can they help? From this point of view the extent to which the great traditions are willing and able to redirect human behavior away from continuing destruction of the biosphere is an important criterion for evaluation.

It would be easy to multiply examples of concerns arising from my philosophical perspective that generate criteria of evaluation. But again, it is obvious that these are not neutral and objective. They express one way of looking at things and seeing reality. They express my deep concern for a decent human survival in a richly variegated context. These concerns are not unique to me, but they are not universal. And there is no neutral, objective philosophical argument why they should be.

The closest approximation a philosopher can propose to such objectivity is to shift from external to internal criteria. Each tradition has its own concerns, intentions, and expectations of itself. Each tradition engages in self-criticism in terms of these criteria. It may be that one could judge with some objectivity that some traditions come closer to measuring up to their own intentions than others.

Even if objective, such a criterion is by no means decisive. From the perspective of one tradition it may be more important to take even a small step toward the realization of its purposes than to take a large one toward realization of other ends. The significance of this criterion would be greatly enhanced only if there are some ends that the traditions being compared share.

One possibility is that these traditions all share the goal of personal transformation in the direction that we can call sanctity. Of course, this has to be examined in detail. Is this important in all traditions, and is what is meant by sanctity sufficiently similar so that the goal can be thought of as the same?

These are difficult questions, but a case can certainly be made that Judaism, Christianity, Islam, Hinduism, and Buddhism all hope and believe that their teaching and practice lead to personal transformation. It is also remarkable that those who are viewed in their own communities as most fully transformed are normally recognizably sanctified in the eyes of others. If so, then one basis for evaluation of the great traditions can be their effectiveness in the nurturing of this transformation. This is a relatively objective and neutral criterion.

Even here, however, there are limits. Unfortunately we know that Christian saints have often acted in destructive ways, preaching crusades, persecuting Jews, denouncing sex, opposing birth control. The recognizably saintly personal character can give support to programs that far less saintly people rightly recognize to be wrong. Within Christianity there is at least a profound tension on this point and even a suspicion against aiming at sanctity. Even if one avowed purpose of most Christians is the encourgement of sanctity, this purpose stands in tension with concerns for society that for many Christians may seem prior.

A more poignant example today can be found among Jews. For many of them, the supreme concern is not personal sanctity but the survival of the Jewish community and tradition. If that survival necessitates actions that are inimical to personal sanctity, then many devout and thoughtful Jews will reject the ideal of sanctity.

One cannot evade this problem by redefining sanctity so as to include all valid concerns of Christians and Jews. If one did so, then the relative objectivity of a shared purpose would disappear. We would have to recognize that each tradition has its distinctive goals by which it evaluates itself, and that while these overlap, this does not make them identical.

My general conclusion is as follows. There are many good criteria by which to evaluate religious traditions. Each tradition generates some and evaluates the others accordingly. Philosophers can also generate some criteria of their own, differing according to the philosophies to which they hold. No one can claim to have found criteria that are objective and neutral.

On the other hand, there are overlaps among the criteria, sometimes extensive and important ones. Further, some newly suggested criteria can be convincing to many. Several traditions, perhaps all, may at some point accept identical criteria as relevant to them. For example, as the threat to human survival grows, some criteria may emerge that make sense to almost everyone. Even so, in each tradition these criteria would be intertwined with others in a way that made the total evaluation different.

There is in the philosophical tradition a drive for universal and detached norms. This is healthy as long as the radically conditioned character of the quest and all its outcomes is fully recognized. The fact that all our judgments about criteria are conditioned, that different conditioning leads to other paths of inquiry, does not deny that what we find has validity and verity. May the quest continue!

8

Christian Universality Revisited

In this chapter, Cobb revisits the way Christians make universal truth claims. It's a revisiting because while in the first part of this book, he was worried about how Christian claims have been absolutized, now he's concerned about how they have been relativized. So what he's after in this essay is how to "renew Christian claims to universality without returning to the arrogant and oppressive role that has characterized Christianity in the past." In other words, how to avoid arrogant absolutism without slipping into mushy relativism. He states clearly why he's so concerned about this watering down of the Gospel: "We live in a time when the world needs Christ as never before."

Cobb detects various forms of this watering-down, or "de-universalizing," of Christianity in recent Christian theology. Along the lines of what we might call liberal theology (both the experiential approach of Schleiermacher/Tillich and the historical approach of Hegel/Troeltsch), Jesus' importance ends up being "only for us." That's an oft-bruited criticism leveled against liberals. But, surprising for some, Cobb notes similar odors of relativism in the conservative camps of Karl Barth and George Lindbeck. For Barth, all religions are relativized insofar as all religions, including Christianity, are of no value; in the end, everyone will be saved by Christ no matter what their religion. For Lindbeck, the truth of Christianity, like that of any religion, is true only within its own "cultural-linguistic system"; any universal claims between systems are ruled out. In both these liberal and conservative perspectives, the body or trunk of Christian truth is affirmed, but amputated are its arms and legs by which it can move and reach out to others.

So Cobb suggests a path beyond both absolutism and relativism that we have seen taking shape in previous essays. "Imagine," he tells us, "that the totality of what is, is very complex, far exceeding all that we can ever hope to know or think." The religious explorers of our history, and the communities that have followed them, have seen something of this amazing complex reality; what they have seen is real, but it is only a part. This means that the messages of the religions are all limited—but they are also all universal! This *is the path that Cobb urges for his fellow Christians: to affirm boldly the universal truth of Christianity—but just as humbly to open themselves to the universal truth of others.*

Cobb recognizes that the "deepest resistance" within many Christian churches to such a suggestion comes from their "understanding of Christ." With pastoral sensitivity (this sermon-like essay is addressed to Christian congregations) Cobb points out that there are two ways to understand Christ as the "Way, the Truth, and the Life": as a blueprint which tells us "all we need to know" and so binds us to the past, or as the Spirit who gives us a Truth that "opens us to surprise and new perceptions." With an understanding of Christ-as-Spirit, Christians can recognize, as they have not sufficiently recognized in the past, that "Christ is not limited to the one historical person." This means, I think, that Christians continue to announce the universal message that truly to know this Christ, the world needs to know Jesus. But they are also open to admitting that for the world to know this Christ, it may also have to know Buddha.

P.F.K.

This chapter is a revision of an unpublished lecture delivered in 1993 at De Pauw University.

I

IN THE CURRENT SCENE the division within Christianity grows wider. On the one side are those who have paid sensitive attention to criticism coming from many quarters. This group has come to see that in many ways Christianity has been arrogant and oppressive. Members of this group are determined not to continue to make the affirmations and claims that have had these destructive consequences. As a result this group is more characterized by its hesitations and negations than by clear positive affirmations of its faith. On the other side are those who have been untroubled by all this criticism. They remain firmly committed to Christianity as they have known it, usually in conservative garb. For the most part they continue to say and do the things that have oppressed others in the past. They continue to make strong claims for Christian universality and to act upon them.

My sympathies are with the former group. I am convinced that faithfulness to Christ requires us to hear about our sins and to repent of them. This is just as true when the sins are collective ones committed in the name of Christ as when they are personal violations of ethical rules. Indeed, there is something particularly distressing about sins self-righteously committed in the name of Christ. We can forgive ourselves for our failure to live up to the high standard of conduct we associate with Christ. But when in the name of Christ we persecute Jesus' own people and oppress women, then we blaspheme the most precious name we have, the name before whom we hope some day that every knee will bow. If we must choose between a lukewarm Christianity that has ceased to do massive evil in the name of Christ, on the one hand, and a self-confident Christianity that continues to be oppressive, on the other, we should certainly choose the former. But surely we can do better!

Frankly, I have little hope for the future of a church that knows only what it does not believe, and then concentrates upon its institutional life. It cannot expect its own children to take it seriously. It cannot win new followers. It can only wither and die. Nothing can be more urgent for the church's theologians than the positive reformulation of the church's teaching in such a way that wholehearted belief can become a truly positive factor in personal and public life.

There are several horizons within which the work of reformulation should be carried on. Today I will talk about the horizon of world religions. There can be no question but that Christians have sinned against other religious traditions and their members in the name of Christ. This has been especially marked in relation to the Jews. But primal peoples have also suffered massively at our hands, and there is hardly a non-Christian religious tradition but that can tell some story of Christian oppression.

Most of this is rooted in our universal claims about Christ. If Christ is the one savior of all the world, we have thought, then our task is to displace all those communities that do not acknowledge this. With so much at stake, hardly any tactic has seemed to Christians too harsh to use. We have justified crusades, pogroms, imperialism, colonialism, and even slavery as instruments of Christian expansion.

Alongside this arrogant imposition of our will on others, there has been serious reflection about how Christianity is in fact related to the other religious communities and traditions. In the past two centuries, many of the church's greatest thinkers have taken the global religious scene as the context for constructing their theologies. In each of the three main responses to which I want to direct your attention, the initial formulations retained strong universal affirmations. In all three cases, the course of thought has led to dropping the universal claims. The reasons for this change have been admirable, but the total effect on the church is troubling. My effort in this chapter will be to suggest a way in which the church can recover the note of universality in its affirmations without renewing the arrogance that has caused so much harm. But first, I want to summarize the three modern traditions that have undertaken to understand Christianity in the context of religious pluralism.

II

Pride of place in modern Protestant theology belongs to Friedrich Schleiermacher. He was the first theologian to order his whole theological program in the context of his understanding of global religion. He depicted Christianity as one religion among others. In this sense, he inaugurated the move toward relativizing Christian faith. But Schleiermacher explained the nature of religion and the forms it could take so as to present the monotheistic faiths as clearly superior, and among the monotheistic faiths he made Christianity appear to be the best. In his hands, the description of diversity became an argument for superiority. His readers were not led to question their whole-hearted commitment to Christ.

Schleiermacher's achievement was a brilliant one, convincing to many. But once Christianity was understood as a religion and was viewed in its relation to other religions, it became important to check his definition of religion and his characterization of the others. His definition of religion as the feeling of absolute dependence did not hold up well under this examination. Other, more plausible, candidates appeared. Early in this century, Rudolf Otto, with more empirical information than had been available to Schleiermacher, concluded that the distinctively religious quality in experience is the sense of the holy. With this judgment, he was able to carry out a program similar to Schleiermacher's. He, too, portrayed Christianity as the highest form of religion.

The last great exemplar of this style of theology was Paul Tillich. For him, what distinguishes religion is ultimate concern. This ultimate concern is truly directed to Being Itself, and on this we are wholly dependent for our existence; so he could capture the truth in Schleiermacher's insight. Also, he believed that the sense of the holy is directly related to our ultimate concern; so Otto, too, was vindicated. And Tillich, like Schleiermacher and Otto, was able to describe the situation in such a way as to present Christianity as the fullness of religion. But in his last years, Tillich had second thoughts. His personal experience with Buddhists in Japan and extensive working with Mircea Eliade led him to see that the situation is more complex than he had realized. He called for a theological approach that took the data of the history of religions more seriously and did not insist on Christian superiority.

Since Tillich, the quest to understand Christianity as a religion has continued, but its leaders have increasingly assumed a rough parity among the great living faiths. The question is now not one of ranking them so as to display Christian superiority, but viewing them as parallel ways of embodying the common religious essence. This effort is often carried on in dialogue with representatives of the other traditions; so the tendency to view all from one perspective is checked. Each is allowed to define itself.

Approaching matters in this way has made it very difficult to discover a common element in all religious experience. There continue to be efforts. But now the commonality is sometimes sought in the religious object instead. Realizing that "God" cannot be acceptable to all traditions as the object of religious concern, other terms are tried, such as "the ultimate," or "the Real." All the religions are then viewed as diverse ways of orienting life to this common reality.

When this approach is adopted, much of what is important to Christians appears quite relative. Not only is Christ seen as one among many ways that people have come to understand the religious object and to orient themselves to it, the same is true of a personal God, and even of anything that can be called "God" at all. This does not mean that we Christians should cease acknowledging the importance of Jesus to us or stop imaging the religious object as a personal deity. But if we follow this line of reasoning, then we know, even as we do this, that Jesus' importance is only for us and that the God we worship is only one possible image or symbol for the religious object. Most of what we care about must be recognized now as belonging to our images of this object and not to the object as such. Clearly no universal claims for Christian faith are involved.

The second great theological tradition that placed Christianity clearly in the global context was initiated by Hegel. Whereas Schleiermacher focused on religious experience, Hegel reflected on the place of Christianity in the unfolding drama of the human spirit or *Geist*. For Hegel, *Geist* had a history, and that meant a linear chronological development. This is the history of civilization understood in terms of basic modes of human self-understanding. Its progress is identified with the emergence and growth of personal freedom and of the institutions that embody it. In Hegel's vision, the beginning of this development of Spirit was in China, the culmination in Christian Europe. Again, but in a different way than for Schleiermacher, Christianity is the final answer.

During the nineteenth century, historical knowledge about other parts of the world increased greatly. The Hegelian story needed to be retold. The task was taken up by a man richly qualified as a scholar and a thinker: Ernst Troeltsch. He, too, thought that he could show Christianity as the culmination, this time because of its peculiar ability to transcend human cultures. But as Troeltsch pursued his research, he made two discoveries. First, Christianity was more culture-bound than he had supposed. Second, certain other religions, such as those of India, were more able to transcend cultural boundaries than he had thought. Troeltsch retained a distinction between the higher religions and the merely tribal ones, seeing the former as able to displace the latter. But he finally acknowledged that, among the higher religions, each was best in the cultural sphere in which it flourished. There was no neutral standpoint from which one could be declared superior to the others.

Since Troeltsch the great majority of the studies of the history of religions has separated itself from theological questions. For this new discipline, the task is simply to understand more accurately, without making judgments of value or truth. This academic discipline has flourished. Insofar as it has theological implications, these are that we should acknowledge that each community has its own forms of life and thought, that each has its own norms and values, that ours are no better and no worse than others. The relativization of Christianity is complete.

The third response to religious pluralism can be called confessional. Karl Barth saw clearly and profoundly the consequences of locating Christianity in the wider context of religion in general or of cultural history. It directed attention away from the content of the Christian faith itself. That faith was in the saving work of God in Jesus Christ. Neither Christian religious experience nor the role of Christianity in universal history can take the place of what God has done and will do. The role of Christians is to witness to God's work rather than to talk about the superiority of our religious experience or our great historical achievements. In this way we can at once be faithful to our scriptures and avoid arrogance.

Barth not only undertook to undercut Christian arrogance but also to soften the excessive concern of Christians with proselytizing. He emphasized that the right witness to what God has done in Jesus Christ is to assure all people that they are already saved in Christ. They are saved whether they believe or not. Of course, many of the advantages of being saved are not obtained until one believes, for unless one believes one will still engage anxiously in the futile quest for salvation. Hence there are reasons for sharing the message. But the motive is not to save souls from hell, a motive that has led to many abuses. Further, in general, members of Christian churches and those outside are pictured in much the same fashion. We are all trying to save ourselves by works rather than accepting the salvation that has already been accomplished for us.

Despite Barth's sensitivity to the implications of the Christian gospel for outsiders and his brilliant formulations, few who have been deeply involved with persons from other traditions are satisfied. Although as individual human beings these persons are neither disparaged nor excluded from salvation, as believers in other traditions they are told that all they hold most dear is worthless and irrelevant. They can not recognize themselves in Barth's account of the anxious efforts at self-salvation. They are offended that once again Christianity alone is depicted as knowing the way of salvation.

Barth's influence continues today, but generally in very moderated form. Negatively, there are many who reject the effort to locate Christianity, as if from without, in the horizon of religion or world history. Positively they agree that the task of the Christian theologian is to witness faithfully to the biblical message. But now that message is not understood as making supernatural or cosmic affirmations about God's activity in Jesus Christ. It is understood as fashioning an imagistic home in which believers can live.

A number of theologians of Barthian background have adopted, from anthropologist Clifford Geertz, the idea of a cultural-linguistic system, and have applied this to Christianity. In their view, the church should be the place where people learn that system and how to operate with it. The problem today is that the language of the church has become merged with that of a secular culture. Christian faith is thereby threatened. We need to intensify the inner life of our congregations by incorporating the people into the cultural-linguistic system that is Christianity.

It should be clear that just as the other moves of which I spoke among the heirs of Schleiermacher and Hegel radically relativized Christianity, this one did so as well. That is, all three give up the effort to show that Christianity is superior to other religions and acknowledge that it is simply one among many.

Still, there is a profound difference between this third, confessional, stance and the others, especially those of the heirs of Schleiermacher. Whereas that development tends to reduce emphasis on what is distinctive of Christianity in favor of the common element it shares with all, this one takes the distinctive reality of Christianity as all that Christianity is. It encourages living in the meanings of the faith, simply avoiding any implication that these are universal meanings. It turns away from the quest to understand Christianity from a transcendent perspective toward immersion within the faith itself. The church ceases to try to explain itself to others in a language familiar to them, and simply lives its own faith.

III

There can be little doubt that of the three options I have sketched, the third is the most promising for the church. It authorizes the church to do its business. Indeed, it frees the church from many distractions to concentrate on its own internal worship and corporate life. This does not exclude social action in the wider community, but that action is to flow out of the church's own understanding as shaped by its own language, not from a secular theory. Surely, this has much to commend it.

Nevertheless, I am not satisfied with this proposal, and I am quite skeptical that it can work in practice. With respect to many ideas, people want to know whether they are true, and the answer that they are Christian does not entirely satisfy. There is in Christianity a thrust toward self-transcendence and self-criticism, so that the confidence that certain things have been asserted in the past, even in the Bible, is often the beginning of the discussion rather than the end. Not everyone is so curious; so the approach will work for some. But I would regret the loss of those among whom the principle of self-criticism is better developed, and indeed I would be one of those who are lost.

The usual answer to this objection of mine is that it is naive, that there is no way of asking about truth outside a cultural-linguistic system. There is no metasystem in terms of which the affirmations of each can be judged. Those who ask about the truth of Christian language, as if there were some higher court of appeal, it is argued, have not yet understood that language. In this view the task is not to answer questions of truth, but to show that when one understands language properly, such questions do not arise.

These questions do not arise, for advocates of this proposal, because Christian affirmations are no longer understood to refer to any objective state of affairs. The meaning of each statement is found in its relation to others and to the pattern of corporate life that is associated with the language as a whole. Questions about the reality of God do not arise, because the meaning of asserting God's reality is exhausted in the way the use of that word is related to the use of other words in the Christian symbol system and to the way people act in relation to its use.

My own opinion is that this strategy cannot succeed. The pattern of behavior associated with the use of these words arose in a period when no one doubted that they referred to objective reality. Believers may have been wrong, but the belief that God existed quite independently of their language and behavior was essential to shaping that language and behavior. Many intellectuals have learned, since the rise of various forms of idealism and language philosophy, to stifle questions about the independent reality of God, but even they find it hard to be consistent. I do not anticipate that ordinary believers will follow suit.

IV

I have outlined three traditions and their current outcomes. I did not take time to criticize the final forms of the first two because, insofar as they are different from the third, they offer little promise for the church. The first relativizes in a way that inevitably depreciates the riches of the tradition, whatever the intention may be. The second objectifies the many religions, viewing them all, including Christianity, from the outside. The third, on the other hand, affirms the full richness of Christian language and liturgy and provides a basis for the church to understand itself and enter into a rich internal life. It is because it is attractive that I have called attention to its limitations. The question I now want to address is whether there is a better way for Christianity to understand itself while recognizing that it is one religious tradition among others. Specifically, can we renew Christian claims to universality without returning to the arrogant and oppressive role that has characterized Christianity in the past?

I believe we can. But this will require that we think of diverse religious traditions and their claims in a fresh way.

Generally, when people encounter highly divergent movements, they suppose that these are incompatible with one another, that, if one is right or true, the others must be wrong or false. In reaction against that, others often move to a radically relativistic position, accepting each in its own terms and denying that there is any perspective from which they can be evaluated objectively. In describing the present scene, it is this relativistic position that I have been discussing thus far. But I believe there is another and a better option.

Imagine with me, if you will, that the totality of what is, is very complex, far exceeding all that we can ever hope to know or think. Now suppose that in different parts of the world at different times, remarkable individuals have penetrated into this reality and discovered features of it that are really there to be found. In some instances, what they learn is merely of intellectual interest, but often it has profound meaning for the way life should be lived. The insight may be into nature, into history, or into what transcends nature and history alike.

Many times, presumably, these insights have died with those who attained them. But in other cases, they were shared, and communities of people developed around what was learned. They have worked out the implications of their respective insights for thought and practice, and they have developed institutions to preserve and carry on what was being discovered. Sometimes further insights emerged in this process and the traditions have received major new stimuli.

When I speak of insights, I imply that something has been seen that is really there to be seen. When I speak of working out their implications, I assume that these implications also have their truth. But all the expressions of the insights and of their implications are also shaped by cultural and historical factors that may illumine, but may also distort. I assume, further, that those who are most eager to defend the new truth are likely to see differing ideas and claims as dangerous to it, and to oppose them, whether or not they directly and necessarily conflict.

But now suppose that times change and that heirs of these several traditions meet and converse in friendly ways, genuinely curious about one another. The fact of difference now does not necessarily mean that they should reject and oppose one another. It may be that the differing insights out of which they have developed their contrasting and conflicting systems are all true! If so, they all have much to learn.

Finding out whether representatives of one community can accept particular ideas important to another is a very difficult task. Initial formulations usually suggest that this is impossible. Consider an example. Christians have a deep appreciation for the personal self. At the heart of Buddhist teaching is the doctrine of no-self, the denial that there is a personal self. Surely, if we do not adopt a complete relativism of the sort I am opposing, we must say that only one can be correct! The other must be flatly wrong.

Yet those Christians who have engaged in dialogue with Buddhists know that we are not reduced to such alternatives. We listen attentively to Buddhists explaining their no-self doctrine. We think long and hard about what is at the heart of our prizing of the personal self. We find many of the points made by Buddhists congenial to ideas of unselfishness and selflessness that have played a role in our own tradition. We recognize that all too often our talk of the personal self has been bound up with philosophical and psychological doctrines that, on reflection, we do not see to be necessary to our Christian faith. Step by step this process leads us to openness to what the Buddhist is saying. On the other hand, the Buddhist may see that the deepest Christian reason for affirming the personal self does not need to be flatly opposed. Eventually, at least for some of the participants, a view of self emerges that is different from either the historic Christian one or the traditional Buddhist formulation, one that affirms the central insights of both without the mutual negations.

This does not guarantee the complete truth of the new belief. But in my view, a belief that contains two distinct insights is closer to the truth than one that affirms one insight to the exclusion of the other. Something may be lost, but the likelihood is strong that more is gained.

Now suppose that Christians, having reformulated our beliefs so as to take account of Buddhist insights, have the opportunity to interact extensively with Native Americans. They, too, have insights into human existence, for example, into the way it is related to the earth. Initially what is heard will seem very different from the Buddhist-Christian anthropology resulting from the previous encounter, even contradictory. But with sufficient patience and good will there is a real chance that ways will be found to do some measure of justice to the deepest insights of Native Americans without giving up either our Christian insights or the Buddhist ones.

I do not mean to suggest that all Christians can devote themselves to endless conversations with persons from other traditions. Christians have other things to do. But if the relation among the beliefs of the many traditions is of this sort, then we do not need to relativize our beliefs. Quite the contrary. We can believe that our own tradition is rich in insights, insights that are true not only for us but for all. This is my central point. We can affirm our insights as universally valid! What we cannot do, without lapsing back into unjustified arrogance, is to deny that the insights of other traditions are also universally valid.

Of course, the awareness that heirs of other traditions have universally valid insights to share with us alters the way we think about our own. We will systematically free ourselves from the sort of universal claims that explicitly or implicitly assert that others have nothing to teach us. We will accent within our own heritage those teachings that point to the future as the time when the fullness of truth will be manifest, and we will tone down those statements that seem to imply that we already have the fullness of truth. Our tradition offers us ample resources for making these moves.

At present, church bodies often acknowledge that they can learn from one another, but they seem to be afraid to admit that Christians can also learn from other religious traditions. This is a sad commentary on the quality of our trust in God and openness to the Spirit who is to lead us into all truth. It expresses our resistance to learn from the New Testament the strength of weakness. Real strength lies not in clinging to what we have already received, but in openness to learn from others. Such openness does not mean that we despise what we now know, or think that we should wait for more before we act on the light we already have. Paul knew that he saw through a glass darkly, but this did not discourage him from speaking with conviction about what he saw. Indeed, what we already know should make us eager to learn more and to grow into a fuller truth. It is the strength of our biblical convictions that presses us toward the fuller truth that is to come.

V

My argument thus far is that we Christians have truths about humanity, about nature, and about God, that are universally valid. We should not be hesitant to claim them and share them. We should shape our lives by them and encourage others to do the same. But we should understand that those truths are but a small part of the whole of truth, that we need the help of

others in advancing toward that whole, that we should honor the universality of their messages as well. In that spirit we could renew conviction and
commitment in our churches. Perhaps we could even persuade our children
that something important is going on there, something in which they would
want to participate. Perhaps the wider public would begin to look to the
church as a place from which it could expect creative thinking and helpful
guidance in the confusion of a relativistic world.

I am letting myself be carried away. In fact the church is resisting this
move. Its leadership seems more comfortable celebrating its particularity in
accustomed ways than claiming its universality, if that claim requires change.
It is easy to interpret this resistance as inertia and defensiveness, and surely
these human weaknesses play a role. But is there more? Are there theological reasons for opposing the adventure on which I would like to see the
church embark?

It may be that the deepest resistance centers around the understanding of
Christ. Christians believe that Christ is the Way, the Truth, and the Life. We
understand that to mean that Christ is all-sufficient. To many it seems that
if we acknowledge that other traditions have universal truths which we need
to learn from them, then we are denying Christ or viewing Christ as but one
teacher among others, rather than as the savior of the world. In the name of
Christ, we are self-protective and close ourselves to others.

But is this biblically and theologically the deepest meaning of Christ? Are
not defensiveness and closedness to truth strange modes of faithfulness to
Christ? Are they not, finally, incompatible with radical faith, which surely
includes, if it does not simply mean, radical trust? Is there not a better way
of understanding Christ?

I believe there is. I do truly believe that Christ is the Way, and that living
that Way is of supreme importance in every generation, but above all today.
What is that Way? It is the Way of Truth and Life, of faith, hope, and love.
Still more concretely, what does that mean? The chief point is to choose
between two images of the Way. One is the image of following a blueprint
already given, or fitting our lives to a fixed set of guidelines. This is the way
of legalism. The second image is that of trusting the Spirit that leads us into
all truth, responding to opportunities as they arise, relating to our neighbors
in love, opening ourselves to individual and collective criticism, testifying to
the truth we have and seeking to learn more. This, I believe, is the Way that
is Christ. Having begun with the Spirit, why do we turn back to the law—
oh, we of little faith?

But with all my talk of the Spirit and the living Christ, am I neglecting the
historical figure of Jesus, and the claim he has upon us? I do not think so. I
think that my talk of Christ and the Spirit is quite continuous with the message
of Jesus and of his cross and resurrection. He did not lay out a practical guide
for future conduct in the church. Where he was original and creative as a
teacher, his role was to break open his hearers, to let them be transformed. The
Way he embodied and offered was one of being open to surprise and new per-

ceptions, not of clinging to established guidelines and inherited patterns. The early church's message of a crucified Messiah likewise was a shock, breaking into deepseated expectations and habits of thought. To think of Christ as binding us to the past, assuring us that we already know all that we need to know, encouraging us to closure, has no basis in what we know of Jesus' life, teaching, cross, and resurrection.

Or the objection may be that I am neglecting the great creeds of the church. Some think that the Christian doctrine of incarnation requires that we claim an exclusive uniqueness for ourselves that prevents us from accepting the truth that others have found. But surely this is not the case! It was not the case in the early church. The conviction that Jesus was the incarnation of the Logos opened many of the church's leading thinkers to believe that the same Logos that was incarnate in Jesus also spoke through the wisest of the Greeks. The church in fact internalized many insights of Aristotle, Plato, Plotinus, and the Stoics.

But perhaps the inclusion of Greek ideas in the development of Christian thought was a great mistake. Perhaps we should have understood the doctrine of incarnation to mean that all truth is to be found exclusively in Jesus, that we are to defend the biblical faith by ignoring all else or treating all else as ignorance and error. We have some basis in the Reformers for moving in that direction. Perhap my proposal involves the abandonment of the greatest insights of the Protestant tradition.

Again, I do not think so. The true insight of Luther was that major insights of the Bible had been obscured in the process of Hellenization. What was most important in his time was the recovery of those insights. In his impassioned work on their behalf, he often overspoke himself in his condemnation of others. To follow Luther rightly is not to adopt straightforwardly his attacks on the papacy, the nobility, the peasants, the Jews, Erasmian humanism, philosophy, reason, and the Epistle of James. It is to learn from him the importance of listening to the Bible openly and honestly, even when its word does not fit our expectation and preference, and to find in it, above all, the message of grace.

The Reformers can help us in another respect as well. They can free us from bondage to Greek formulations of Christian beliefs. Those who resist learning from Buddhists, or from representatives of primal communities, often, without realizing it, base their resistance not on biblical insights but on Greek thought. For example, it has been Hellenized thought, much more than biblical teaching itself, that has made it difficult to accept the insight in the Buddhist doctrine of no-self. This does not mean that in our eagerness to learn from Buddhists we should lose the insights we have gained from the Greeks. But it may help us in the process of honing the formulations of our present beliefs, to recognize how often we have confused the biblical insights with their Hellenized expression. Truly to recognize that what we know as Christianity is a Hellenized, and subsequently modernized, form may enable us to open ourselves to Buddhized and primalized forms as well, and to look for the fullness of truth through all and beyond all.

Let me finally say directly what I mean by "Christ." I mean the incarnation of God in the world. That God is in the world, and the effect God's presence has in the world we know in and through Jesus. The way God was present in him was unique. But Christ is not limited to the one historical person. When Paul spoke of the Christian life as being "in Christ" he could not have said, with identical meaning, "in Jesus." Christ was alive in the church. The church was, or could be, a continuing incarnation of God, the body of Christ. God is incarnate in the world as well. Our task is to discern Christ in our neighbor and to see what Christ is doing in the world today, to join in that work, and to let Christ be in us as well.

I am affirming that God is present in the world at all times and places, that we Christians know this presence as Christ, that Christ is the creative, redemptive, life-giving power in the world. Those are strong, universal affirmations. Do they return us to the arrogant, exclusivistic, and oppressive theology from which it is so important to separate ourselves?

They need not, and they must not. To affirm the truth of God's universal presence arrogantly, exclusivistically, and oppressively is to falsify it. It is to turn good news into bad news. To avoid that, we must think through, and learn to articulate, the crucial point, which is that the truth of this universal assertion by Christians does not exclude the truth of the universally relevant insights of others.

Consider the Buddhist claim that Gautama is the Buddha. That is a very different statement from the assertion that God was incarnate in Jesus. The Buddha is the one who is enlightened. To be enlightened is to realize the fundamental nature of reality, its insubstantiality, its relativity, its emptiness. To realize that is to be liberated from all attachment and all illusion, and to live in perfect compassion. This enlightenment is in principle open to all. But what enlightenment really is, that is made known in and through Gautama.

I hope my point is clear. The Buddhist claim is extremely different from the Christian one. It is based on very different interests and very different insights. Many doctrines that have been developed in support of these different insights are in conflict. But the basic insights themselves do not contradict one another. That Jesus was the incarnation of God does not deny that Gautama was the Enlightened One. In that vast complexity that is all that is, it may well be that God works creatively in all things and that at the same time, in the Buddhist sense, all things are empty. Perhaps we will understand God's creative and redemptive presence better when we also understand that all things are relative and insubstantial. Indeed, I believe that is the case. To affirm both that Jesus is the Christ and that Gautama is the Buddha is to move our understanding closer to the truth. To learn from some primal people that the earth is alive, that human beings are her children, that in wounding her we wound ourselves as well, will carry us still further toward the truth.

Learning from others in this way certainly requires *extensive* rethinking of our received faith. That is the task of theology in every generation. But it does not threaten or relativize our faith. It is because of our faith that we open ourselves to others, and the resultant growth is at once in understanding and in faith. Our confidence in the universality of Christ grows as living in Christ, that is, trusting the creative and redemptive work of God, expands the horizons of our understanding.

VI

I speak with pain and passion. We live in a time when the world needs Christ as never before. We are all lost, and Christ is the Way. I think I see what it would mean to follow that Way, to trust Christ, to be led by Christ toward all truth. I think it would mean once again knowing the Life that is so hard to discern in our churches now.

I see us, instead, trying to decide between two options, both deadly. One is to relativize our faith and with it Christ, abandoning confidence in the universal saving power that is the Way, the Truth, and the Life. The other is to identify Christ with past forms of the tradition that we now know to have been profoundly oppressive.

I fear that we are already far down the paths that lead to death. But today, again, God sets before us the great choice, the choice between Death and Life. May we hear once more the words of Moses as reported in Deuteronomy: "Therefore choose life." And may we obey!

9

Proclaiming Christ in a Pluralistic World

This essay carries forward the concerns of the previous one. As he surveys the Christian churches and the status of interreligious dialogue, Cobb makes a clear, and perhaps startling, assessment: "the pendulum has swung too far from proclamation." That this pendulum needed to swing away from the arrogant and often imperialistic way in which Christians have "proclaimed Christ" Cobb recognizes and affirms; but now he feels it has gone too far. In their relations with persons of other faiths, Christians are no longer acting like Christians—because they are no longer proclaiming Christ.

In a move already familiar to us from previous essays, Cobb takes us on a quick walk through contemporary Christian theology and points out how theologians, in their effort to move away from the "arrogance" of proclaiming Christ to other religions, have ended up proclaiming something else that is equally, if not more, arrogant. Liberal theologians such as Schleiermacher, Otto, Tillich, and more recently John Hick, move away from talking about Christ as their norm, but end up with their own philosophical and psychological norms which they proclaim under the camouflage of universal experience; instead of Christ they talk about "absolute dependence," or "ultimate concern," or "the Real." People in the perennial philosophy camp—like Huston Smith—do basically the same; they proclaim a mystical norm which they purport to be universal but which is really rooted mainly in Hindu terrain. Finally, Cobb detects this same subtle but dangerous move to replace the proclamation of Christ with the proclamation of something else within the post-liberal school of George Lindbeck; here the new norm is drawn not from philosophy or mysticism but from the kind of cultural anthropology that insists that language is the ultimate horizon of our existence; language determines (not just influences) what is real and true. For some religions, that's just as much an imposition as to tell them that they are saved only by Jesus.

So Cobb's appeal is that "Christians should think as Christians about the global religious situation and in relation to the diverse traditions that make it up." In other words, Christians should be upfront about the perspective from which they view other religions—Christ; and they should be upfront about why this perspective can be of value also to others. Cobb is certain that such proclamation need not lead to imposition or arrogance if it is truly a Christian proclamation—that means, done in love. Love requires one to always respect those to whom one is proclaiming. But respect means valuing them and recognizing that they, too, have something to proclaim to us. Thus, proclaiming Christ calls Christians not only to witness to others, but to be witnessed to by them—and so to clarify, expand, correct what they know in Christ.

He ends this essay with a fascinating example of what this kind of proclamation of Christ can mean in the Christian dialogue with Buddhism. There is much to be proclaimed—and learned—on both sides.

P. F. K.

This chapter is a revised version of an unpublished lecture delivered at the Graduate Theological Union in Berkeley in 1995.

I

I HAVE CHOSEN as my title a rhetoric that many will find troubling, if not offensive. They have good reasons for that concern. Proclamation suggests a monologue in which there is little sensitivity to the diverse experiences and needs of the hearers. I have chosen this title, however, because the pendulum has swung too far from proclamation. Few of us today are in good position to "proclaim," but it should be our goal to prepare for the time when we can again proclaim in good conscience.

The spread of Christianity throughout the Mediterranean world and far beyond was largely accomplished by proclaiming Christ. The same is true of the nineteenth-century missionary movement through which Christianity became truly a global community. The great revival movements of the eighteenth century in Great Britain and North America were also ways of proclaiming Christ. Proclamation has played a large role in Christian history.

Qualifications are in order. Many of the proclaimers were very sensitive people. The most effective proclamation was by those who well understood the people to whom they spoke and were able to address their real needs in ways that were effective and convincing. Sometimes this entailed serious study of other cultures and religious traditions.

Furthermore, proclamation alone did not produce the church. That required organization and formation. Usually the interaction of believers in small groups either as congregations or within congregations has been crucial to formation. Teaching and counseling have always been important adjuncts of proclamation.

The proclaimer has been important to the proclamation. The Christ who is proclaimed can have some convincing power even when the proclaimer does not embody the graces that Christ bestows. But the message is far more powerful when the one who speaks also lives and embodies it. Christ is proclaimed in deed as well as in word.

We now recognize that the power of the proclamation was often ambiguous in its effects. The truth of Christ was always mixed with the dross of human error. Especially in modern missionary activity, the cultural norms of the proclaimer have often been confused with the gospel. The separation of them is at best difficult, and often little thought was given to its achievement. As a result, much of value in existing cultures and religious communities was destroyed. In other cases this confusion blocked the acceptance of Christ altogether.

We have now learned also that many of the cultures in which we proclaimed Christ had religious traditions of great sophistication which we erroneously treated with indifference and even contempt. We acted as if we brought Christ for the first time to a world from which God was absent. We did not nurture the work that Christ was already doing even where the name was not spoken.

We see also that although the way we proclaimed Christ was liberating in part, it was also oppressive. It sometimes disempowered the converts, establishing missionary control over them. At times it was closely bound up with political and economic colonialism.

I will not rehearse further this litany of evils. Some of this evil is inherent in the project of bringing a new message to those who have not heard it. This is inevitably disruptive of traditional homogeneous cultures. No wisdom and virtue on the part of missionaries could have made the spread of Christianity painless. In this sense, Christ came to bring not peace but a sword. We must judge whether the gain is worth the pain. That is not always easy to do.

Many of the evils resulted from particular historical circumstances in which a truly wise and loving solution would have required genius of a high order. We should not be too critical of the failures of the missionaries. It is not clear that even in hindsight we can be much wiser.

On the other hand, we must also acknowledge that racism and cultural chauvinism played a role in the proclamation of Christ and the establishment of churches. Much of the evil stemmed from this. Probably on the whole the missionaries were less bound by these vices than the sending churches as a whole, but that the missionary movement was deeply distorted by them can hardly be doubted. The "heathen" to be converted were not really viewed as humanly on a par with the Christians who set out to convert them. One reason why the word "proclamation" is difficult to reclaim is its close tie to the arrogance of those who thought themselves superior human beings to those to whom they preached.

II

The missionary movement itself contributed to a major effort to understand the other religious traditions. At the scholarly level this effort characterized much of the theological work of the nineteenth century. The World Parliament of Religions, just over a century ago, led to a much wider recognition that the "heathen" were sometimes people of religious depth and wisdom. From that time on in the United States there has been increasing uneasiness about "proclaiming Christ."

Missionary work continued, but proclamation played a declining role. In the context of the social gospel, witness to Christ through medical and educational institutions, agricultural work, and social reform seemed a more appropriate emphasis. Since churches were already established almost everywhere, missionaries could work in and with them. Authority was turned over more and more to indigenous people, and most of the work of proclamation was put in their hands. It was hoped that in that way it would be less distorted by cultural differences and Western arrogance. After World War II the world mission of the church moved to the periphery of the church's consciousness and interest.

Meanwhile proclamation also declined in the United States. Partly this was due to the success of the nineteenth-century mission to the frontier. The country was covered with churches, so that proclaiming Christ to those who were beyond the churches' influence ceased to be a major task.

However, the decline was also because there was less confidence that we knew what it meant to proclaim Christ. During the heyday of the social gospel this was not true. To proclaim Christ was to call people into the work of building the Kingdom. This had quite concrete meaning. But when the social gospel declined, nothing replaced it in the actual life of the old-line churches. Theologians introduced Barth's proclamation of Christ, but this did not strike deep roots on this side of the Atlantic. Indeed, the association of the proclamation of Christ with a complex imported theology only served to remove it from the actual consciousness of ordinary Christians.

The recognition of the positive value and the religous wisdom of other traditions was only one factor in the decline of proclamation. But it was, and is, an important one, and it is our topic here. The energy that once went into proclaiming Christ increasingly has gone into efforts to understand the global religious situation in all its diversity. This has led to widespread interest in comparative religions and the history of religions.

This emphasis was fostered also by the separation of church and state. Those who recognized that it is not healthy for a whole nation to be ignorant of religion found this a way in which religion could be taught in public schools and state universities without violating this separation. By now there are millions of Americans who have been given some introduction to the religions of the world. Often their instructors have leaned over backwards to be appreciative of other traditions while feeling free to be more critical of Christianity. This exposure has not supported for the renewal of proclamation.

III

In addition to the appreciative description of other religious traditions, there have been intensive efforts to understand what religion as such is and how its diversity is to be understood. These reflections are usually more explicitly normative, with direct implications for how believers in the several communities should understand themselves.

Often those who seek this understanding are Christian theologians. They are motivated by their faith to understand the relation of Christianity to other traditions. But the work of identifying the essence of religion is not viewed as itself a theological task. An important tradition of such reflection goes back to Schleiermacher.

Schleiermacher himself taught that religion is the feeling of absolute dependence, that is, God-consciousness. From this definition he went on to show that different religious traditions were more and less successful in embodying the essence of religion. The hierarchy he derived culminated in Christianity.

A century later Rudolf Otto took up the task with far greater scholarly knowledge of the world religions. He identified the experience of the numinous or the holy as the essential characteristic of religion. In his case also, Christianity appears, although less blatantly, as the finest form.

Paul Tillich is the most recent widely influential practitioner of this approach. For him "ultimate concern" is the mark of religion. The issue is whether ultimate concern is directed to what is ultimate. The symbol of the cross for Tillich is the ideal way of opposing every tendency to idolatry.

These approaches to the understanding of religion all testify to their theistic origins even when they avoid narrowly theistic language. There has been another set of responses that come from the more mystical traditions. These writers distinguish popular religious practice in all the traditions from the truly religious experience that grounds and inspires the tradition. The more devout members of any of these traditions become, the more they seek and find purer religious experience. This is typically experience of unity with the divine.

Aldous Huxley culled the literature of many religious traditions to display that those who lived from mystical experience at first hand had much to say in common. Huxley named this common teaching of the world's mystics the "perennial philosophy." Because it arises quite directly out of personal experience, it can be trusted.

Huxley understood that this was the position of modern Hindu Vedantism. Hence it is not surprising that when one defines true religion in this way, its purest expressions are to be found in particular forms of Hinduism. This counterbalances the tendency of the tradition stemming from Schleiermacher to favor the theistic communities and especially Christianity.

Huston Smith who has been the nation's leading teacher of world religions has a similar view. He also has been particularly influenced by Hinduism. Hence the esoteric religion that he favors as truly authentic, although discoverable elsewhere as well, is particularly well embodied in Hinduism.

It is striking that, at least in Huxley's case, Buddhist quotations are conspicuous by their absence. At first glace this seems strange. Buddhism is very much a religion of first-hand, unmediated experience. However, this first-hand experience does not take the form of unity of the self with ultimate reality. Buddhist enlightenment is the experience that occurs when one realizes that there is no self and no ultimate reality with which to merge. There is only emptiness.

Buddhist voices stemming from this experience have also proposed ways of understanding the essence of religion. For them, of course, it is the realization of emptiness. They, too, find that this experience has its witnesses in Christianity and other world religions as well as in Buddhism. But it is hardly necessary to say that the greatest clarity about this experience is given in Buddhist texts.

My point, of course, is that plurality reasserts itself at the point of defining the essence of religion. Even though those who engage in this act conscientiously undertake to transcend the biases of their traditions and to do their work objectively as students of world religion, what they see is what they have learned to see as they have been formed in their own traditions.

In each case their conclusions allow a place for a highly muted proclamation. But what is proclaimed is not likely to be Christ even in the pro-Christian instances. What one is led to proclaim by these analyses are ultimate concern about the ultimate, the possibility of unity with ultimate reality, or emptiness. One proclaims them in a way that emphasizes their relative independence of any one tradition.

The most recent new undertaking to define religion objectively and neutrally is that of John Hick. He explicitly refuses to affirm the superiority of any one. To avoid such favoritism he focuses on the change effected by religious traditions in their members. He identifies this change as from centeredness in the self to centeredness in the Real.

The leaves open whether the Real is the personal God of the Judaic traditions or the impersonal ultimate of Vedanta and Buddhism. Hick points out that the personal transformation effected is much the same in both cases. He takes the "Real" to be a neutral term, and he affirms that it is apprehended personally in some communities and impersonally in others. It is itself purely noumenal and so untouched by such distinctions.

The strength of this position is apparent. It points to a commonality in many of the "higher" religions, that is, the freeing of people from self-preoccupation and orienting them to a larger or more fundamental reality. It avoids favoring any one tradition.

Unfortunately, its success is bought at a high price. It offends all equally. It posits a noumenal reality available only to the philosopher that is beyond, or more fundamental than, the personal or impersonal ultimates of the religious traditions. This is particularly offensive to Vedantists and Buddhists. The Brahman whose identity with Atman is realized is already beyond all such distinction as personal and impersonal. Since it can in no way be conceived or imaged, it is misunderstood when it is treated as one culturally informed way in which the noumenal Real is apprehended. For the Buddhist, the same must be said of Emptiness. It is not the way that something else is apprehended. The noumenal Real is just that kind of ground whose reality Buddhism denies.

Some Christians will not object to recognizing that the personal deity is the way of apprehending a mystery that is beyond all such distinctions. Some formulations of the Trinity suggest that beyond the three persons there is Godhead itself. But Hick would have to deny that this Godhead is the Real. In order to maintain balance, he must assert that it is simply the culturally conditioned way in which Christians have apprehended the Real. Meanwhile other Christians will be deeply offended at this relativization of the personal God.

This completes my fragmentary survey of the efforts to view the field of religion objectively in order to discover the religious essence and interpret the several traditions in light of their diverse embodiments and developments of that essence. My judgment is that the effort has failed and that it necessarily fails. Let us consider why this may be so.

One explanation of the failure of all such undertakings is offered by those who are most influenced by the linguistic turn in philosophy. This is the turn away from thought, experience, or objective reality to language. The most thoroughgoing advocates of this turn take language to be the horizon of our existence. For them we live in, and only in, a linguistic world.

It is possible to draw the conclusion that the analysis of language can free us all from those mystifications that constitute religion. But it is also possible to recognize a variety of language worlds of which none can be privileged. Religion can then be free to function as a language game, and one can go on to think of each religion as a separate language game.

This way of thinking has been more fully developed recently under the influence of Clifford Geertz. He speaks not of multiple language games but of cultural-linguistic systems. George Lindbeck has developed this idea for theological use. Applied to the problem of religious pluralism, it implies that each religious community is constituted by its cultural-linguistic system. The meaning of each element in that system is found in its role in the system as a whole. Its references, in other words, are not to a neutral and independent reality outside the system but to other parts of the system. Thus, within the system the liturgical acts and symbols and assertions make sense. They make no sense when abstracted from the system.

Viewing the religious traditions in this way throws light on the failure of the quest for the religious essence. It is understandable that those who are informed by the Buddhist cultural-linguistic system, however richly informed by the study of other traditions, interpret all that in terms of their own system. It is equally understandable that this happens also with Hindus and Christians. But this should caution us not to use our cultural-linguistic system beyond its borders.

The lesson offered here is that there is no transcendent perspective from which to understand the cultural-linguistic systems that constitute the several religious traditions. They are simply different and are only understood from within. Learning to live with differences is our task. Proclaiming Christ makes sense within the Christian cultural-linguistic system. It does not provide an appropriate approach to persons who live outside it.

Although these conclusions are very different from those of John Hick, my objections are quite similar. Whereas Hick goes to metaphysics to establish the point of view outside all religious traditions from which their truth and limits are described, Lindbeck goes to cultural anthropology. This discipline, or particular findings from it, are offered, not as one perspective among others, for example, alongside the perspectives of the religious traditions, but as a basis of pronouncing what all the religious traditions are and are not. What is said of them in no instance corresponds to their self-understanding.

Now it may be that Lindbeck is correct and the great majority of believers in all the traditions are in error. But he provides little evidence for this possibility. The Buddhists have a theory of language and its relation to experience that overlaps with Lindbeck's at some points but leads to quite different conclusions. My own judgment is that it is far more richly developed and more plausible than the one Lindbeck derives from Geertz. Would it make sense for Buddhists to abandon their traditional theories and adopt Lindbeck's version of Geertz's? They are free to do so, but my expectation is that they will, and should, continue to work with their own theory. Buddhists have reasons internal to their own self-understanding to be open to learning from the natural and social sciences. But they also have reasons to be critical of what is offered to them. It is inappropriate to ask them to relativize their own self-understanding in order to fit into a theory that was developed with extremely little attention to their wisdom.

Lindbeck, of course, did not develop his theory with Buddhism in view. Hence my critical response is unfair. Nevertheless, the implications I have drawn from it are very much in the air. They seem to follow from the linguistic turn when it is combined with the recognition of the diversity of linguistic systems and their close associations with religious communities. If language never expresses prelinguistic experience or refers in any way to a nonlinguistic reality, then these conclusions follow. But all of the religious communities have taught otherwise. To declare them all wrong in order for them to live together in their differences is not an adequate strategy.

IV

I have taken this long route to come to a point which I could have asserted quite simply at the outset. In my opinion, Christians should think as Christians about the global religious situation and in relation to the diverse traditions that make it up. If I had said that to start with, however, you might not have realized that I am proposing a quite radical shift away from what has been occurring for a century or more.

Most people seem to assume that if Christians think as Christians (and Buddhists, of course, as Buddhists) the results will be biased, one-sided, and parochial. Hence, in order to avoid these limitations, Christians, or Buddhists, must put on another hat—that of the historian of religion or philosopher of religion or cultural anthropologist, for example. Only after they have done their objective work in that way, it is supposed, can they return to their role as Christian and Buddhist thinkers and carry out the much narrower tasks suited to that role.

I have gone to some length to show that this does not work. When Christians take these steps, one of two things happens. *First,* they may in fact carry their Christian perspective with them without acknowledging this fact. They then pretend to a neutrality they do not really attain. This leads to supposedly neutral judgments that are covertly Christian.

Suppose, now, that Schleiermacher, Otto, and Tillich had made their proposals explicitly from a Christian point of view. The consequences would have been quite different. They could have invited representatives of other traditions to consider with them how successful these definitions were in clarifying their self-understanding. They would have learned that not all felt comfortable with them. If they still thought that these definitions illuminated Christian and some other experience, they could have continued to use them in this qualified way. But they would have avoided the scholarly imperialism of defining others in Christian terms. They would have avoided the largely circular argument of declaring ourselves the best because we do best what we regard as most important to do.

Or, *second,* they may adopt a position that has its justification in a particular philosophical or scientific field and impose it on all religious communities. If philosophy or social sciences were themselves free from human bias and perspective, then this might be justified. But the philosophical position Hick develops is idiosyncratically his own, and Geertz, for all his wisdom, is not the final authority on language and religion.

When I say that Christians should approach these questions as Christians, I certainly do not mean that we should ignore philosophers or cultural anthropologists, or specifically either Hick or Geertz. We have Christian reasons for seeking help in understanding ourselves and others from whoever seems to have help to offer. But since as Christians we will not start out with the commitment to establish an essence of all religion and the equality of the major traditions, we will not adopt a philosophical position chiefly because it achieves those goals. Similarly, we will not accept simply on the authority of a cultural anthropologist that our language is unaffected by experiences that are partly independent of language. We will hear that as an interesting, if extreme, hypothesis, to be tested against our own Christian experience of how language functions, as well as against evidence we can gain from others. If the philosophical and cultural-anthropological views are presented as alternative perspectives alongside Christian and Hindu ones, we will certainly enter into dialogue with them. But when they are presented as objective truth whereas the views of religious traditions are seen as having no purchase on such truth, we find this one-sidedness arrogant and unacceptable.

If Lindbeck had approached Geertz for help as a Christian thinker, he might well have found assistance in understanding the way in which various Christian groups shape their symbols and their linguistic systems. He could have appropriated that help. Other theologians could have discussed with him the strengths and limitations of the theory he had adopted in terms of their Christian undersanding. But he would not have been disposed to make universalistic statements about religions in general with strong implications for how they should relate to one another and change. If the topic of other religious traditions had been important to him, he could have offered a theory that he found useful for his Christian purposes to see whether thinkers in other traditions also found it useful. But he would not have presented it as universally valid unless, again and again, he found support for it in the other traditions.

I am calling for Christians to think as Christians. I hope that my meaning becomes clear as I register my complaints about what Christians have in fact done. In one sense, whenever Christians think, they think as Christians. When Lindbeck turned to Geertz, he was a Christian, and when he pronounced Geertz's view normative, he was still a Christian. But this does not satisfy my requirement of thinking *as* a Christian. My complaint is that he formulates his arguments and presents his position as if it were not an expression of his Christian perspective but something more objective or scientific. Thus, what I mean by calling for Christians to think as Christians is to ask them to acknowledge that all their thinking is informed and directed by their Christian faith. I am asking them to stop pretending that at times they step out of their role as Christian thinkers and speak from some more universal perspective based on science or philosophy.

Thinking as a Christian is not only a constant recognition of the perspective from which we approach all questions but also a continuing critical reflection on that perspective. Being a Christian is not a fixed condition. It involves openness to the Spirit and that is also openness to wisdom wherever it may be found. My Christian perspective now is not the same as my Christian perspective when I was an adolescent. I hope it has matured. The perspective of twentieth-century Christians is not the same as that of thirteenth- or seventeenth-century Christians, and among twentieth-century Christians there are great diversities. Hence one cannot spell out once for all for oneself, much less for all Christians, the detailed character of the Christian perspective.

We *can* say that a Christian perspective is one that is formed primarily in that history of which Jesus is recognized as the center. One may also say, at least provisionally, that it is a perspective for which Christ is somehow normative. Of course, the meaning of "Christ" can vary greatly, as can the way Christ norms the Christian. Every particular Christian perspective has far greater specificity and richness, but from my Christian perspective, I do not believe that I should prejudge other perspectives as not Christian if they have come into existence in the ongoing history of the Christian movement, with its recognition of the centrality of Jesus and the normativity of Christ.

In many instances I consider such Christian perspectives to be distorted, idolatrous, even perverse. I consider it my vocation as a Christian to criticize many of the more influential Christian perspectives. I do so in the name of the centrality of Jesus and the normativity of Christ as I have come to understand these through my participation in the ongoing community of faith. I expect others to try to correct me as they see me missing the mark.

There are other instances in which I am skeptical of the claim that a perspective is Christian. I see some putatively Christian perspectives as informed more by participation in national life than in that of the community of faith. I see some as using the symbols of faith to support and advocate beliefs that are in fact derived from quite different sources.

The issue of derivation from other sources needs clarification. Actually, most of my own beliefs are derived at least partly from sources that are at least partly independent of the formative Christian events. Much of the way I think about psychology, for example, is learned from psychologists. Many of them are somewhat influenced by Christian traditions, but much of what they say is largely independent of those traditions. To think about human psychology only in ways that are demonstrably derived from the New Testament or the church fathers would be foolish. From my point of view, it would not be Christian. As a Christian I am not only free to learn wherever I can, I am called to do so. The fullness of truth is only gradually realized by Christians and it will be realized only as we are open to its presence everywhere.

But the Christian does not accept every idea that is offered. The Christian selects critically. The basis of selection is found in the Christian perspective. When I express skepticism about the source of some beliefs that are supported by artificial use of Christian symbols, my concern is not that relevant information was gleaned from outside of traditional Christian sources. My concern is that these beliefs express the self-interest, class interest, or cultural bias of the person who is claiming Christian authority. To think as a Christian is to be critical of such distortions. When no such criticism is taking place, and when the thinker in question refuses to engage in it when called upon to do so, I am left with the impression that Christianity is being exploited for alien purposes.

V

Now it is time to ask the question: When one approaches the pluralistic situation from a Christian perspective, what happens? Does one simply proclaim Christ regardless of all the problems with that approach? I think not. For me, the Christian perspective requires attention to criticisms and changes in light of them. We have learned that proclamation that is not sensitive to those to whom it is directed does as much harm as good. We cannot then simply continue it.

How then do we approach persons from other religious traditions? The answer should always be, in love. But what does it mean to love others? In the past it has often meant telling the others about the saving truth of which we have assumed they were ignorant. Today we are repenting of having spoken too much and listened too little. Love requires that we take the others seriously, and that now requires us to listen to what they have to say. Often that is painful, since Christians who have not listened have inflicted enormous suffering, especially, but not only, on the Jews. Even when we think we understand our collective crimes, listening to the particular pain and accusations of the individual others is painful. Sometimes we feel that their charges are unfair, that we are unjustly accused, and perhaps we are. But again, after so many centuries of self-righteous proclamation, it is time to listen. Christian love requires it.

Next, Christian faith calls us to repent. We are not here thinking so much of private and individual repentance. Our sins are collective and our repentance must be collective, too. But we can repent collectively only as we individually acknowledge our collective sin and do all we can to turn away from it both individually and collectively. The Christian community is collectively repenting of its anti-Judaism. But this must be an ongoing process over a long period of time. It is not enough to say that we are sorry for this or that act or doctrine. The longer we listen the more we realize that our whole heritage is permeated with beliefs and practices that are implicitly anti-Jewish. Ours will be a very different community when we have finished the process of repenting.

Listening is not only hearing about who we have been from the perspective of others. It is also hearing from them what they have come to understand through their quite different histories. This need not be painful. It can be exciting. Ideas and possibilities are brought to our attention to which we had heretofore been blind. In short we can learn not only in the sense of gaining information, but in the more important sense of having our horizons extended and our consciousness raised. Again, we accept only what we as Christians perceive as true wisdom. But there will be much of that. And the Christian perspective from which we learn will change as we learn.

Love that takes the others seriously will not only listen, repent, and learn. It will also speak. When we have listened, repented, and learned, we will know much better what we have to offer. We can then speak the truth in love responsibly. As we have listened from our Christian perspectives, we will not only have learned wisdom, we will also have noticed gaps and omissions. Sometimes we will perceive dangers in the emphases and ideas that are presented to us. Sometimes we will find that those who rightly criticize us do not notice similar weaknesses and failures in their own positions. If we have been shaped in ways for which we are grateful in our own tradition, we will want to explain this to the others.

In love, we will speak tentatively, feeling our way. Sometimes the gaps we think we have observed are already well filled in the other traditions. Sometimes the self-criticism we missed will come quickly to the fore once the concern is brought out. But some of our honest sharing of what we think we have to offer will turn out to be of real value to the others. Some of the wisdom we have gained from our heritage will commend itself to them. Some of our tentative criticisms will hit home, and we will be encouraged to develop them more fully.

In all this I have not spoken specifically of Christ. But because I understand Christ to be the norm of all that I think as a Christian, I will in fact be sharing Christ. It is not usually best to begin with the name. The others will have heard it, and it will be laden with meanings that may distract from matters at hand. It is better to begin quite concretely with those gifts of Christ that are relevant to these particular others.

But in the end it is also appropriate, even imperative, to proclaim Christ. If that language is offensive, then we can say first that it is appropriate to witness to Christ, to state our conviction that the wisdom that we have shared is Christ's gift, that we discern that Christ has already been present in and with the others, and that we receive their wisdom as Christ's gift to us through them.

The others will listen to us from their perspectives. They may distinguish between Christ and those features among Christ's gifts that they want to appropriate. They may think that our attributing these to Christ is an unnecessary interpretation. But if we have spoken confessionally, they will not resent our having told them how we understand Christ. They want us to be as honest with them as they have been with us. They will respect our devotion to Christ, even if they do not share it.

We should not assume, however, that this is always the end of the matter. Two other results are possible. One is that some who hear us proclaim Christ in this way will want to enter that community in which Christ is most fully known. Individual conversion is possible and, in most instances, a positive outcome of the proclamation of Christ.

But the positive outcome of listening and proclaiming is likely in most instances to be change within traditions rather than switching from one to another. This change can include the affirmation of Christ in traditions other than the Christian one. Indeed, this has already happened in many ways.

There are Jews who have accepted Jesus as Christ and yet remain Jews. Why should they not? True, they are a fringe movement, but that does not negate the value of this move. More important is the possibility that as Jews become more free from the fear of Christianity and of cultural assimilation, especially in the state of Israel, they can appropriate Jesus and Paul into their own history and tradition. Indeed, to some extent this is already happening. We will have much to learn from them when this process has gone further.

Jesus already plays an important role in Islam. The results of listening and sharing with Muslims may be to heighten that role and enrich the understanding of who Jesus was. Muslims may not need to become Christians in order to accept Christ.

There is nothing in Hinduism that prevents the recognition of Jesus as a holy man, even an incarnation of the divine. There are Hindu movements that have given to him a very high status. But from my Christian perspective, appropriating Jesus into the Hindu religious vision does not allow Jesus' distinctive person and message to be experienced in all its power. As we witness to Hindus, they may come to appreciate the meaning of their reverence for Jesus in new ways, and Christ may become more central in their religious life.

VI

In all of this I have spoken only formally of Jesus and of Christ. I have not provided a Christology that would give content to my assertions. I want to conclude with a discussion of Buddhism in which I indicate, however sketchily, what the results of listening and proclaiming can be for Christians and for Buddhists.

The heart of Buddhist insight and wisdom centers on enlightenment. Enlightenment is freedom from all illusion and distortion and openness to all that is as it is. Enlightenment brings freedom from all the suffering that results from having wants that can never be permanently satisfied, from having aims that can never be permanently fulfilled, from having guilt about which nothing can be done. It leads to serene acceptance of what is, moment by moment, without anxiety or regret.

Speaking thus of its results certainly does not plumb its depths. It is a mode of being in the world to which few have fully attained and to which even approximation is not easy. But such approximation is nevertheless real and leaves its mark in the lives of many. That of which Buddhists speak is reality. Christians can benefit greatly from listening. By now, many have listened, and many are practicing Buddhist forms of meditation so as to participate in the movement toward enlightenment that meditation makes possible. Christian learning from Buddhists continues, and it has transforming effects.

But after we have listened and learned, have we something to say? Yes, we have. Buddhists, at least those in China, Korea, and Japan, have had little responsibility for the social and political lives of their countries. They have developed little social analysis or political ethics. They offer little resistance to what Christians perceive as idolatrous forms of nationalism.

Even in personal life they have focused on the attainment of a certain spiritual state that is beyond good and evil, and accordingly they have not developed a rich sense of genuinely moral responsibility. They are rightly confident that enlightenment involves wisdom and compassion, and there are many beautiful stories of how that compassion is expressed. But the meaning of the goal of compassion for those who have not yet attained enlightenment is not worked out.

These criticisms require careful qualification, but they rightly suggest that from the Christian perspective Buddhism is incomplete. It has analyzed the path to enlightenment in great detail. It has not given equal attention to the issues of justice and righteousness that are so central to Christian faith.

This is connected to the fact that Buddhism focuses on features of the human situation that are present at all times and places. It draws attention away from those features that change. With regard to them it makes few judgments as to whether changes are for the better or for the worse with the exception, in some Buddhist traditions, of judging the greater difficulty of attaining to enlightenment as the temporal distance from Gautama increases. In short, history plays a negligible role in Buddhism. From my Christian perspective, this is a major weakness closely related to the lack of social analysis and of a passion for justice and righteousness.

These limitations of Buddhism are acknowledged by some Buddhists. The solution might seem to be simply to add them to existing Buddhist practice. But one cannot simply incorporate fruits one wants while ignoring the trunk and branches that have borne them. There is a close relationship between the basic Buddhist analysis of reality, intimately connected to the quest for enlightenment, and the absence of the social, ethical, and historical dimensions from its central self-understanding. If the proclamation of Christ in these ways is to have any result other than making some Buddhists feel uncomfortable about their limitations, it needs to be presented in a way that is closely integrated with the heart of Buddhist teaching. I believe this is possible.

Consider the standard Buddhist analysis of reality as empty. It is empty of substance. But this means not that there is nothing at all, only that nothing exists in itself. There is no self-existent being. The existence of each thing, or, better, event, is a function of the existence of others. What comes into being is a joint product of everything else. This is called "dependent origination" or *pratitya samutpada*.

I read all this through eyes informed by the philosophy of Alfred North Whitehead. Whitehead had the same interest as early Buddhists in overcoming the substantialist view of things, and his way of doing so was quite similar. The similarity is great enough that Whitehead's account can serve as one valid rendering of *pratitya samutpada*. Whitehead wrote of the many becoming one. There is not first an entity, or a happening, an occurrence, or an event that is then related to others. The event *is* the coming together of the others. It can have no independent existence. The event is misunderstood if it is conceived as the one that is the result of the many. The many are ingredient in it.

Both Buddhists and Whiteheadians know that it is difficult to experience and think of the world in this way in the face of ordinary sense experience and the substantialist bias of the Indo-European languages. Buddhists know, indeed, that one cannot attain true insight by thought alone. Hence they have developed complex and demanding meditational methods to free the mind from all conceptualizing and to allow it to realize that it is in fact nothing but the many becoming one. They have known, as Whiteheadians would otherwise hardly have guessed, that this realization, in distinction from intellectual opinion, is radically transforming. It *is* enlightenment.

As a Christian, especially as a Whiteheadian Christian, I see no reason to dispute any of this. In my opinion, the Buddhists know whereof they speak, and that is to know a great deal. This is wisdom we cannot find in any other tradition, certainly not in our own. It is to be gratefully learned. Such learning will have a transforming effect upon the whole of our perspective.

Nevertheless, it is possible to examine events further to discern features that have been largely neglected in the Buddhist analyses. Equally remarkable with the fact that every moment of my experience is an instance of the many becoming one is that every moment also has a measure of transcendence over the many that constitute it. It is not a mere product of that many. It is not part of a wholly deterministic system. There is a feature of each personal event that can be identified as freedom or decision. In each moment there is an act, and not only a passive reception.

In Whitehead's analysis this is because in every momentary occasion there is a "mental pole" as well as a "physical pole." The physical pole is constituted by the inflowing of the many events of the past. The mental pole is constituted by an aim to build upon that past and to become what it is possible to be, given that past. This means that there are alternatives among which the occasion can choose and a call to realize the richest alternative. This requires of the occasion a decision.

This supplementation of the past world that introduces transcendence or freedom into each new occasion involves the inflowing of another "one." Although it is one of the many, it is not simply that; for its contribution differs from the others. It contributes novelty, alternatives, freedom, and in human occasions, the dimension of morality and responsibility. Whitehead calls this "God," and I call the incarnation of God in each occasion, as one of the many that become one, "Christ."

The basic analysis of *pratitya samutpada* does not exclude the possibility that among the many that become one, one plays a distinctive role of this sort. Nor does it intend to deny that there is decision in each moment. Some of its rhetoric presupposes this. But freedom and decision are not thematically considered in the Buddhist literature. And the tone of the analysis does not encourage one to ask about different roles played by different ones among the many.

If one introduces such elements into the analysis, one will be led quite naturally to ask also about how the many in one moment differ from the many in another. That they do differ Buddhism has never questioned. But that these differences are affected by public events and constitute a history has hardly been considered. It is Christ who brings these differences to life, because Christ calls us to decisions that are informed by these differences.

Pratitya samutpada is also called Buddha-nature. For Christians to include Buddha-nature in their interpretation of the world and to learn to experience themselves in these terms will involve a profound change. Yet I hope that Buddhists continue to call us to realize our Buddha-nature. There is no reason for us to avoid that terminology. It connects what would otherwise seem an abstract metaphysical point to the one who, through its realization, attained a unique wisdom and compassion. It thus enables us to appreciate the depth of religious meaning and possibility we would otherwise ignore.

As we listen and learn and are transformed by Buddhist wisdom, we also are freed to proclaim Christ to Buddhists. We could describe what we believe transpires in less evocative language. But that leads to the neglect of its meaning and importance. By calling God's presence in our lives "Christ," we connect it to the unique event of Jesus and to the whole biblical history of which he is for us the center. We see that our life with God centers in our receipt from God in Christ of our calling, our freedom, our very life. We see also that our response involves responsible righteousness and love in the concrete context of history. And we have a picture of what it means to live from God and for God. There should be nothing offensive to Buddhists in our proclaiming Christ.

A Buddhist who understands who and what Christ is may want to become individually a Christian. There is nothing wrong with such conversion. We should welcome the new believer. But the Buddhist who remains a Buddhist may also come to have faith in Christ, just as persons who remain Christians may engage in the arduous practice of Zen meditation as a means of realizing their Buddha-nature.

If we think as Christians about other religious traditions, we will approach them one by one and listen. We will not try to develop a theory of what they all are and then hear only what fits that theory. We do not want to be dealt with in that way. We want to be able to define ourselves. To listen to others is to allow them in love the freedom we also want.

It is my expectation that as we deal with other religious traditions one by one, we will come to some generalizations about them, but I doubt that these will describe what is most interesting in any of them. What will be more impressive will be their differences, just those differences that the quest for an essence of religion obscures. But such judgments should arise out of experience, not be imposed a priori. If the other traditions turn out to have more in common than I now think, so be it. If, at what each recognizes at its core, there is identity, so be it. My concern is not that my own judgment of deep diversity be vindicated. It is that as Christians we allow each religious tradition to define itself rather than impose our definition upon it, and that we learn to proclaim Christ concretely in relation to the needs in each religious community.

10

Can Comparative Religious Ethics Help?

Here Cobb continues his critical, yet creative, dialogue with the current postmodern preoccupation about how language seems to define the way we view reality and then locks us within that view. He was asked the question: Might a common concern for the global issues confronting us all provide the religions with bridges across their incommensurable linguistic divides? Or: "Can comparative religious ethics help?" Hints and musings that we heard in previous chapters suggest that Cobb would answer that question positively— for example, when he wondered if all religions can affirm "the wider framework of the liberation of the whole of creation" (chapter 2), when he proposed for all an "ultimate concern that we leave to our descendants a habitable planet" (chapter 6), and when he suggested that from these concerns "some criteria may emerge that make sense to almost everyone" (chapter 7). Yet his answer to the question of this chapter is qualified: "Yes, but only in part."

The reasons for his "yes" seem to be twofold: Cobb recognizes not only that for all religions such ethical issues have an urgency and an immediacy that doctrinal or speculative questions do not have, but also that all religions feel they have valuable answers for these questions insofar as "all religious traditions have encouraged social behavior favorable to the continuation" of either their own community or (in the case of the axial religions) of all humanity. And he admits that he finds himself "astonished" at the way issues of "human rights" or "equal rights" between women and men or the menu of issues in the "Declaration toward a Global Ethic" have been able to rally and animate dialogue between religious communities.

Still, his "yes" limps with reservations. They spring from the postmodern caveat that our different cultural-linguistic systems will never allow a common reading of these global, ethical issues, much less a common response. So Cobb, with seeming reluctance, concludes with a message we have heard in previous chapters: the best way to bridge and learn from our differences is to talk to each other out of a recognition that each of us has something to say but none of us can say it all. But he doesn't think it makes much difference whether we start our conversations with ethics or with doctrines. Global issues are "simply another way of getting into the conversation."

Somehow, that last sentence doesn't seem to square with the astonishment that Cobb experienced when assessing how productive an ethical starting point can be. Nor does it resonate with the passion to confront global suffering that he expressed in chapter 6. I suspect his reservations really stem from the exaggerated claims or agendas that some have raised for a globally oriented or ethically based dialogue. For Cobb, a dialogue that starts with ethical issues will not, and cannot, reveal an already given ethical consensus among religions; rather, it reveals a "commonality" in the way all religions can change as they try to respond to these issues. So the goal of an ethically based dialogue should not be to find "agreement on a global ethics," but rather, to keep the religions talking to and learning from each other—and thus, cooperating in their communal concern about common, global challenges. I suspect that Cobb would agree that an interreligious dialogue grounded and inspired by the "ultimate concern that we leave to our descendants a habitable planet" is one of the most effective, because one of the most urgent, ways we have to keep the interfaith conversation alive and fruitful.

P.F.K.

This chapter is a revised version of a paper delivered at the American Academy of Religions annual meeting in 1994.

THIS CHAPTER TAKES UP the question whether a comparative religious ethics might be a way of bridging the gaps between what some members of the postmodern academy call the "incommensurabilities" that exist between different religious language worlds. Such an ethics starts with the fact that we live in a common world and face common problems. By seeing how different traditions respond to common problems, we may be able to find points of contact with our own that will enable us to understand some features of an otherwise incommensurable way of thinking and being. The point, I think, is that action more obviously relates us to a common world than do ideas.

There is a tension between the belief that there is a common world of any kind and the belief that the languages of the several traditions are incommensurable. The latter belief grows out of a tendency to follow the linguistic turn to the conclusion that language constitutes the horizon of human being-in-the-world. In this view, words and phrases have their meaning only in relation to other parts of the language or to the linguistic system as a whole. They do not refer to elements in other language systems or to a world outside of language. The consistent conclusion is, indeed, incommensurability.

This conclusion is supported by the long history of *mis*interpretations that have occurred when Western scholars have undertaken to interpret religious ideas of other cultures in terms of ideas already established in their own. In *The Buddhist Nirvana and Its Western Interpretations*, Guy Richard Welburn provides an overview of nineteenth- and early twentieth-century Western scholarship along these lines. The extreme difficulty faced by Western scholars lends support to the doctrine of incommensurability.

If Christianity is understood to be forever what it has been in the past, fixed in its own language and system of meanings, and if Buddhism is thought of in the same static way, no terms of one system can be translated adequately into the terms of the other. This fact, which I accept and affirm, is often what is meant by incommensurability. For scholars who stand outside of both traditions, this is a convenient way of viewing matters. They then are able to present each system in its own terms without translating them into a common language. It is another question whether they, in this way, achieve an understanding of either.

But this static view, favored by scholars, is not the only or, in my opinion, the most accurate view of either Christianity or Buddhism. In studying nineteenth-century Western treatments of Buddhism, I was struck by the fact that Arthur Schopenhauer came closest to understanding Nirvana despite, or because of, his limited scholarship. As a radical speculative thinker, he was not bound to the linguistic and conceptual system accepted by the Western scholars. Instead he was struggling to understand what that system did not allow him to name. His creative reflection led him to view the phenomenal world as a creation of the will and to a desire to extinguish that will. Reading Buddhist texts with this concern, he found them authentically meaningful.

When we think of living Christians and Buddhists not as embodiments of static linguistic systems, but as dynamic thinkers seeking answers to questions that are often not adequately expressed within their inherited linguistic systems, we can understand that in fact their thinking is not simply incommensurate. But this implies that existing linguistic systems are not the final contexts of life and meaning. They deeply affect our experience of the world, but that experience can also raise questions about their adequacy. We can grope for ways to express aspects of our experience that are obscured by the language we know. Sometimes we find help in the language of other traditions.

I want to be concrete about this claim, and such concreteness can be attained only by examples. One central Buddhist term is *pratitya samutpada*. Obviously this term is explained within Buddhism by reference to many other features of the Buddhist linguistic system. It has no equivalent in Western languages. Also many of the other terms employed in explaining this one have no equivalent. Furthermore, it gains the fullness of its meaning through meditational practices which, in their turn, are affected by the language. But does all this mean that it is simply closed to the Western Christian apart from becoming a Buddhist, learning Sanscrit or Pali, and practicing Buddhist meditation?

It does not. I speak dogmatically because I have observed the term becoming useful to those who engage in sustained dialogue with Buddhists. I believe I have gained some understanding myself. Of course, we Christians do not understand *pratitya samutpada* as well as some Buddhists do. But as we grow dissatisfied with the dualist and substantialist ways of thought built into our own language, and as we grope to express a more fluid, relational, and processive vision of reality, we find this and other Buddhist terms illuminating and helpful. No two of us understand them exactly the same way. That is true for the Buddhists as well as for the Christians. But after years of occasional, but serious, dialogues, there is no radical hiatus between what we Christians mean when we incorporate this term into our language and what the Buddhists in the group mean. Communication with and about the term is real. Christian thought has grown by its incorporation of this important Buddhist term without in any way ceasing to be Christian.

This could not happen if linguistic systems were not embedded in larger natural systems or if experience in no way transcended language. But it *does* happen, and for me that confirms the reality of a horizon that extends beyond language. Every effort at dialogue *also* confirms the extent to which language shapes our apprehension of that larger world and how difficult it is to communicate effectively between the great traditions.

For this communication we need all the help we can get. Our current task is to consider whether comparative religious ethics can help. One way it can do so is by breaking the stranglehold of exaggerated assertions about the all-embracing reality of language. When we talk about the Holocaust, few dare to say this is a linguistic event which has reality only as it comes to speech. Jewish suffering and death on a mass scale took place, whether we say so or not. That raises ethical issues, and we can ask about the different responses to these issues on the part of Christians and Jews.

The combined consequences of the population explosion, the exhaustion of resources, and global pollution seem to some of us to force thoughtful people to face ineluctible dangers that are not erased by refusal to acknowledge them in language. Since these will affect all peoples in much the same way, they offer valuable opportunities to the student of comparative religion. Asking how the several traditions respond to this threat *can* help.

On the other hand, the gain would be easy to exaggerate. Even within the West, among people who live in extensively overlapping languages, there are almost incommensurable ways of perceiving and responding to the situation. For some, as in my case, the statistics and realistic projections indicate that we collectively as a species are heading for disaster, that we should make massive efforts to change direction. Others deny that resources are exhaustible, assert that technology can solve the problem of pollution, and believe that the growth of population provides the brainpower to develop such solutions.

Are we responding to the same facts? Yes and no. Yes. There are common elements in what we perceive to be the facts. For example, we agree that

global population is growing rapidly. We agree that the now available sup-
ply of certain raw materials is declining. We agree that automobiles emit
unhealthful chemicals in their exhausts. But also No. Even at this level of
"facts" our words do not have identical meanings to us. We have learned that
all facts are laden with meaning and interpretation. But I pass over this point
since in this case the issues do not hinge upon it. The real problem is at the
level of interpretation of these "facts." I place them in my world of understanding, certainly a linguistic one. The proponent of the optimistic view
places them in a quite different world of understanding. Our ethical responses
are to these facts as mediated through these linguistic worlds.

The differences in the experience of the facts may be even greater if the
perceivers and interpreters are Christian and Buddhist. I am not sure. Often
differences on such current issues cut across the traditional lines. But I will
illustrate possible differences anyway.

Our senses of time and history are quite different. As a Christian I consider the heightened suffering from widespread starvation and poisoning
much worse than the suffering of daily existence in a relatively secure and
hopeful society. Some Buddhists, on the other hand, may accent what is common to both situations as long as people remain attached. As a contemporary Christian I find myself immediately called to analyze the situation so as
to determine both the causes of what is happening and the reasons for the
lack of adequate response. I then analyze my own capacity to act in relevant
ways and try to do what such analysis calls for. Some Buddhists, on the other
hand, *may* believe that they already know the deepest causes and reasons for
whatever is or will be wrong. These are found in attachment. They may,
therefore, not need to go through the analyses I find important. The response
will be to practice detachment and lead others in the middle way.

If this happens, will we have a bridge to mutual understanding? Yes, to
some extent. Buddhists can understand why we Christians respond as we do,
and we Christians can understand why they respond as they do. But I am not
sure that understanding contrasting responses will be particularly easier in
this public ethical domain than when we discuss our interpretations and
responses to suffering in general, or the meaning and role of faith, or the relation of theory to practice, or of experience to language. In every case we find
deep differences, but both sides are able, in considerable measure, to explain
their views to the other. Whether the focus is on ethics or on theory, if the
assertion of incommensurability means that there can be no growth in
mutual understanding through conversation, or that we can learn nothing
from one another, then it is false. If it means that there is no set of facts or
experiences or beliefs or concerns that is common to the two, such that from
this common foundation their differences can be defined and adjudicated,
then it applies correctly to ethical matters as much as to any others.

There may be exceptions to this. All of our traditions are having to come
to terms with the legacy of the Western Enlightenment. The concept of
human rights, for example, is not a part of earlier traditions, but we are

forced to deal with it. It seems that leading representatives of many traditions are willing to go a long way together in their affirmation of these rights.

Hans Küng has given remarkable leadership in this area. As a result of his tireless work, the Parliament of the World's Religions has issued a "Declaration toward a Global Ethic." I am myself astonished by how extensive an agreement has proved possible. I am astonished also by the extent to which it is the much-criticized Enlightenment that has provided the agreed-on understanding.

What does this mean? Does it mean that the ethical implications of the several traditions are, after all, quite similar? Is the fact that something like the Golden Rule is found in many of them more significant than we have supposed?

The answer must, in part, be Yes. But only in part. All the religious traditions have encouraged social behavior favorable to the continuation of the group. The axial traditions all tended also to extend the group to include all human beings. There is value in spelling out what this means in contemporary language and in relation to contemporary problems.

Of particular interest is the agreement on equal rights and partnership between women and men. Quite conspicuously, such a doctrine has been absent from most, if not all, of our traditions. Yet now leaders from many traditions are prepared to subscribe to this. That is a remarkable fact in the history of religions, showing, in my view, the dynamic character of all religious traditions.

Of course, those who signed this declaration represent one side of a debate that can be found in all the religious traditions. Women have forced this debate in recent decades on a global basis. Studying how each tradition is divided in its response to these demands for justice and reform can provide one of the most interesting bridges for understanding one another. It focuses attention on how traditional systems, linguistic and otherwise, change. And there may be more commonality in the way they change than in the systems themselves as givens.

But the differences are still very great. For some of us, our treatment of other human beings, and perhaps of other creatures as well, is the heart of the matter. For others, this is a preliminary matter, paving the way for what is truly critical. For still others, our relations are primary, but the kind of humanistic teachings here agreed upon are subordinate to others more centrally featured in their faith.

This means that agreement on a global ethic may provide a largely illusory bridge toward mutual understanding. If we really want to understand one another, we may do better to ask what role each sees for such an ethic, how central it is to each tradition as now constituted, and what is meant by key terms. This might, practically speaking, be a bridge toward real understanding. But it is simply another way of getting into the conversations that have been going on all along in dialogue.

I have been asked to end my presentation with questions or statements that may encourage discussion. I will offer ten theses that partly grow out of what I have said, partly are presupposed by it, and partly go beyond it.

1. All living linguistic and religious systems evoke, or relate to, a world beyond language.

2. The actuality of a world beyond language does not mean that it is known in ways that are unaffected by language. It does mean that experience of the world also affects language.

3. Every system highlights some aspects of the world beyond language and obscures other aspects of that world. Most systems are open to revision as experience of the world comes into tension with them.

4. Interaction with persons shaped by different systems is a major factor in leading to expanding experience of the world and changing linguistic systems. Much of this change is unsought and unacknowledged, but it can also be consciously sought and developed. Some systems encourage that seeking more than others.

5. Being changed by, or learning from, those who live from a different system is not especially helped by finding commonalities among systems. What is important is that members of the other community can point to features of reality one has not clearly noticed before, name them, and thus allow them to grow in clarity and influence.

6. Although commonalities are not the basis for mutual understanding, they exist. No two systems are likely to be without overlapping features. But since no part of a system is unaffected by the rest, the overlap can be misleading. And at the points at which some overlap others will differ.

7. It is important to approach representatives of a different system with minimal assumptions and maximum willingness to be informed. Normally one *can* expect that the more understanding one gets, the more one will be aware of differences. These differences are not to be plotted in terms of the conceptuality with which one enters the conversation. They can be understood only as they are allowed to change that conceptuality.

8. The emphasis on difference and not imposing pregiven concepts on what one encounters should not lead to talk of incommensurability. What is incommensurable *before* interaction becomes in some measure commensurable through interaction. The transformed views of each dialogue partner have elements of commensurability absent before the interaction occurs.

9. The language of incommensurability is associated with the view of static linguistic systems rather than dynamic traditions. Intentionally or not, it encourages conservatives who falsely think that faithfulness to a tradi-

tion is expressed by refusal to learn from others or to respond creatively to new challenges. This is a central point in the contemporary church struggle between liberationists and conservative traditionalists.

10. The academy should not lend its support to an inaccurate understanding of religious traditions that blocks progress in religious communities.

11

Hans Küng's Contribution to Interreligious Dialogue

We've decided to include this essay in this collection not so much because of what it says about Hans Küng (it says a lot) but for what it tells us about John Cobb and the development of his thought that we have been tracking throughout this book. In singing Küng's praises as an ecumenical theologian, Cobb sings, even more loudly, his praises for Küng's recent "global project" (Weltprojekt)—Küng's proclamation that the most urgent item on the agenda of interreligious dialogue must be the ethical challenge of saving humanity and the earth from self-destruction.

Contemplating Küng's global project, Cobb declares, at the end of this essay, "I have been converted." And he humbly confesses that "in the past my work in interreligious dialogue has not been . . . ordered to making a real difference in the real world." In view of such a confession and in light of Cobb's enthusiastic endorsement of Küng's project, perhaps I am on track in judging Cobb's reservations about a comparative religious ethics in the previous chapter to be more tactical than substantive. That the religions of the world must gather together in shared concern for the sufferings and anguish of all beings, Cobb is in full-hearted and clear-headed agreement. But he is concerned about the way Küng and others go about exploring this new ethical landscape—and just what they want to achieve and construct on it.

In his conversation with Küng, Cobb spells out more clearly what some of these tactical reservations are. Küng illustrates the dangers that Cobb signaled in the previous chapter—the danger of forgetting that even when religions agree on common ethical issues, they will see those issues differently. So, Cobb is critical of the presupposition that seems to undergird Küng's call for a global ethic—that there is a secular, supra-religious and univocal reading of the global situation which all religious persons can affirm before they put on their religious glasses. Cobb again reminds us that although all religious communities feel the challenge of global suffering and danger, each will view it through their own glasses. So Cobb gently chides Küng for not realizing how Christian—and how European and First-World—his assessment of global issues really is.

But in reminding us that the same global issues will have many readings, Cobb is also affirming, it seems to me, two things: that all religions need to respond to these global issues, and that the different responses will challenge and fructify each other. He's not saying that all religions have in the past taken up such ethical challenges; but he is saying that now they can. And if they do so, they will have much to talk about, fruitfully, with each other. Again, Cobb is wary of setting up a neatly formulated "global ethic" as the goal of such conversations; he seems to prefer a global project that is always in process, that will keep interreligious conversation and cooperation going.

When he reminds Küng of how dangerously First-World his contribution to a global ethic is, Cobb does seem to advance some rather universal judgments. However different the religious readings of our global predicament will be, they will have to agree on two issues: that the interreligious efforts to fashion a global ethical discourse will have to move away from the anthropocentrism that now characterizes the global market, and it will have to be critical of the given economic system and its "individualistic and dualistic anthropology." Cobb seems to be presuming—or requesting—that all religions agree on these two issues.

In the end, Cobb's endorsement of Küng's project clearly outweighs his reservations. The "conversion" that he speaks about in his essay indicates the path along which John B. Cobb, Jr., will continue his efforts to negotiate between absolutism and relativism—and so to enable a dialogue of religions that will transform both the religions and the world.

P.F.K.

This essay is the original English version of a chapter published in a German-language Festschrift for Hans Küng in 1993.

I

NO CHRISTIAN HAS CONTRIBUTED more to interreligious dialogue than Hans Küng. Whereas such strong statements are dangerous to make in many fields, in this one they are safer. Although interreligious dialogue has occurred in earlier generations, it has been primarily a phenomenon of the post-World War II period. Hence competitors with Küng for this honor are his contemporaries. Comparisons are, therefore, easier.

Contributions to such dialogue occur at many levels, of which I will distinguish five. (1) There is Christian theological reflection that shows that in principle a dialogical relation to other religious communities is appropriate. (2) There is actual participation in such dialogue and promotion of it. (3) There is reflection about what happens in dialogue and how it can be improved. (4) There is the interpretation of other religious communities that encourages

dialogue and shares its fruits. (5) There is clarification of the role and importance of dialogue in the total human situation.

There are others who have given more concentrated attention and leadership at one or another of these levels. For example, some have written more
extensively, and perhaps more rigorously, on the Christian reasons for
engaging in dialogue. A few have devoted more time to actual participation
in dialogue or to promoting dialogues. Certainly some have gone further
in particular dialogues with Jews, Muslims, Hindus, or Buddhists. Others
would compete with Küng in terms of reflection on what actually happens
and can happen in dialogue. There are historians of religion who have provided more information about other communities of faith. But there is no one
who has done all of these as extensively, as effectively, and as influentially as
Hans Küng. Hence, my original statement, far from being exaggerated, is not
strong enough. Hans Küng has contributed *more* than any other Christian
to interreligious dialogue.

I have made this assertion without commenting on the fifth level of dialogue as identified above. It is here that his contribution is most distinctive.
Most Christians who engage in dialogue do so to share and to learn and to
express solidarity with representatives of other religious communities.
These are laudable motives, and Küng supports them. The World Council
of Churches promoted dialogue chiefly for practical purposes of cooperation on shared goals, tending to contrast these purposes with specifically
religious ones. Küng agrees that dialogue has profoundly important social
purposes.

But Küng understands the purpose of dialogue in a broader context than
either of these. This context is nothing less than the total global situation of
the present. He presents interreligious dialogue as an indispensable element
in dealing with this situation. But he shows that it can work in this way only
if it engages in genuinely religious interaction of the sort of which the World
Council has been suspicious. When this contribution to interreligious dialogue is included, Küng's leadership is without peer.

This leadership is not merely an intellectual and scholarly one. Küng is recognized in the public and political world as a spokesman to whom it is wise
to listen, one who can speak for the wider religious community rather than
only for one tradition. Furthermore, as he identifies needs, he shows how
they can be met and, indeed, does himself much of what is needed. No other
Christian plays an analogous role.

What is distinctive in Küng's contribution comes to expression most
clearly in *Projekt Weltethos* (1990). This has been translated into English
and given the less accurate title: *Global Responsibility: In Search of a New
World Ethic*. This builds on work that Küng had been doing since the mid-
sixties (perhaps earlier) and announces programmatically a whole new project, one of daunting proportions! This essay will take this book as its focus
for interpreting Küng's most distinctive contribution to dialogue among the
religious communities.

In different books, and often within the same book, Küng writes from two perspectives. As a Christian theologian he describes these as "external" and "internal." This book is written primarily from the external perspective, but with important sections in which the internal perspective is explicitly adopted.

The external perspective allows Küng to survey the global situation as objectively as he can. What is happening, and what role is being played by the religious traditions? He does not justify the focus of attention on these traditions by his own participation in one of them or by any special pleading. His arguments for their importance are quite objective. First, religions are crucially involved in some of the most intractable international problems, problems recognized by politicians everywhere. Second, instead of contributing as religions do to the difficulties faced by political leaders, they are capable of making a fundamental and indispensable contribution to the solution.

The role of religion in causing problems is too obvious to require much of Küng's time or ours. More important is his analysis of the positive role that religious communities can play, and indeed must play, if there is to be a viable future for humanity. The dilemma is that societies cannot exist without a shared ethos, and yet most national societies are now religiously pluralistic. The democratic state is expected to remain neutral on those matters on which the religions disagree. The danger is that where there is no common ethos, the state must exert raw power. The alternative is that the religious communities work together to form the needed common ethos.

The problem is even more acute because so many of the decisions that must now be made are global rather than national. All peoples must agree on certain principles and directions if catastrophe is to be avoided. Hence the need is not only for a shared ethos within nations. It is for a world ethos.

The problem is still more complex. Although historically the religious traditions have shaped the ethos of their several communities, today tens of millions of secular people are little affected in their own values and commitments by the pronouncements of religious leaders. The world ethos that is required must commend itself on secular as well as religious grounds.

This might suggest that the task is to get from philosophy a neutral, rational system of beliefs and directives. But this will not do even if agreement were reached among philosophers. First, religious communities will not accept a secular ethos imposed upon them. Second, secular ethics does not have the depth and power needed to redirect human thought and life. That depth and power reflect the religious dimension of human experience.

Küng does not suppose that all the religious traditions overlap in their ethical teachings in such a way that all that is needed is to bring their historic agreements to the fore. He knows that differences run deep. He knows also that for the most part they have historically resisted some of the teachings that are now indispensable if they are jointly to aid humankind in its crisis. The required agreement among them must be forged out of the present situation, not merely discovered in their sources.

Simply to have identified this urgent need and to have called for dialogue that would help to respond to it would have been a distinctive and important contribution. But Küng did not stop there. On the contrary, at least since 1984 ("What is True Religion? Toward an Ecumenical Criteriology," a lecture delivered at a conference at Temple University and published in Leonard Swidler, ed., *Toward a Universal Theology of Religion*, Orbis Books, 1987, pp. 231–50), Küng has proposed that the needed ethos can be developed from the idea of the *humanum*. All religious traditions, he is convinced, as well as secular people, are committed to human well-being and fulfillment. Their ways of relating their ultimate commitments to this ethical one differ. But a shared ethos can nevertheless be developed. Küng had an opportunity to try out this important proposal at a UNESCO meeting in 1989, and he was encouraged by the response of representatives of many traditions.

Once again, this is a contribution of enormous importance. Küng could well have offered his proposed solution to the world and encouraged study by representatives of the several traditions to test their readiness to accept it. But once again, Küng has not stopped here. Instead, he has launched a whole new program. He will survey the several great traditions himself to examine their present situation, especially as it relates to the possibility of joining in the support of the urgently needed world ethos.

Coming from some other scholar nearing his sixty-fifth birthday, such an announcement might have been greeted with skepticism. Surveying the present situation of any one tradition would be considered by most scholars as more than a lifetime's work! But Küng does not affirm the kind of academic sensibilities that call always for more detailed studies of particulars and draw attention away from the larger picture. He knows that it is the larger picture that shapes decisions about the future. And he is convinced that there are responsible ways of providing this larger picture. Furthermore, he has repeatedly demonstrated his gifts in this respect.

II

This whole program swims against the stream, not only of university scholarship in general, but also of trends in current Christian theology. Küng is fully aware that in both Catholic and Protestant contexts, the trend is conservative, where he is unabashedly progressive. But even among those who are seeking new responses to the changing context, most are moving in one of two directions, quite different from Küng's.

One group, sharing Küng's enthusiasm for interreligious understanding and mutual respect, is superficially similar in its desire to identify what is common to the great traditions. But it differs in two respects. First, although Küng spends much of his time viewing matters from the external perspective, as in the analysis of the actual and possible roles of the religious communities in the global situation, he enters dialogue always as a believing Christian committed to Christian truth. Second, he eschews all a prioristic theories of what is common to the traditions, working instead with great care individually with each. Among his most impressive writings is *Christianity and the World Religions* (1986). Here he listens to scholarly accounts of Islam, Hinduism, and Buddhism and then provides a detailed critical response to each as a Christian theologian. He followed this up with *Christianity and Chinese Religions*, a similar response to Julia Ching's scholarly accounts of the religion of Chinese antiquity, of Confucianism, of Taoism, and of Chinese Buddhism. These volumes contain the most extensive and wide-ranging Christian criticisms of the other religious traditions that exist anywhere. If Küng had written nothing else, these books would have established him as a major and distinctive contributor to dialogue.

More than any other theologian, Küng has worked theologically with the whole range of religious traditions. He deals with each in its particularity. This means that when Küng indulges in generalizations about all these traditions, as he occasionally does, he has earned the right to do so! And in any case, the commonality he hopes to find is the capacity to support a shared ethos, not already existing support.

The other group more obviously diverges from Küng. Many thoughtful Christians, especially Protestants, finding themselves in a situation in which Christendom no longer exists as political establishment and is fading as a cultural one, claim this situation as an opportunity for a truer faithfulness to Christ. They see this faithfulness as a renewal of the distinctive Christian ethos, its language, beliefs, symbols, and practices. They eschew negative statements about those who do not share this faith. But they want to renew the congregation and deepen its immersion in a pattern that was greatly weakened by the church's internalization of Enlightenment values. Precisely the way Küng affirms the *humanum* is, for many of them, the sort of influence of the Enlightenment from which the church should free itself.

From Küng's perspective this movement can only be seen as a retreat from public responsibility at a crucial time. But from the point of view of these theologians, Christians cannot make their proper contribution to society except out of the particularities of their distinctive heritage. The whole effort to find common ground either with the secular world or with other religious communities belongs to the Enlightenment or to the modernity that is now dying.

This is a profoundly different reading of postmodernity from Küng's. I mention it here, not to support it, but to indicate the obstacles among Protestants to gaining support for Küng's project. Instead of progressing in the direction in which Küng calls us, much of the best of Protestant energy is directed toward undercutting all such projects! A generation ago support would have been more readily forthcoming.

III

Although I do not participate in this current trend and hope that it will not go too far, I do see a related weakness in Küng's characteristic formulations of the inner and the outer perspectives. They seem almost disconnected and at times even in tension. When he writes from the outer perspective, he seems to claim perspectival neutrality in the manner of objective discourse. He pronounces on the strengths and weaknesses of the several traditions as a scholar and a humanist. Then he shifts somewhat abruptly to the profession of his own faith. In that context he makes rather startling statements to the effect that Christianity is *the* true religion.

Both voices are offensive to some who believe themselves to be truly reflective of the new, postmodern situation. The first is offensive since it seems to ignore the social location of the writer and the way that affects what he sees. The second is offensive since, despite all qualifications, it sounds arrogant.

Much can and should be said in defense of Küng against these criticisms. He knows, of course, who and what he is. But the emphasis on one's social location easily leads to the relativization of what one says and, indeed, to avoidance of bold analyses and overviews of the sort he offers. It may be better to get a clear proposal before persons in other social locations for their response than to modestly limit oneself to reflecting on one's own perspective. In particular, white male Europeans too easily abdicate the responsibilities that go with their social location by emphasizing what that social location is.

In response to the charge of arrogance, we can see that in the same paragraphs in which Küng affirms that for him Christianity is *the* true religion, he affirms that there is truth in others as well. Throughout his account he emphasizes the importance of self-criticism in all traditions, and he engages in a great deal of criticism of Christianity. His affirmation that Christianity is *the* true religion does not lead to harsher criticisms of others or any lack of appreciation for their contributions either to Christianity or to the world situation as a whole. Küng is anything but a Christian chauvinist.

Further, many people will be able to deal with his book more easily, given the sharp distinction of the two perspectives as he presents them. For example, secular people will be interested in his overall analysis. Many of them will be able to take it more seriously because it presents itself as a secular view of the religious role in global affairs. They can discount the sections clearly labeled as "internal" in perspective.

More important, many representatives of other traditions will be able to share the overall account. Then, when they come to the sections that are specifically Christian, they can substitute their own, specifically Muslim or Hindu perspectives, for example. This will enable the proposal to get a good hearing from those to whom it is especially directed.

IV

Despite my recognition of all of these arguments in Küng's favor, I share in the discomfort felt by some as a result of the sharp distinction of the inner and outer perspectives. Even though I recognize that there are practical advantages in writing in this way, I wonder whether, in the long run, it will not cause more problems than it solves. And from the point of view of full intellectual honesty, I believe it distorts somewhat the real situation.

I believe that ultimately Küng engages in the study of the global situation as he does because he is a Christian. That does not mean, as I see it, that his being a Christian introduces a bias that he could escape by putting on the hat of the objective scholar. On the contrary, I believe that his Christian passion causes him to see features of the global situation that persons lacking that perspective—however scholarly and objective they claim to be—consistently neglect.

Indeed, there is no scholarly, objective, or "external" perspective as such. There are academicians with diverse interests and convictions and with varied social locations who examine the same world situation. Each highlights particular features. Most underestimate the importance of religious traditions. Some underestimate the importance of the ethos in general. Others overestimate the capacity of secular rationality, or of some philosophical tradition, to provide the needed ethos.

Küng makes none of these mistakes. In my view, that is, from my perspective, his depiction is more accurate precisely because he brings to bear what he knows and feels as a thoughtful and learned Christian. But one does not have to share his Christian perspective to recognize the truth of what he says. The fact that one's special perspective enables one to discern what others have not seen does not mean that they cannot see it when it is pointed out to them.

Hence, to acknowledge and emphasize one's perspective is not to relativize what one sees. Economists see some features of the situation more clearly than do those without that training. That does not, or should not, cause us to deny that what they see is there to be seen. The same is true of cultural anthropologists, political scientists, and ecologists. The total situation is so complex that no one analysis begins to exhaust it. For particular purposes, some correct analyses are more useful and more important than others. Küng's is extremely important for all those who hope for a happy future for humanity. To say that it attends to some features of the situation rather than others, and that his selection is affected by his Christian faith, does not diminish that importance.

I doubt that I am saying anything here that Küng denies. My point is only that, perhaps for practical purposes, he does not make this Christian theological character of his whole analysis explicit. That may be a prudent decision, but it has a price. It gives the reader the impression that Küng remains very much the child of the Enlightenment in respects that postmodern thought has rightly criticized.

It also makes the transition to the internal perspective uncomfortably abrupt. In my opinion, just as what Küng thinks of as the external perspective is informed throughout by the internal one, so also what he affirms in the internal perspective is informed throughout by the external one. Just as there are Christian reasons for his highlighting of particular features of the global situation, so there are external reasons that he finds truth in his Christian faith. It is better to think of two poles in one continuous mode of thinking rather than of two perspectives.

I picture my own situation, which is similar in many ways to his, more as follows. I can engage in study and reflection only where I now am. I am formed by my Christian history and my repeated decisions to affirm my Christian identity. Hence all my thinking is affected by my Christian perspective. But one of my reasons for reaffirming my Christian identity is that it motivates me to be as honest and open to evidence as possible, and especially to evidence that is critical of the Christian position I have adopted. If I found that being a Christian inhibited openness and honesty, I could not remain a Christian. This is not because I am more committed to openness and honesty than to Christ, but because I understand commitment to Christ to involve commitment to openness and honesty.

I also find that being a Christian enables me to discern aspects of the real situation that other perspectives do not clarify. Of course, I see that others discern aspects that I miss. But it has seemed to me that my Christian perspective does not inhibit my learning from them. As I learn from them, my Christian understanding expands and deepens. Whether any other perspective allows those who embody it to learn as freely from others as I think my Christian one does, I do not know. I am quite sure that some do not, including many that call themselves "Christian." But I can confess the liberating and illuminating power of Christ without making negative statements about others.

From this point of view, I am uncomfortable with the statement that Christianity is *the* true religion. I am quite comfortable in saying that Christian faith opens me, in principle, to all truth. Of course, that is not to claim that I am free from defensiveness, but it is to assert that I experience that defensiveness not as faith but precisely as idolatry and lack of trust in Christ.

None of this means that Küng should make no distinction between what he is saying when he talks about Christianity in much the way he talks about other religious traditions and what he says when he confesses or describes his reasons for repeatedly reaffirming his Christian identity. But the distinction seems to me overdrawn and misleading in some of Küng's formulations.

On the one hand, I hesitate to make this criticism. Küng is moving ahead on an extremely important project. We theologians have the habit of criticizing one another's projects in such a way as to inhibit any bold undertaking. It is easier to show some limitation in another's formulations than to launch one's own initiatives. And once one has criticized, one can excuse oneself from giving the support the project deserves! My criticism is not intended in that spirit. Even if I am correct, this does not invalidate Küng's project or reduce the reasons for supporting it.

On the other hand, my quarrel is not a trivial one. Indeed, from my perspective the long-term ability of theology to support the kind of project Küng advocates depends on undersanding that project as Christian and theological. Küng could be read as saying that the definition of his project is purely secular. This secular project is then brought to the attention of believers in the several traditions. At that point he will put on his theological hat and work on the Christian response.

If the book is read in this way, it is not an invitation to other theologians to share in this venture or to engage in similar ones. The theological task is limited to the internal thinking that appears at certain points in the book. The tendency is for theologians to limit themselves to the theological task; so the survey of the global situation and the identification of the role religious communities need to play will be left to others.

I believe, in contrast, that Christians, and especially those who are set aside as professional theologians, are called to identify the most important needs of God's creation, to clarify what they are, and to propose ways of responding. Küng is a model of this kind of theological work. But his distinction between the external and the internal perspectives obscures this fact. It is because I want much more of theology to follow in the direction Küng has pioneered that I am so critical on this point.

V

Perhaps related to this formal criticism, which at a deeper level is intended as support, are some material criticisms. I wonder whether the *humanum* is today an adequate basis for the ethos that is needed. I am not at this point raising the question of the relation of the *humanum* to ultimate reality, a topic deftly treated by Küng. My concern is with the relation of the *humanum* to the other creatures.

Küng is himself quite sensitive to environmental issues, and many of his statements indicate that he has transcended the anthropocentrism of the Enlightenment. Yet the choice of the *humanum* as the basis of the needed ethos does not transcend anthropocentrism, even when the relation of human beings to the other creatures is emphasized. Indeed, much of the discussion of the *humanum*, even in this book, accents its close relation with the Enlightenment.

Küng is surely correct that the gains of the Enlightenment, such as the emphasis on the dignity of every human being, should not be abandoned in postmodernity. But the need now, I think, is to affirm human dignity without the anthropocentrism of the Enlightenment. It is also to avoid the individualism so characteristic of the Enlightenment. Other religious traditions, such as Hinduism and Buddhism, and certainly the primal religions, can help us find ways to do that.

At this point my criticism *is* directed to Küng's specific proposal. *This* criticism *is* a reason for not supporting that proposal in its present formulation. But I do not want to be primarily negative. In my book with Herman Daly, entitled *For the Common Good*, we criticized the Enlightenment model that has dominated economic theory, and we proposed the model of person-in-community. We went on to clarify that the community in view is not only the human one but also includes other creatures.

This could be viewed as simply a proposal as to how to understand the *humanum*. I would argue that even if it is only that, there would be some gain in formulation. It would work against an individualistic understanding of the *humanum*. However, more is involved in including both human community and other creatures from the outset rather than only later in the process of unpacking what is meant by the *humanum*.

I make my proposal hoping that, should it be accepted, it would not slow down or inhibit the important work of involving the several traditions in moving toward a common ethos. It is my opinion that the weaknesses in the focus on the *humanum* stem from its connections with Enlightenment individualism and dualism, and that these have not had comparable effects in other traditions. The notion of persons-in-community-with-one-another-and-with-other-creatures is not alien to the other traditions or to our own. Today this communitarian character of personal life and its embeddedness in the natural context are gaining recognition both in religious communities and in secular ones. Many of the principles Küng advocates follow more directly from this model than from focus on the *humanum* alone.

VI

The issue of social location comes out more clearly on another point. Hans Küng writes, inescapably, as a citizen of the First World. There is nothing wrong with that. It is probably easier for affluent people to think in global terms than for those who struggle to survive; so First World people have a special responsibility to give leadership in this direction. Furthermore, what happens in the First World is of utmost importance for what happens throughout the planet. And Küng writes as a citizen of the First World who is deeply concerned not only with that world but with the Third and Fourth Worlds as well.

However, there *is* a problem with developing a *world* ethos that generalizes so clearly from the problems and situation of the First World and does not acknowledge this slant. Even when it refers also to the problems of the Third and Fourth Worlds, it discusses them from the perspective of the First World. This is where explicit acknowledgment of social location would help. We could then be assured that as the global problematic is developed other voices would be heard, so that other features of that problematic would find their place.

One way in which the First World orientation shows itself is in the minor attention given to economics. The writing sometimes implies that after the Second World is lifted to First World standards, something like this can happen in the Third and Fourth Worlds also.

But in fact this is impossible. Already our affluence is overtaxing the global biological and chemical systems. If the inhabitants of the Third and Fourth

Worlds consumed at current European rates, the collapse of the biosphere would be rapid indeed!

In any case no serious proposal has been made that would even lead in this direction. The only proposal before the global community that deals with economic growth in the Third World is the Brundtland Commission report. That calls, for understandable reasons, for a five- to ten-fold increase in production in the Third World. But it envisions achieving this goal by a similar increase in the size of the economies of the First World! The absurdity is patent.

When the only proposal before the global community for alleviating the suffering of the Third and Fourth Worlds is patently absurd, and while that suffering deepens year by year because of the "restructuring" of the economies of many Third World countries required by the International Monetary Fund and the World Bank, the suggestion that First World business people, by subscribing to a better ethics can make a great difference, seems simplistic. We desperately need a new ethos. But unless that new ethos expresses itself in new economic theory and practice, it will do half of the world's people little good.

One reason for my great concern about the nature of the ethos that the religions will support is that the economic theory and practice that is destroying the Third and Fourth Worlds stems from an individualistic and dualistic anthropology. As a result, for the sake of increasing Gross National Product, it has systematically assaulted traditional community and exploited the other creatures, animate and inanimate. Current policies and proposals are no different in these respects. I see little hope for Third and Fourth World peoples unless this changes. Nothing said about the *humanum* in Küng's book indicates that it would give significant support for the needed change. If we order economic development instead to the strengthening of human communities in their natural contexts, there is a chance for real improvement even though the GNP will not be much affected.

Küng's profound analysis and responses are ordered to making a real difference in the real world. That is why I take them so seriously. I am forced to confess that in the past my work in interreligious dialogue has not been informed by a full understanding of what is at stake. I have been converted.

But just for that reason a critique of the details of the analysis and response is not a merely academic exercise. If Küng's proposals are taken seriously, and he is in a better position than anyone else to promote them, the results will be of world-historical importance. It would be tragic if they did not genuinely help the Third and Fourth Worlds as well as the First.

CONCLUDING REFLECTIONS

JOHN B. COBB, JR.

Paul Knitter has performed a great service to me personally. He has helped me understand myself better and to become aware of how certain deep-seated convictions have both shaped my thinking and led to significant tensions within it. Now he offers me a chance to reflect again about these and where I stand with respect to them.

Two important concerns have shaped much of my work in the past thirty years. One of them has been the understanding of Christian faith in the context of religious pluralism. The essays in this volume express that concern.

The other has been the global crisis focusing on what is happening to the natural basis of human existence and to those human beings who have been most directly dependent on this. I was awakened to this crisis in 1969, and I have spoken and written on ecological theology, organized conferences, and agitated in various other ways. In the past twenty years I have become absorbed in economic theory and practice, believing that this is a key to human degradation of the Earth. This concern shows up at the fringes of some of the essays in this book.

During most of this period I found that my concern to relate to and learn from other religious communities required bracketing my environmental and libertionist concerns. I engaged in interreligious dialogue, especially with Buddhists, but also with Jews and Muslims, and to a lesser extent with Hindus. My experience was that each dialogue had a quite different character, that the issues and topics were determined by unique historical and theoretical commitments, that one needed to enter each dialogue in genuine openness to what seemed most important to the dialogue partner. For many years in no case did my partners regard the global crisis as I experienced it as the appropriate topic or even context of our conversations. For that matter, few of my Christian colleagues did so.

This did not mean for me that the dialogues in which I was involved, or the reflections on Christian theology to which they contributed, were irrelevant to the healing of the Earth. I found much in Buddhism, for example, that could counter elements in traditional Christianity that have contributed to the crisis. For this and other reasons I have called for the transformation of

Christianity through the appropriation of Buddhist wisdom. I have argued that such transformation is entirely faithful to Jesus Christ, indeed, that the attempt to hold on to past formulations of the faith when we are confronted by previously unknown wisdom is an expression of lack of faith.

For me the primary purpose of dialogue for Christians is to learn from others in transforming ways. Certainly, the fact that we need so to learn in order to cease being a threat to our planetary home adds urgency to this call. But Christians have reason to hope that others can benefit from our wisdom as we benefit from theirs. And the global situation adds urgency to sharing our wisdom as well. Accordingly, I have hoped that in the dialogue Buddhists were being brought to think more historically and systemically about themselves and our shared world, and that this would enable them to make the important contributions they could offer. But even if Buddhists lacked the sense of urgency that the Christian experience of time and history has inculcated in me, and even if they decided that appropriating that understanding would, from their point of view, do more harm than good, I would still wish to pursue the dialogue, focusing it, perhaps, on the perceived dangers of thinking too historically.

One of my motivations for dialogue, therefore, was to increase the likelihood that both communities would become more effective in countering the forces that endangered the future. But I understood this as a particular form of normal Christian motivation. I believed that Buddhists might take part in dialogue with other purposes. We did not need a common goal in order to converse and to benefit from that conversation.

Discussions with Jews and Muslims had a very different character. Their connection to environmental and economic issues was still more indirect. Political issues, on the other hand, were always in the back of all our minds. These included the painful tensions in Israel/Palestine, but also the oppressive rule in many Muslim states and the tendency to demonize Islam in the popular American mind. To achieve the kind of mutual understanding that might help to ease these tensions seemed eminently worthwhile for the salvation of the planet, but the political concerns could be approached only indirectly through discussion of our several traditions and doctrines.

Here again I suspected that the motivation for taking part in this dialogue differed among Jews, Christians, and Muslims, as well as among the members of each group. I might be alone in locating this work within the context of the global crisis as I understood it, but this did not prevent the conversation from being productive. We did not require a common formulation of purpose in order to learn about and from one another.

This openness to others without the requirement of common ground or common purpose is a theme that Knitter identifies throughout my essays. This does not mean that I want to deny, a priori, that there are common elements in all the major traditions, even important ones. (One line in Knitter's introduction to chapter 2 could suggest that.) To deny that there are such common elements in advance of conversation and study is surely as bad as to affirm that they exist. What I do deny is that identifying such common elements is a condition of dialogue. My hypothesis is also that if there are such common elements, they do not constitute what all the traditions regard as most important. Thus far, my conversations with various traditions have led me to this hypothesis and tended to confirm it. My study of the proposals of a common essence has thus far led me to the conclusion that these proposals involve the imposition of the beliefs of the writer on others, and that the facts belie their claims.

During the nineties there have been remarkable changes. The shared concern about the future of the planet that seemed to me lacking in the seventies and eighties has come into being. It is now quite possible to bring together representatives of the several religious communities around discussion of the global crisis. The two concerns that I had experienced as pulling in somewhat different directions have now merged to a greater extent than I had thought possible.

During the same period there have been increasing efforts to bring the great traditions to common statements on the issues that face us. My essay on Hans Küng acknowledges my initial skepticism and my excitement at the extent of his success. Steven Rockefeller is doing splendid work in developing an Earth Charter with input from all traditions. These achievements are important both for immediate political purposes and because the possibility of agreeing on many formulations reflects the growth or transformation that is taking place within all the traditions as the global situation worsens.

Knitter rightly notes, however, that I have reservations as to what this means. We have all taken part in committees charged to come up with consensus statements. We know that our agreement to certain formulations in that context does not entail that we mean just the same thing as others in the committee. We know that we do not all attach the same importance to the document as a whole or to its several parts. That we can come to a consensus statement is important, and our views may mature in the process of working on it. Also, the document may influence others in a positive way. But the differences among signers is also important, and it will often show up at the point of implementing the consensus. If there is to be continuing collaboration and growth, conversation must continue.

Furthermore, this conversation cannot limit itself to ethical issues. Indeed, the separation of ethics from its religious context is itself a Western, Enlightenment, mode of thought. The Enlightenment still has much to teach us all, and the possibility of building consensus on its basis is remarkable. But it is also highly vulnerable to criticism from a variety of perspectives. Unless commitment to certain principles of action is rooted deeply in each tradition rather than grounded only on recent developments within them, it will not grasp the masses of believers or survive serious critical attacks. At this point the particularity of each tradition reasserts itself. And at this level we still have much to learn from one another as well as from the recent history of Western ethical thought.

I will illustrate my concern here from personal experience. I have been privileged to supervise the dissertations of two Buddhist students. Both were interested in clarifying the way Buddhists could, and should, approach social issues. One was from the Pure Land tradition, the other, Zen. Both wrote fine dissertations. But they were very different. The resources in these two Buddhist traditions for entering into serious involvement with the social issues of our day differ greatly. I believe this kind of work needs to be done in many traditions, and that it is advanced through dialogue. I also believe that Christians can learn much from the formulations of others. Our own history of social action is far from ideal!

Knitter wants clearer criteria of what constitute the strengths and positive values of religious traditions. I make no secret of the fact that I have passionate ideas about this, although these ideas are muted in the essays in this book. Contributing to the indivisible salvation of the whole world is what I would like everyone and every community to be about. And I have many ideas as to what we need to be saved from and what the positive nature of such salvation would be. But I recognize that this passion comes from my Christian faith and especially my hope for what Jesus called the *basileia theou*, the world in which God's purposes are realized.

As a Christian I can, and do, evaluate other communities and traditions by this norm. That means, further, that I evaluate them by my judgment as to what most contributes to this goal. But it is important to me that I say it here "as a Christian." This is part of my confessional Christian theological work. I want to share it with other Christians. I want people from other communities to know how I see the world and what I hope for and how that affects my evaluation of their contribution. I want them to know also that I believe that Christ has saving meaning for them as well.

But as a Christian I also affirm that there are other points of view than the Christian one which may establish different goals and judge quite differently how Christianity and other traditions contribute to them. I am grateful when representatives of those other points of view share with me their way of thinking and hoping, including their critique of my Christian one. Conceivably they may convert me. More likely, they will lead me to refine my own thoughts and hopes to take account of concerns to which I have been blind.

For me as a Christian, it does not seem necessary that others share my hope for a world in which God's purposes are fulfilled in order to contribute to the coming of that world. There are Zen masters who give little thought to such broad historical concerns who nevertheless keep alive and transmit a mode of existence that I regard as very precious. I believe they contribute quite positively to the movement toward the world for which I hope.

Further, for me as a Christian, love requires that I accept the right of others to work for goals that are different from mine, to formulate different criteria of what is desirable, and to evaluate Christianity and other communities in those terms. This is why I am so hesitant to speak of criteria outside a confessional context. I do not deny in advance that there are shared criteria. I have even made some tentative suggestions of what these may be. But they are very modest indeed in comparison with my confessionally Christian criteria. I think Knitter is calling on me to emphasize my confessionally Christian criteria more and my relativization of these as Christian less!

On the other hand, for me as a Christian, there are also movements, some of which claim to be Christian, that seem to work against the coming of the *basileia theou,* at least as I understand it. I should be open to careful listening to correct my negative impressions, but if that listening does not change my judgment or revise my understanding of the goal, then I must oppose these movements. More cautiously still, I should oppose movements arising in other traditions when I judge them contrary to the fulfillment of God's purposes. To be open to wisdom everywhere is not to affirm everything or to abandon all negations!

Perhaps this may help to clarify my failure to provide criteria for what is to be learned from other traditions. In his preface to chapter 4 Knitter asks how we can know whether what we have learned from someone else is true. Here the problem is partly terminological. One may, of course, speak of learning errors, but I do not use the word "learn" in that way. Hence for me the question I confront as a Christian when I hear what is new to me is whether it is true and important and, if so, how I can learn or appropriate it. My judgment of its truth and importance will be based on my total understanding at the time, an understanding that is deeply formed by my history and my Christian faith. There is no neutral standpoint from which to make such choices, but my Christian faith calls on me always to be as open, as objective, and as neutral as I can in making these judgments.

The judgments remain fallible. I may appropriate as true and important what is in fact trivial or false. The result may be to deform rather than to transform my Christian understanding. But I do not believe this happens much in interfaith conversation. The problem is much more resistance to an alien wisdom than uncritical openness to an alien error. Each of our traditions provides safeguards against sheer gullibility. Each opens us in differing ways to learning from the wisdom of others. What we can appropriate depends on who and where we are.

Knitter points out that my statements about openness to learning and transformation are sometimes quite extreme. As a Christian I believe that in principle I must recognize that my openness to the wisdom of others could lead me to cease to center my own life and understanding in Jesus Christ. It has certainly done so for some others. Many of the finest Buddhists I know were once Christian.

This factual statement, of course, is not shocking. But some Christians might think that one should enter dialogue with safeguards to prevent that from happening. One should be open to what does not threaten one's basic faith but not to what does. One should, perhaps, predefine some essence of Christian faith that one should not allow dialogue to question. It is my rejection of any such a priori limitations on openness that leads me to make shocking statements. For me, faith in God as we know God in Jesus Christ requires that I be open to truth wherever that may be found and wherever it may lead. If that leads me to deny God's reality or reject the centrality of Jesus Christ, then in faithfulness to God and to Christ, I must go there too.

But my own judgment and experience does not lead me to expect anything of this sort. In fact the loss of faith is much more likely to happen if one associates it with defensiveness. If one supposes that Christians are required to assert a particular set of doctrines and to negate all that seems to conflict with these, then life experience is likely to lead one away from Christianity. This has happened on a mass scale in Western society. There are dangers to faith in trusting the God of truth, but they are far less. A healthy, confident Christian faith is much more likely when we recognize that we do not know what we will believe in the future, but that we know that for now God in Christ calls us to learn all we can.

Knitter has difficulty with my talk of multiple ultimates as ontologically given. This is an important part of my understanding. It is not so important in Jewish-Christian-Muslim dialogue, although it plays some role there. But it is very important when we enter conversation with Hindus, Buddhists, and Taoists.

Perhaps the term "ultimate" is so identified with the idea of a single ultimate reality that I need to find other language to express my point. Perhaps I could express my view better by saying that there is no one ultimate but that different features of the totality have been viewed as of supreme importance in the several traditions and sub-traditions. Nevertheless, in this further effort to explain myself, I will continue with the language I have used in the past.

By an ultimate I mean that at which a line of questioning ends. In the Medieval Aristotelian tradition, several lines of questioning ended with God. God was the ultimate in the line of efficient causes, formal causes, and final causes. But God was not the ultimate in the line of material causes. The ultimate in that line was "prime matter." In my terminology, this established two ultimates: God and prime matter.

Named in that way it would be hard to imagine religious interest centering in the latter. "Matter" is understood to be purely passive. The principle of act is form. Understandably, religious interest in the West centered overwhelmingly in the ultimate in the line of efficient, formal, and final causation.

But consider what this other ultimate is. It is that which, without possessing any form, is subject to taking on any form. It is the formless. It is that which all entities, that is, all instances of formed matter, have in common, that apart from which they would not be at all.

Now consider also that in the twentieth century matter is no longer understood to be passive. Instead, it is reconceived as energy. It may be described as pure activity or as creativity. It is now form that is passive. "Prime matter" has been transformed into the act of being, Being Itself, dynamically understood as that which gives being to all that is.

The ultimate "material" cause does not thereby become also the ultimate efficient, formal, or final cause. But seen in this way, it is understandable how religious interest can be attached to this. Brahman/Atman seems to be the ultimate in this line of reflection. The goal in some forms of Vedantic practice is to realize that at the deepest level I am what all things are, Atman is Brahman. This realization brings release. Questions of efficient cause, formal cause, and final cause belong to a subordinate sphere.

Within Hinduism those who focus on Brahman/Atman are an influential but small minority. Most Hindus focus not on Brahman/Atman as such but on the divine embodiments of this ultimate reality. Often this is done polytheistically, and then it is difficult for a Westerner to speak of an ultimate. But Hinduism can also have a strongly monotheistic character, sometimes identifying Ishvara as the one God. The one God appears as the supreme personal expression of Brahman/Atman. We have here the intimate relation of what in the West have been called Being Itself and the Supreme Being. Both are ultimate, but they are not identical. The former is realized in mystical union as identical with the deepest self. The latter is adored, beseeched, and obeyed. The effort to identify them in the Thomist tradition has broken down in the twentieth century.

Today in the West there is another religious spirit at work, a reverence for the Earth and the cosmos. It, too, takes many forms. It has deep roots in many cultures. Much of primal religion has this form. It expresses itself in some forms of Taoism. Western pantheism has sometimes had this character. Surely we cannot deny that in some sense the totality of the things that are is ultimate as well! But it is not just another way of conceiving of Being Itself or of the Supreme Being, of Brahman or Ishvara.

Reflection on these matters has led me to speak of three ultimates. Perhaps there are others, although at present I have no idea what they might be. Thinking of these three has helped me understand the diversity of religious traditions more deeply.

The charge of polytheism, sometimes directed against this affirmation of multiple ultimates, is misplaced. Being Itself is not God, and the cosmos is not God. There is only one God. But not all religions are theistic. To claim that in fact they are directed to God when they say they are not is one more expression of religious imperialism. To claim that all are directed toward an ultimate that lies behind or beneath these three, disparages all the religious traditions with the claim to know directly what all of them relate to only indirectly. It reflects the Western passion for unity and metaphysical tidiness which should be respected but not allowed to dominate.

But though these three are distinct they are not separate from one another. The universe reverenced as ultimate is the embodiment of Being Itself or Brahman and is pervaded by God. That this is so is often attested unintentionally in the rhetoric of those who find meaning in appreciating their part in this whole.

God is also an instance, an embodiment, an expression of Being Itself, and is unthinkable apart from the world for which God functions as the ultimate efficient cause, formal cause, and final cause. Language about God often draws on what is strictly true only of Being Itself and also refers to the totality.

Being Itself does not exist at all except in God and the creatures. Very little is said of Being Itself or Brahman that does not hint at characteristics that actually belong to God. Being Itself, being the being of all things, is also closely associated with the thought of the whole.

That much religious language blurs the distinctions and relates to more than one of the three ultimates is understandable and unobjectionable. But when this is taken to deny the distinctions, confusion results. That confusion has been more characteristic of the Western tradition than the Indian one.

I have been led to this way of understanding matters as a Christian by my study both of Christianity and of other religious traditions and by philosophical reflection. Although Whitehead made no such proposal, my thinking is here as everywhere deeply indebted to him. I certainly accept the fact that there are other ways of understanding and that, indeed, few share mine. I continue to push it forward against great resistance because I believe it helps those who accept it to acknowledge the deep differences among religious traditions without denying that each has its truth.

When we understand global religious experience and thought in this way, it is easier to view the contributions of diverse traditions as complementary. This approach reduces the tendency to reinterpret what others say to make it fit into what one already believes. It avoids the need to assert that behind the realities to which the traditions attest there is another that unifies them. Until I encounter what seems to me a better hypothesis, I will continue to employ this one and recommend it to others.

Paul Knitter and I have been in debate and dialogue ever since, in *No Other Name?*, he critically described and evaluated my position. Much of the difference between us is a mixture of temperament and philosophy. I am a process thinker who believes the most we can do is to deal with the conditions of the present with what wisdom we can muster, always recognizing the particularity of our perspective. Knitter finds locating ourselves simply in the flux unsatisfying. He wants more fixity, more detachment, more closure. These are tendencies on our parts, not settled positions. And Knitter's willingness to deal seriously with my work again and to present it with such remarkable insight and generosity shows that, at least on his part, my own ideals of dialogue have been realized.

For the most part we are even closer than this exchange may suggest. We share a passion for the Earth and its poor and oppressed people. We believe that interreligious understanding can contribute to saving the world. Our ideas of what such salvation involves are certainly compatible. And I rejoice that, at last, what Knitter has long called for—dialogue among the religious traditions centering on the practical needs of the world—is happening. No doubt he is correct that I should have called for this earlier, as he did! He deserves major credit for this change. He deserves major credit, as well, for opening many Christians to the creative transformation that can come when we recognize how much others have to teach us. Not only I, but all of us are in his debt.

Index

Abe, Masao, 104
absolutism, 5-8, 39-40, 42-48, 73, 102, 165-66
academia, limitations of, 48, 98-103, 107, 111-12, 125-26, 171
acosmic religion, 120-24
"anonymous Christian," 25, 38
Aquinas, Thomas, 20, 55

Barth, Karl, 23, 36, 128, 132-34
Beyond Dialogue (Cobb), 84
Buddhism, 28-29, 46-47, 136-37, 146-47, 155-58

certainty, the quest for, 51-52, 97, 110
Christ: interpretations of, 36, 47, 79-85, 129, 138-41, 157-58; proclaiming, 76-91, 138-41, 142-45, 152-55
Christ in a Pluralistic Age (Cobb, 1975), 7, 71
Christianity: Christian perspectives, 90-91, 130-41, 151-55, 182-84; conditioned, 139, 173-74, 177-78; imperialism, 8, 96, 105, 120, 150, 185; internal history, 80-85, 138-41; mission, 30-31; radical pluralism, 68-75, 182-86; secular, 24, 102 (*see also* ethics); transformational capabilities, 38-39, 68-75, 90, 128-41, 155-58; universalism, 25, 27, 35-36, 38, 76
Christianity and Chinese Religions (Küng), 172
Christianity and the World Religions (Küng), 172
Christocentrism: catholic, 7686
Cobb, John B., Jr.: Christian superiority, 72-75, 128-41; on creative transformation, 46-48, 90, 110-11, 155-58, 179-83 (*see also* Christianity, transformational capabilities of); motivations, 2-11, 99-101, 139, 143

common ground: discovery of *vs.* positing, 10-11, 34, 56, 77; global challenges and, 56, 126-27, 144-47, 159-66, 177-81; quest for, 40-48, 96, 10-35, 110-12, 126-27, 128-36 (*see also* essence of religion)
conceptual relativism, 61, 66-67, 97-98
Confucianism, 18-21, 56-57, 63-64
consciousness-raising. *See* deconstruction
conversion, forms of, 154
cosmic religion, 120-24
cultural-linguistic systems. *See* language theory

deconstruction, 96, 1069
"dependent origination" (*pratitya samutpada*), 156-58, 161-62
dialogue, interreligious: dangers of, 15, 95-96; ethics and, 7-11, 52, 186; examples, 86-87, 89-90, 136-49, 155-58; methods, 44-48, 72-77, 136-41, 163-66, 181-86; philosophical model, 119-27; purpose, 37-48, 66-68, 80-90, 169, 180; radical listening, 5, 86-91, 100-102, 165; self-definition, 39, 48, 79-87, 131, 136-41, 158
dualism, 162, 176-78

enlightenment (Buddhist), 69-70, 140, 147, 155-56
Enlightenment (European), 21-24, 163-64, 172-74, 176-77, 181
epistemology of religion, 114 27
essence of religion: abandoning quest for, 40-44, 128-35, 162-66, 169-71, 176-78; identification, difficult, 16-17, 22-27, 10-35, 146-49, 158; whether able to unite peoples, 24, 54-60, 62-66, 126-27, 146-49; and

Other Titles in the Faith Meets Faith Series